A Selection from John Keats

LONGMAN ENGLISH SERIES

This series includes both period anthologies and selections from the work of individual authors. The introductions and notes have been based upon the most up-to-date criticism and scholarship and the editors have been chosen for their special knowledge of the material.

General Editor Maurice Hussey

*Available in paperback

A Selection
from John Keats

*edited with an introduction
and notes by*

E.C. Pettet

Longman

Longman
1724-1974

Longman Group Limited
London
*Associated companies, branches and
representatives throughout the world*

First published 1974
ISBN 0 582 34149 3

Printed in Hong Kong by Sheck Wah Tong Printing Press

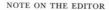

NOTE ON THE EDITOR

E. C. Pettet is Head of the English Department, Goldsmiths' College,
London University. He has published studies of Shakespeare and Vaughan
and in the present selection returns to the subject of what is possibly his
most important book, *On the Poetry of Keats*.

Preface

The selection from Keats's poetry offered in this volume has been divided into four distinctive groups, which, it is hoped, will prove of some help to the reader, especially to someone exploring that poetry for the first time. But their distinctiveness does not mean that they are exclusive. They obviously overlap in many respects; and several chosen poems (the *Ode to Psyche* for one example) might perhaps have been assigned to some other section than the one in which they have been placed.

In each group the poems and extracts are printed in chronological order, and the text for them has been taken from Miriam Allott's admirable complete edition of Keats's poetry in the Longman 'Annotated English Poets' series, where the poems are presented chronologically. Only on two occasions has the present editor deliberately departed from that text. He is convinced that the eighth line of the sonnet *On Visiting the Tomb of Burns*–'All is cold beauty, pain is never done'–should end with a heavy punctuation mark, semicolon or full stop, and that a question mark is preferable to an exclamation mark after 'it' in line 12.

Each group of poems is followed by a selection of relevant letters and extracts from letters. These, too, are printed in chronological order, though in the selection coming after 'Poems Various' the letters dealing with Keats's observations on poetry are all printed before those illustrating his descriptive powers.

The text of the letters and letter extracts, taken from the editions of M. Buxton Forman and Hyder E. Rollins, has been modernized slightly, particularly in respect of Keats's highly individual punctuation. These punctuation changes always run the risk of distorting or misinterpreting the meaning, but it is hoped that, if any such blunders have been perpetrated, they will be more than counterbalanced by a greater ease of reading.

It is hardly necessary to add that the Notes, whose extent often depends on previous discussion of a particular poem (or not) in the Introduction, owe a very great debt to the work of previous editors, Miriam Allott certainly included. But here and there the present editor trusts that he may have added a trifle or two to their invaluable labours.

Contents

LIST OF ILLUSTRATIONS

A NOTE ON THE ILLUSTRATIONS

The mythological illustrations reveal that, like Wordsworth with Constable, Keats found a special affinity with Titian, and Claude Lorrain. Many of the greatest Titians were shown in London in Keats's time and Claude, the French artist whose best work is in England, provided that blend of classicism in myth and architecture with romanticism of external nature that gave Keats, a keen student of art, a set of visual symbols that run through poem after poem.

Introduction

In *Sleep and Poetry*, a comparatively early poem written towards the end of 1816, Keats sketched something of a programme of his future poetic activity. This section of the work begins with the lines:

96   Oh, for ten years, that I may overwhelm
Myself in poesy; so I may do the deed
That my own soul has to itself decreed.
Then will I pass the countries that I see
In long perspective, and continually
Taste their pure fountains. First the realm I'll pass
Of Flora and old Pan: sleep in the grass,
Feed upon apples red and strawberries,
And choose each pleasure that my fancy sees;
Catch the white-handed nymphs in shady places
To woo sweet kisses from averted faces,
Play with their fingers, touch their shoulders white
Into a pretty shrinking with a bite
As hard as lips can make it, till, agreed,
A lovely tale of human life we'll read.
And one will teach a tame dove how it best
May fan the cool air gently o'er my rest;
Another, bending o'er her nimble tread
Will set a green robe floating round her head,
And still will dance with ever varied ease,
Smiling upon the flowers and the trees;
Another will entice me on and on
Through almond blossoms and rich cinnamon,
Till in the bosom of a leafy world
We rest in silence, like two gems upcurled
In the recesses of a pearly shell.

From this passage, admittedly more of an illustration than a definition, we can readily appreciate the nature of the 'poesy' in which Keats longed, so unhesitantly and intensely, to overwhelm himself for another ten years. It was, most obviously, a mellifluous kind of verse continuously evocative of delightful images and pleasurable sensations, these 'luxuries', as he often called them, constituting in their ideal totality 'loveliness' or 'beauty'. Much of it sprang from fancy and 'imaginings' (line 71), especially those stemming from desires, aspirations, and dreams of life as we might wish it to be. It also included a mild, sentimentalized, and often prettified, erotic strain.

All Keats's early poetry (most of it contained in his first published volume, *Poems 1817*) was predominantly 'poesy' of this sort; and for at least another year, through 1817 and into 1818, that is to say, such 'poesy' remained his constant objective. However, what is important in the programmatic section of *Sleep and Poetry* is not the implicit definition of the verse he was then writing but his vision of a poetry of very different possibilities, for immediately after the lusciously sensuous elaboration of his ten years' wish he suddenly arrests us with the lines:

122   And can I ever bid these joys farewell?
       Yes, I must pass them for a nobler life,
       Where I may find the agonies, the strife
       Of human hearts.

One or two commentators have suggested that these lines specifically refer to Keats's known ambition to write poetic drama. But whatever form this poetry of a 'nobler life' was to take, whether dramatic or not, is of minor importance. What chiefly matters is Keats's clear-eyed conception of a poetry beyond and superior to the 'poesy' of which he had been speaking—a poetry not of delectable 'imaginings', but of human life as we experience it, especially in its struggles, conflicts, and suffering.

However, if his initial emphasis is on 'agonies' and 'strife', this more significant poetry that he has in mind was not to be entirely an expression of human heart-ache. He goes on to symbolize the poetic imagination (a power very different from fanciful imaginings) as a heavenly

charioteer; and the varied figures who pass before the
charioteer clearly represent all the mixed stuff of human
experience, its joys as well as its sorrows:

142 Lo! how they murmur, laugh, and smile, and weep—
        Some with upholden hand and mouth severe;
        Some with their faces muffled to the ear
        Between their arms; some, clear in youthful bloom,
        Go glad and smilingly athwart the gloom;
        Some looking back, and some with upward gaze.
        Yes, thousands in a thousand different ways
        Flit onward—now a lovely wreath of girls
        Dancing their sleek hair into tangled curls,
        And now broad wings.

Perhaps the last line or two of this passage—a passage
which may have influenced Shelley's description of the
pageant of humanity in his great poem *The Triumph of Life*—
returns us to the 'poesy' of his earlier wish. But taken as
a whole, and with the rest of the paragraph in which it
is included, it constitutes an impressive vision of a kind of
poetry far more ambitious and incomparably more demand-
ing than anything Keats was then composing. This vision
was probably the 'vast idea' that he later refers to in line
291. It may also have prompted him to speak (lines 245–7)
of

                the great end
        Of Poesy, that it should be a friend
        To soothe the cares and lift the thoughts of man.

As he had more or less forecast in *Sleep and Poetry*, Keats
did bid farewell to these joys of his early 'poesy'—and very
much sooner than he could have guessed when he proclaimed
his wish. The important critical question that arises is
when, and to what extent, in the three short years of active
life that remained to him (1817–19), he approached the
poetry of 'nobler life' that he had envisaged.

   This question immediately raises the problem of *Endymion*,
which, in his effort to 'make 4000 lines of one bare circumstance and fill them with poetry' (letter to Bailey, 8 Oct.

3

1817), occupied him fully through most of 1817. If, like the present editor, we read *Endymion* as a straightforward narrative poem, containing some reflective passages but chiefly composed of lavishly sensuous descriptions, flights of exotic fancy, erotic day-dreams, and delighted, expansive retellings of what in his Preface Keats called 'the beautiful mythology of Greece', then it is still 'poesy' of the sort indicated in *Sleep and Poetry*: ten years of it superabundantly crammed into one. If, on the other hand, like many eminent twentieth-century critics, we insist on reading it as a fairly complex, neoplatonic allegory, based on the theme of the poetic soul in search of ideal Beauty, then already in 1817 Keats had moved some distance from the 'poesy' of such pieces as 'I stood tip-toe upon a little hill' and *Sleep and Poetry*.

The Changes of 1818
Whichever way we choose to take *Endymion*, there can be no doubt that a perceptible change comes over Keats's poetry in 1818. It is the change that he himself records in an often quoted letter to Reynolds, in which he describes human, and particularly poetic, experience, as a progress through various chambers:

> We no sooner get into the second chamber, which I shall call the chamber of maiden-thought, than we become intoxicated with the light and the atmosphere. We see nothing but pleasant wonders, and think of delaying there for ever in delight. However, among the effects this breathing is father of is that tremendous one of sharpening one's vision into the heart and nature of man—of convincing one's nerves that the world is full of misery and heartbreak, pain, sickness, and oppression [3 May 1818].

This change in Keats's poetry, a growing maturity, cannot of course be totally explained. Like all such crucial developments in a writer it inevitably leaves a certain sense of mystery. On the other hand, it is by no means entirely inexplicable, for it is obviously closely related to the known or reasonably surmisable facts of Keats's life in 1818. To begin with a simple, though not unimportant point, we may well believe that the long composition of *Endymion*–the indulgence of it, we might be tempted to say–had glutted his appetite, temporarily at least, for the 'poesy' of enticing 'white-handed nymphs' and so on that he had described in *Sleep and Poetry*. Again, there was his intent, deeply pondered reading of certain major poets whose work was the antithesis of such 'poesy'–of Shakespeare and Wordsworth from 1817, and of Milton and Dante (in Cary's translation) in 1818. Further, including his reading of these poets and plainly evident in his letters of 1818, there was his greatly intensified search for knowledge, though of course this impulse was as much an effect as a cause in the change of his poetic direction.

For Keats such knowledge meant a deeply felt experience of life as well of books, and in 1818 life, in its 'misery and heartbreak, pain, sickness, and oppression', bore upon him with a severity he had almost certainly never experienced before. This was the year in which his much loved, youngest brother, Tom, died from tuberculosis (1 December); and for Keats his brother's long, painful illness must have been particularly harrowing during the last three or four months when he acted as Tom's constant bedside nurse. Apart from the close contact with suffering, this experience must also have sharply raised–or, more probably, revived in him–the mystery of things. Why should one so young and so lovable be suddenly struck down in this terrible, seemingly inexplicable, way? Why, again, as he had asked in an early letter of 1818, 'should woman suffer? Aye, why should she? . . . These things are, and he who feels how incompetent the most skyey knight-errantry is to heal this bruised fairness is like a sensitive leaf on the hot hand of thought.'

There was another aspect of Tom's death that made it a singularly distressing experience of 'heartbreak'. The three orphan Keats brothers, who had been living together in lodgings since November 1816, had always been most intimately united. Now, with Tom's death, this bond, which must have meant a great deal to Keats for the stability and shared affection it provided, was completely broken, for earlier in the year, in June, his other brother, George, had emigrated to America with his newly married wife.

It was mainly in the hope of carving out a fortune for

5

himself and his brothers that George had decided on the American venture; and financial worries, persisting to the end of his life, were another of the burdens Keats had to bear in 1818. Further, and possibly more serious, there were the first obvious signs of physical weakness in himself, apparent when he returned from the exhausting summer tour, on foot through Scotland, with his friend, Charles Brown.

The change that appears in the poetry of 1818 was neither sudden nor decisively final. We may perhaps discern something of it in *Isabella*, Keats's chief work in the first part of the year. Certainly this sad tale of ill-fated love and death contrasts noticeably with the happily-ending love story of *Endymion*. It might also be taken to some extent to embody a central conception of Keats which, though by no means new to him, had now become a steady and intense conviction—that of the close, inevitable intermingling of joy and sorrow in human life. But the first part, describing the dawning love between Lorenzo and Isabella, is unquestionably 'poesy' of the old sort, while the second part is probably much more effective in its expression of horror, of the Romantic *frisson* of the beautiful-loathsome, than of grief and suffering. Keats himself acutely diagnosed the fundamental limitation of the poem when he wrote: 'There is too much inexperience of life and simplicity of knowledge in it.'

Several short poems written in the first half of 1818, notably the sonnet *On Sitting Down to Read 'King Lear' Once Again* and the later one, *On Visiting the Tomb of Burns*, with its haunting line,

All is cold beauty, pain is never done...

afford a glimpse of the conflict in Keats at this time over the direction his writing should take. But for our understanding of his development none of these shorter pieces compares with his more extensive verse epistle, *To J. H. Reynolds, Esq.*, though this rapidly written, impromptu poem of 25 March was never intended for publication and in fact was not published during his lifetime.

After a short introductory passage of a comic, slightly

6

satirical sort, the epistle begins with an elaborated, freely adapted description of Claude's painting, 'The Enchanted Castle'. One or two humorous touches apart (these perhaps indicating some degree of detachment from the kind of verse Keats was writing), this description is essentially an exercise 'in fair dreaming wise', a deliberate indulgence in the old 'poesy' of loveliness and delight:

49   The doors all look as if they oped themselves,
      The windows as if latched by fays and elves—
      And from them comes a silver flash of light
      As from the westward of a summer's night;
      Or like a beauteous woman's large blue eyes
      Gone mad through olden songs and poesies.

Nevertheless, in spite of Keats's intention to cheer the spirits of his sick friend, he somehow cannot resist the impulse to confess something of the 'horrid moods' that have been lately afflicting him; and in the second part of the poem he goes on to describe his vision of the 'eternal fierce destruction' in nature:

                    I saw
93   Too far into the sea—where every maw
      The greater on the less feeds evermore...
      But I saw too distinct into the core
      Of an eternal fierce destruction,
      And so from happiness I far was gone.
      Still am I sick of it; and though today
      I've gathered young spring-leaves, and flowers gay
      Of periwinkle and wild strawberry,
      Still do I that most fierce destruction see:
      The shark at savage prey, the hawk at pounce,
      The gentle robin, like a pard or ounce,
      Ravening a worm.

These two, widely divergent parts of the poem are bridged by an important commentary passage (lines 67–81), which should be read side by side with his 3 May prose letter to Reynolds. Some of the details of this passage pose teasing problems of interpretation. But there is little or no obscurity

7

about its central lines:

> Oh, never will the prize,
> High reason and the lore of good and ill,
> Be my award.

On the one hand, as in *Sleep and Poetry*, he is expressing a desire to reach out beyond the old poesy of 'fair dreaming' to a poetry inspired by knowledge (in his own wide sense of the word) as well as sensation, and intent on assimilating and accepting all the mixed contraries of human experience, its joy and sorrow, its happiness and its suffering. On the other hand, though his 'never' may be discounted as a momentary exaggeration of despair, he plainly feels that such poetry is beyond his present scope; and at the end of the poem, after an arbitrary dismissal of his 'horrid moods', he writes:

110   Do you get health–and Tom the same–I'll dance,
     And from detested moods in new romance
     Take refuge.

In Keats's vocabulary 'romance', the antithesis to the 'bitter-sweet of this Shakespearian fruit' that he speaks of in his *King Lear* sonnet, was a near synonym for the kind of 'poesy' in which he had wished to overwhelm himself for ten years. The new romance he refers to, as a refuge, was *Isabella*.

'*Hyperion*'

In spite of all this uncertainty and conflict of poetic impulses so plainly evident in the verse and letters of the first half of 1818, by the end of the year Keats had almost completed a long poem of close engagement with 'the agonies, the strife/Of human hearts'. This poem, his first major work (though often underrated), was *Hyperion*.

In some ways this decisive break from the earlier 'poesy' presents something of a paradox. For his subject Keats turned once more to the remote world of Greek mythology– to the story of the overthrow of Saturn and the first Titan race of gods. Again, as his letters to his friends Dilke and Reynolds show (21 and 22 September), at the beginning of composition he seems to have regarded the work as a

8

'feverous relief', an escape into a world of 'abstractions' away from the misery of nursing his dying brother. But though some of the mainly descriptive writing—his elaborate picture of the palace of Hyperion for an obvious example—probably did serve him in this way, as a whole the work he finally produced is in no fundamental sense of the word an escapist one. Quite the contrary, for whether by deliberate choice or irresistible compulsion, what he principally expressed through this potentially remote classical myth was an experience of pain and suffering, of agony and strife—that and the perennial question of how such unhappiness was to be endured, and how, if in any way, it was to be explained. Further, as he explicitly states in two of the key passages of the poem, this *cri de coeur* is essentially a human one. Saturn and his fellow Titans have lost their godhead, have been reduced to a mortal level, precisely because, in their downfall, they have abandoned themselves to desperate mortal feelings, including hope for the impossible. Echoing the earlier words of Coelus in Book I (lines 329–336), Thea clearly expresses this truth:

II.*92* There saw she direst strife—the supreme God
At war with all the frailty of grief,
Of rage, of fear, anxiety, revenge,
Remorse, spleen, hope, but most of all despair.
Against these plagues he strove in vain; for Fate
Had poured a mortal oil upon his head,
A disanointing poison.

Apart from its descriptive passages, including the incomparable opening (lines 1–14), most of Book I is an expression of giant agony and strife—of Saturn in all the anguished dejection of his overthrow, of Thea in her impotence to minister any kind of comfort to him, and of Hyperion, still the original sun-god but torn with dark premonitions of his own impending doom. The Book also voices something of Saturn's frantic, bewildered questioning why such misery should be, a questioning that is resumed in Book II.

In the second Book, in the long central speech of the old sea-god, Oceanus, Saturn is offered an answer to his questions. Oceanus is an embodiment of 'thought and

9

musing', who even in his dethronement, as Saturn recognizes, has somehow preserved a 'severe content'. His speech, lucid and beautiful in many ways, follows two main lines. In the first place, to explain what has happened to Saturn and the first race of gods (himself included), he propounds an idea of inexorable evolutionary process. Just as they, the Titans, were superior to all that had preceded them in the mysterious creation of the universe, so Jupiter and the new race of gods are indubitably superior to them. And in this inevitable process of nature, Jupiter and his fellow gods may in their turn be superseded:

> For 'tis the eternal law
> II.228 That first in beauty should be first in might;
> Yea, by that law, another race may drive
> Our conquerers to mourn as we do now.
> Have ye beheld the young God of the Seas,
> My dispossessor . . .
> I saw him on the calmèd waters scud,
> With such a glow of beauty in his eyes,
> That it enforced me to bid sad farewell
> To all my empire.

The second main purpose of Oceanus's speech is to advocate, for the endurance of their fate, an attitude of undelusive, all-comprehending acceptance, a return to the calm, the serene composure of spirit, that had been their essentially divine attribute:

> II.203   to bear all naked truths,
> And to envisage circumstance, all calm,
> That is the top of sovereignty.

One problem immediately leaps at us from this speech. The prime determinant of these progressive, evolutionary stages of superiority is 'beauty', that complex, elusive concept that we find in so many of the most important passages of Keats's letters, to say nothing of those cryptic and endlessly debated lines in the *Ode on a Grecian Urn*:

> 'Beauty is truth, truth beauty'—that is all
> Ye know on earth, and all ye need to know.

But though Oceanus's affirmation of the superior beauty of the new race of gods is emphatic enough, there is little or nothing in the speech itself to indicate what constitutes this 'fresh perfection'. Perhaps Keats intended that his later account of their poet-god representative, Apollo, should afford the answer to our question.

This one major difficulty apart, Oceanus's speech poses no serious problems–so long as we take it as a purely dramatic utterance in the context of the myth that Keats originally intended to retell, which included a second war between the two generations of gods. In a debate modelled on that between the fallen angels in Book II of *Paradise Lost*, Oceanus is presenting one way of regarding historic change (a possible theme of the poem, and one of undoubted interest to Keats, that several commentators have strongly stressed); he is also offering *one* sort of counsel, which the Titans may ignore to their cost. His words receive some support from Clymene but are derisively dismissed by the bellicose Enceladus, who seems to speak for most of the Titans. Saturn, curiously silent, gives no indication of his response.

But in what ways, if any, and to what extent, may Oceanus's speech be regarded as a reflection of Keats's own developing ideas and attitudes, particularly if we relate it, as to some extent we must, to the much more subjective, and in some ways confused, third Book?

In answer to that question one important point seems fairly clear. Granted the obscurity of the word 'beauty' in that emphatic statement,

'tis the eternal law
That first in beauty should be first in might,

it seems likely that Oceanus is expounding a belief about general historical change that Keats himself entertained at this time: namely, that all the suffering and distress involved are to be seen, and accepted, as part of a progressive evolutionary process. At least there is no reason for thinking the contrary. But obviously, so far as the afflictions of individual experience at any stage of historical development are concerned, such a belief could have meant little for that 'lore of good and ill' which he always saw as his supreme goal. It contained nothing to explain or justify the fate of a beloved brother painfully dying before his eyes as he wrote the poem.

Again, we may fairly certainly take it that Oceanus's speech expresses what Keats would have considered a 'philosophic' response to the agony and strife of the Titans—and of humanity as well. This was a sort of attitude that increasingly attracted him, as we may see from his letters of 1818, from such a statement as: 'An extensive knowledge is needful to thinking people. It takes away the heat and fever, and helps, by widening speculation, to ease the "burden of the mystery".' On the other hand, since the rest of the poem, the fragmentary third Book, is devoted to Apollo, who was certainly intended to represent the ideal poet, it is obvious that he conceived of a poetic response to the mystery of things, which, while it might have much in common with the philosophic, is nevertheless distinct from it.

The third Book concludes with a description of Apollo dying into the life of a new authentic godhead; and there can be little doubt that this episode symbolizes the transformation, foreseen in *Sleep and Poetry,* from one kind of poet into another, higher kind. But about the nature of the poetic ideal embodied in the transformed poet-god Keats has comparatively little to say. His adumbration of it comes in the brief passage describing the vision that Apollo sees in the face of the silent goddess Mnemosyne:

III.*111*   Mute thou remainest—mute! Yet I can read
    A wondrous lesson in thy silent face:
    Knowledge enormous makes a God of me.
    Names, deeds, grey legends, dire events, rebellions,
    Majesties, sovran voices, agonies,
    Creations and destroyings, all at once
    Pour into the wide hollows of my brain,
    And deify me, as if some blithe wine
    Or bright elixir peerless I had drunk,
    And so become immortal.

It might, just possibly, be argued that this passage carries no more than a limited, purely narrative reference: that Apollo is merely learning of the 'dire events' and 'rebellions' that have preceded the triumph of the new gods. But from some closely parallel lines in *The Fall of Hyperion,* in which Keats is speaking of the transfigured Poet, not of Apollo—

i.*302*   there grew
         A power within me of enormous ken
         To see as a god sees, and take the depth
         Of things as nimbly as the outward eye
         Can size and shape pervade—

it seems probable that the spectacle seen in Mnemosyne's face, like the human pageant witnessed by the charioteer in *Sleep and Poetry,* again intimates a poetry of comprehensive assimilation and acceptance of life, especially of its sorrow and of the pain that is 'never done'. But, if we are justified in reading the passage in this way, it hardly establishes any significant distinction between a philosophic and a poetic response to life, though perhaps, along the always dubious lines of implication, we may discover two differences: first, between an attitude of detachment and one of imaginative involvement, and secondly, between confronting suffering as and when it occurs and being perpetually conscious of it. This second difference, the poet's cross and glory, could certainly be supported by some lines Keats later wrote in *The Fall of Hyperion:*

i.*172*   Every sole man hath days of joy and pain,
         Whether his labours be sublime or low—
         The pain alone; the joy alone; distinct:
         Only the dreamer venoms all his days,
         Bearing more woe than all his sins deserve.

Though we have no confirmatory evidence on the point, Keats could, with some truth, have regarded the first two Books of *Hyperion* as a substantial achievement, for the first time, of the kind of poetry that is probably intimated by Apollo's 'lesson'. He, too, in a crucial break from the old 'poesy', had seen, and poetically expressed, a vision of 'agonies, Creations and destroyings' (*Hyperion* iii.116)— much of it with an unmistakable human application. On the other hand, we must also take into account a long passage in the third Book, probably written three or four months

13

after the first two, which presents a weeping Apollo very different from the finally deified figure:

III.*86*   For me, dark, dark,
And painful, vile oblivion seals my eyes.
I strive to search wherefore I am so sad,
Until a melancholy numbs my limbs;
And then upon the grass I sit and moan,
Like one who once had wings.

All the biographical evidence supports the view that this confession of Apollo–of numbing melancholy, uncertainty, frustration, loss of poetic inspiration, and, as the outburst goes on, of frantic escapism–is essentially a confession of Keats's own actual state in the deeply troubled weeks between late February and early April of 1819. There is also some evidence from other poetry of the time, notably from that painful, enigmatic sonnet 'Why did I laugh to-night?', that clearly reveals how far he still was from a firm, assured grasp of his poetic and spiritual ideal.

Finally, in any comment on Book III, the composition of which was much broken and spread over two or three months, something must be said about the lyrical, richly sensuous apostrophe to Apollo that occurs at the beginning (III.10–41). It is probably not difficult to account for the inspirational impulse behind this passage. It almost certainly served to express a life-affirming reaction from all the deprivations of the recent death-shadowed months of nursing Tom, as well as the spirit of a new-found love–whether for Fanny Brawne, or, just possibly, Mrs Isabella Jones. In these respects the apostrophe is probably to be linked with Keats's main work of early 1819, *The Eve of St Agnes*, which, for all its sombre notes, is certainly one of the most joyous poems he ever composed. Also the ideal of poetry that he always had before him was one embracing the joys as well as the sorrows of human life. But in *Hyperion* this glowing and beautiful address to Apollo, coming abruptly after the sad opening lines (which may refer to Tom's recent death), and followed by the account of a weeping Apollo, must, to some extent at least, strike as an intrusion, if not as a discordance. In other words, it is yet another element in

14

Book III that testifies to the conflict and confusion that lay behind the fitful and—in comparison with the fluent writing of Books I and II—laboured composition of that short Book.

There were probably several reasons to account for Keats's abandonment of his projected epic. But, from the evidence of Book III, it seems likely that the main one was that he was no longer in an assured spirit to continue it—for the time being at any rate.

The Odes of 1819

The four odes, *To a Nightingale, On a Grecian Urn, On Melancholy,* and *On Indolence,* which in a renewed upsurge of creativity Keats rapidly composed in late April-May of 1819, are an expression, incomparably more vital than almost anything he had achieved before, of an intense and often ecstatic sensuousness. But if, in this obvious respect, they take up the strain of his apostrophe to the golden Apollo—

> Let the rose glow intense and warm the air,
> And let the clouds of even and of morn
> Float in voluptuous fleeces o'er the hills—

they also resume the relentless questions and uncertainties of the other, weeping Apollo. In their own distinctive way, they mark a return to the quest for the 'lore of good and ill', though now, without the writing becoming obtrusively subjective in the common Romantic manner, this good and ill is regarded much more in personal terms, particularly of the stresses arising from love, poetic ambition, mortality, and a feverish spirit. Under all of them, like some palimpsest, are those words from the *Nightingale* ode that speak of an ineluctable human reality:

> The weariness, the fever, and the fret
> Here, where men sit and hear each other groan;
> Where palsy shakes a few, sad, last gray hairs,
> Where youth grows pale, and spectre-thin, and dies;
> Where but to think is to be full of sorrow
> And leaden-eyed despairs;
> Where Beauty cannot keep her lustrous eyes,
> Or new Love pine at them beyond to-morrow.

15

No one is likely to underrate the supreme aesthetic qualities of these odes–their innumerable, memorable felicities of phrase, their verbal music, the immediacy and vitality of their imagery, the packed density of the writing, their structural beauties and their convincing communication of the feelings, attitudes and moods that inspired them. It was on such qualities as these that the older critics based their admiration. What we may however question is whether (excluding the later ode *To Autumn*) they contain the insights and illuminations, the depth, so to speak, that many twentieth-century critics have found in them–whether they in fact mark any very notable advance in Keats's aspirations towards the 'lore of good and ill', or whether they are not to be read as essentially another poignant *cri de coeur*, the poems of an anguished Apollo rather than of the transformed, deified one. And there are at least two considerations that make this a necessary question to raise. In the first place, though these odes (omitting the *Ode on Indolence*) were included in the *1820 Poems*, there is nothing to suggest that Keats attached any exceptional importance to them; and indeed he may have regarded them as something of a byproduct to his main poetic activity. In the second place, in the opening vision of *The Fall of Hyperion*, written several months later, he was to describe all his previous poetry (possibly with the exception of *Hyperion*, which he was hoping to continue) as the work of a feverish, indulgent dreamer. Probably this self-condemnation is excessive, like his later declaration, 'I have left no immortal work behind me'. But at least Keats knew better than any critic what his poetic goal was and how far he had truly advanced towards it; and though we may wish to modify the judgment expressed in *The Fall of Hyperion*, we cannot entirely ignore it.

Of these late spring odes probably the most highly admired has been the first, the *Ode to a Nightingale*. There is no need to comment in detail here on its superlative exhibition of those aesthetic qualities of the odes that have already been generally indicated–on, for one instance, the compressed simplicity and precise image of lonely desolation in Ruth as

> sick for home,
> She stood in tears amid the alien corn,

followed shortly, without any discordance, by the freely
suggestive fancy, the rich verbal music, and, if one may
use an unfashionable word, the sheer enchantment of the
lines,

> Charmed magic casements, opening on the foam
> Of perilous seas in fairy lands forlorn.

Nevertheless, for all these beauties, what most of the ode
essentially communicates is a series of hectic whipped-up
entreaties to escape, through 'fancy' (Keats's own word),
those painful human realities so truthfully described in the
third stanza. Wine, Poesy, finally 'easeful Death', are all
in turn desperately and vainly evoked as means to attain
the happiness and beauty that seem to be suggested, as
human possibilities, by the song of the nightingale. But
these wilful flights of fancy are, as Keats finally admits,
the beguilements of a 'deceiving elf', never more so than
when, carried away by a momentary death wish, he indulges
in the imagined 'luxury' of a flower-smothered, sensuously
experienced condition of death similar to the one he had
pictured for the mythical Adonis in *Endymion* (ii.407–27).

In other words, with its 'Away, away! For I will fly
to thee' motif, the ode still retains much of the escapist
sentiment of the Keats-Apollo in *Hyperion* who had cried
out feverishly to Mnemosyne:

iii.96   Are there not other regions than this isle?
> What are the stars? There is the sun, the sun!
> And the most patient brilliance of the moon!
> And stars by thousands! Point me out the way
> To any one particular beauteous star,
> And I will flit into it with my lyre,
> And make its silvery splendour pant with bliss.

But, having said this, one must hasten to add that the ode
is certainly not a poem of jejune unqualified escapism.
For one thing, at a crucial turning-point the indulgent
death wish is decisively rejected in a realization of the

probable nature of death:

> Still wouldst thou sing, and I have ears in vain—
> To thy high requiem become a sod.

For another, as has already been indicated, the poem ends with a rejection—or at least, to include the last two lines, an agitated, deeply troubled questioning—of the validity of fancy and its dreams:

> Adieu! The fancy cannot cheat so well
> As she is famed to do, deceiving elf.

There is a further, if paradoxical, point, with some relevance to the other odes as well, that must be made about the *Ode to a Nightingale*. Granted that much of its dynamic is one of dream indulgence, even perhaps of evasion, it nevertheless provides rich imaginative sustenance through its grasp of substantial actuality, particularly of a joyous physical kind. The second stanza provides a good example of this continual paradox. Of course we cannot ignore the effete immature sentiment of fading away into the forest dim, etc.; but the effect of this is almost cancelled out by the vital gusto of the preceding lines:

> Oh, for a draught of vintage that hath been
> Cooled a long age in the deep-delvèd earth,
> Tasting of Flora and the country green,
> Dance, and Provençal song, and sunburnt mirth!
> Oh, for a beaker full of the warm South,
> Full of the true, the blushful Hippocrene,
> With beaded bubbles winking at the brim,
> And purple-stainèd mouth,
> That I might drink, and leave the world unseen,
> And with thee fade away into the forest dim.

The *Ode to a Nightingale* was immediately followed by the *Ode on a Grecian Urn*, a poem commonly interpreted as a celebration of the enduring beauty of art and of its solace amid all the painful flux of transient human life.

Though open to several objections, this interpretation may have some validity. But, whether we accept it or not, it is surely much more satisfactory to see the *Ode on a Grecian*

Urn as yet another reflection of what an American critic, Newell Ford, once called Keats's 'blissful imaginings'. After the first stanza, which probably owes something to works of art with which Keats was familiar, the main part of the poem (stanzas 2–4) consists of a series of images, the poet's own invention, that embody a dream of ideal felicity, of life if only it could 'to the will/Be settled'–an eternal springtime of unfading natural beauty, perennial youth, unfailing poetic inspiration, and–in stanza 4–a vision of a pacific, harmonious society. Some of these images might, conceivably, symbolize the timeless beauty of art, but it is hard to see what is symbolic, or spiritual or philosophic, about the enraptured fancy of

> More happy love, more happy, happy love!
> For ever warm and still to be enjoyed,
>   For ever panting, and for ever young.

Further, it will be noticed that several of the images that Keats depicts on the side of his invented urn are closely and significantly related, as opposites, to those painful human actualities that he had described in the third stanza of the *Nightingale* ode.

For all their obvious interconnections and similarities, these first two May odes record very different inclinations and experiences in Keats. In the *Ode to a Nightingale* he is striving desperately, at times (as in his attitude to death) confusedly, to escape from the 'weariness, the fever, and the fret' of mortal life; in the *Ode on a Grecian Urn*, momentarily at least, he has achieved a satisfying state of escape. Nowhere in the *Grecian Urn* is there the note of 'Away! away! For I will fly to thee'. Keats *is* there, in his imagined world of bliss; and the ode is much more joyous and assured than its immediate predecessor. There are no reversals, uncertainties, questions; and the poem closes with a ringing, emphatic affirmation:

> 'Beauty is truth, truth beauty'–that is all
> Ye know on earth, and all ye need to know.

Whatever else that interminably discussed aphorism means, it must surely be taken as a confident assertion that the kind of beauty represented by the urn images has a validity that, in a way, constitutes its 'truth'.

Nevertheless, in spite of this assurance, Keats could not rest content with an idealized beauty that excluded pain and the intermingling of joy and sorrow; and in the next ode, *On Melancholy*, he engaged himself once more with the 'burden of the mystery':

> Beauty that must die;
> And Joy, whose hand is ever at his lips
> Bidding adieu; and aching Pleasure nigh,
> Turning to poison while the bee-mouth sips.

Unfortunately, as a whole, the ode fails to justify the impressive seriousness of these lines. For the most part it is a kind of poetic recipe for the cultivation of some exquisite, artificial 'melancholy', not an imaginative engagement with the 'pain that is never done'; and F. R. Leavis was certainly not over-severe in his strictures when he spoke of its 'perverse and debilitating indulgences'. Even 'perverse' is not too strong a word for the lines,

> Or if thy mistress some rich anger shows
> Imprison her soft hand, and let her rave,
> And feed deep, deep upon her peerless eyes.

Little need be said here about the last of the May odes, *On Indolence*. It, too, has its moments of sensuous beauty and verbal perfection, and though it was excluded from *Poems 1820*, one might argue that it is not notably inferior to the *Ode on Melancholy*. It is also interesting for what is probably Keats's most striking poetic expression of that complex mood of 'indolence' that was one of his chief reliefs from the distresses of life–a mood, not to be simply described as escapist, which, if it offered no answer to the problems that left him like 'a sensitive leaf on the hot hand of thought', seems often to have recharged his poetic energies:

> Ripe was the drowsy hour;
> The blissful cloud of summer indolence
> Benumbed my eyes; my pulse grew less and less;
> Pain had no sting, and pleasure's wreath no flower.

of an agonizing and exhausting love-affair, it is a disturbing poem to read in the context of Keats's general development– first, for the hankering it appears to reveal after the old thoughtless 'poesy' (lines 10–17), and secondly, for its attitude to the 'monstrous region' in which he imagines his brother and sister-in-law to be living. His description of the harsh, inimical features of the American landscape, implicitly contrasted with his own 'realm of Flora and old Pan', ends with the line, 'And great unerring Nature once seems wrong'. The attitude behind this passage is not one of acceptance but of the old obstinate wish that life *could* 'to the will/Be settled', while he also dreams of a peace of mind that may be gained by *banishing* thoughts of this hateful land. It never occurs to him that it may be his own attitude, not Nature, that is wrong.

So far, in this sketch of Keats's development, several important poems, like *Lamia,* have been ignored or lightly touched on, though they certainly have some relevance to what has been discussed. The reason for this omission is that most of these poems are much more concerned with the intermingling of joy and sorrow in the 'bitter-sweet' of love and with Keats's conflicting attitudes to love than with human experience in general.

As we survey Keats's love poetry, from the sugary superficial sentimentalities of some of his earliest verses (illustrated in this volume by the 'Happy is England' sonnet) to the late sonnets 'The day is gone' and 'Bright star!', there is no mistaking its strong, uninhibited affirmation of the joy of sexual love, especially on the physical side. His first large-scale poem, *Endymion*–unless we choose to read it as a neoplatonic allegory–is essentially a young man's sustained, unquestioning dream of erotic pleasure; it also, in the important speech on happiness (lines 777–842), asserts the claim, never to be repeated, that sexual love is both the height of human felicity and a force making for general good. But *Endymion,* though a better poem than some critics would have it, fails in convincing imaginative impact (among other reasons for the 'mawkishness' that Keats himself discerned), and it is *The Eve of St Agnes* that stands as his supreme affirmation of the joy of love. As

Middleton Murry wrote of this poem in his book *Keats and Shakespeare*: 'It has the rapture and enchantment, the rich and deep and right sensuousness, of complete surrender to the god.' In these respects we might also couple the *Ode to Psyche* with *The Eve of St Agnes;* but from the commentaries of several eminent critics it is obvious that this ode is open to other possible interpretations.

Middleton Murry goes on to qualify his account of *The Eve of St Agnes* with the necessary admission that, even if much of its impulse springs from the ecstasy of the first days of Keats's love for Fanny Brawne, it is not a poem of entire and overwhelming joyousness. However obliquely, our response to the 'opulent and triumphant love' of Porphyro and Madeline must to some extent be modified by those notes of mortality, of old age and death, that are struck so chillingly at the beginning and end of the poem and never entirely forgotten throughout. Even the more youthful *Endymion*, though predominantly an expression of delighted eroticism, is full of the pains and griefs of love, not only in the main narrative of Endymion's long frustrated quest for Cynthia but also in many of the pendant love-stories.

One particular note of sorrow in some of the later poems is that of the brevity of love, especially of the satiation that time inevitably brings with it. This note is heard through a long passage in the poem *Fancy* (lines 69–76) and in the *Ode to a Nightingale* when Keats speaks of the world

> Where Beauty cannot keep her lustrous eyes,
> Or new Love pine at them beyond to-morrow.

It recurs in the *Ode on a Grecian Urn*, in his vision of an ideal love that is

> All breathing human passion far above,
> That leaves a heart high-sorrowful and cloyed,
> A burning forehead, and a parching tongue.

A similar reflection is expressed in *Lamia*–in the final comment on the god Hermes and his nymph–

> Into the green-recessèd woods they flew;
> Nor grew they pale, as mortal lovers do–

and again, more cynically, in the curious opening to Part
II, which concludes with the lines,

> too short was their bliss
> To breed distrust and hate, that make the soft voice
> hiss.

The Fatality of Love
However, the most striking feature of Keats's love poetry,
and what more than anything else gives it an individuality
of its own, is the continual representation of love as a
destructive force. How soon this major theme enters his
work may be a matter of some dispute. At most we can only
regard the sonnet *On a Leander Gem* as an intimation of the
theme, and though a considerable part of the third Book
of *Endymion* is concerned with the baneful enchantment
of Circe, it might well be contended that she represents
the force of lust, not of love. *Isabella*, on the other hand,
is certainly a tale of true love that brings death to the two
lovers involved; but here again it might be argued, if not
convincingly, that Keats was drawn to this story simply
because it happened to be one of the best in Boccaccio's
Decameron.

Whatever hesitations we may have about these earlier
poems, there can be no doubt at all about the prominence
of this theme of love's fatality in the poetry of 1819. It is
most hauntingly epitomized in one of the finest of Keats's
shorter poems, *La Belle Dame Sans Merci*, a poem which,
though it may lend itself to some possible secondary interpretations, is obviously and centrally a symbolic representation of the irresistible enchantment and ultimate ravage
of sexual love, love of a strongly sensuous kind no doubt
but certainly not Circean lust. Shortly before *La Belle Dame
Sans Merci* Keats had started *The Eve of St Mark*, and there
is much to be said for D. G. Rossetti's surmise that this
uncompleted poem would have shown the remorse of the
heroine, Bertha, for the suffering, leading to death, that
she had inflicted upon her lover. If this is mere speculation,
there is no missing the significance of another poem of
this period, the sonnet 'As Hermes once', in which Keats
imaginatively identifies himself not with the living and

27

mainly happy Paolo and Francesca of Leigh Hunt's poem but with the two sad spirits of Dante's vision in the *Divine Comedy*, destroyed by their passion and borne in a whirlwind around the second circle of Hell. In one of his letters of the time Keats confessed of the fifth canto of *Hell* (the first part of the *Divine Comedy*) that it 'pleases me more and more'; and no doubt he had pondered those lines which in the translation that he used read:

A thousand more he show'd, and by name
Pointed them out, whom love bereaved of life.

Later in 1819 came *Lamia*, and this work, which Keats seems to have regarded as the finest of his narrative poems, is largely an extended variation on the theme of *La Belle Dame Sans Merci*—on love as a blinding, overwhelming enchantment leading to disillusion and destruction. But *Lamia* is most certainly a variation on, not a repetition of, this theme. Filled from end to end, in its subsidiary as well as its main parts, with impressions of false-seeming, hallucination and deception, it emphasizes, even more strongly than *La Belle Dame Sans Merci*, that love is quite literally an enchantment. Again, however we are intended to take the lady of the ballad, the heroine of *Lamia* is a much more human figure, and in the main she is a helpless, involuntary agent of the destruction that her love brings with it. Further, *Lamia* is a poem of considerable complexity, with many ambiguities and contradictions that often create serious uncertainties in our response to it.

At the same time as he was engaged on *Lamia* Keats was also writing, in collaboration with his friend Charles Brown, the play *Otho the Great*. This, too, for all the bewildering complications of its entangled plot, is basically the story of an infatuated lover, Ludolph, ravaged by his love into utter disillusionment and madness. But here the woman concerned, Auranthe, is an unambiguous figure of evil, treacherous and faithless, while in the latter part of the play, through Ludolph, there is an expression of the anguished doubts, suspicions, and jealousy of love that is not to be found in *La Belle Dame Sans Merci* or *Lamia*.

When every allowance has been made for dramatization

and purely imaginative experience, the fact remains that Keats as a love poet was always close to Keats the man; and the man, as we may plainly see from his letters, was always divided, in a 'gordian complication of feelings', in his attitude towards women, and always divided–and apprehensive–about sexual love. There is a confession to his sister-in-law, when he is writing about his reactions towards 'Charmian' (Jane Cox) that comes near to epitomizing this fundamental ambivalence: 'I should like her to ruin me, and I should like you to save me' (14 October 1818). So far as *Lamia* and *Otho the Great* are concerned, there can be little doubt that these two works, like the later and entirely personal poems, 'I cry your mercy' and *To [Fanny]*, reflect the devastating conflict of this time between the irresistible attraction he felt towards Fanny Brawne and the intuition that, for him, this love was destructive. Sentence after sentence in his letters to Fanny point straight to *Lamia* and the play, as, for instance, the confession: 'You have ravished me away by a power I cannot resist; and yet I could resist until I saw you; and ever since I have seen you I have endeavoured often "to reason against the reasons of my love"' (13 October 1819).

One further point: if one of the central features of Keats's general attitude towards life was, from the beginning, a continuous sense of the juxtaposition of joy and sorrow, nothing in his work more evidently expresses this conviction than his love poetry, though admittedly, after *The Eve of St Agnes*, it is the pain and havoc that predominate. On the other hand, right at the end, there are the sonnets 'The day is gone' and 'Bright star!' that return to the mood of *The Eve of St Agnes;* and possibly, had Keats lived to write more poetry, he would have modified that vision of the devastation of sexual love that is so prominent in the compositions of his last productive year.

Immediacy of Language
At the beginning of his review of Keats's poems and letters (1880), included in *Essays in Criticism: Second Series*, Matthew Arnold wrote: 'No one can question the eminency, in Keats's poetry, of the quality of sensuousness. Keats as a poet is abundantly and enchantingly sensuous; the question,

with some people, will be whether he is anything else.'

Partly because the impression does, to some extent, still persist that Keats was above all else a poet of sensuous experience, a poet who early in his career once proclaimed, with an unfortunately misleading word, 'O for a life of sensations rather than of thoughts', this introduction has so far been devoted to the question Arnold raises. (Arnold's own answer, not unsatisfactory as far as it goes, is that Keats's poetry is important for its perception of 'the necessary relation of beauty with truth, and of both with joy'.) But it is time now to redress the balance somewhat and meet–half way at least–the judgment of the anonymous reviewer in *The Times Literary Supplement* who recently, nearly a hundred years after Arnold's essay, spoke of 'the fleshly, sensuous, pictorial, unreflective nature of Keats's verse'.

Almost any randomly opened page of this volume will readily demonstrate the truth of the second and third of those adjectives; and, in spite of its pejorative connotation, even 'fleshly' is a fair and obvious epithet for *Endymion*, a poem that constitutes nearly a quarter of Keats's verse. But there is certainly one interesting critical problem that confronts us in this sensuous quality of his writing, and it arises, implicitly, from Arnold's word 'eminency'. Sensuousness in various forms is, after all, a basic constituent of most poetry, as Arnold reminds us when he quotes Milton's dictum that poetry should be 'simple, sensuous, impassioned'. Why then should so many critics, Arnold included, feel that Keats is almost unparalleled for the sensuous impact of his verse?

One obvious answer to this question is to be found in Arnold's comment on the sheer abundance of Keats's sensuousness. However, in other comparable poets such abundance is frequently the cumulative effect of extensive passages of writing, and what is so particularly remarkable about Keats's mature style is the richness of sense impression and sensation that he continuously compacts into a few words–into such characteristic lines as

'Mid hushed, cool-rooted flowers, fragrant-eyed,
    Blue, silver-white and budded Tyrian,

or

> The coming musk-rose, full of dewy wine,
> The murmurous haunt of flies on summer eves.

For this reason density is probably a better word than abundance to explain something of the special sensuous effect of his verse.

The two brief quotations from the odes just offered clearly illustrate one outstanding and persistent feature of this density, that is, the variety of diverse sense impressions, often in swift succession, that are so frequently evoked. In the first quotation, for instance, just thirteen words, there are references to colour, shape, scent, coolness, and even an odd, but characteristic, suggestion of silence. For a more extensive example of this variety there is a notable passage in *Lamia*, where, in turn, all four senses of sight, smell, touch, and taste are most powerfully stimulated:

II.*173*   Of wealthy lustre was the banquet-room,
> Filled with pervading brilliance and perfume:
> Before each lucid panel fuming stood
> A censer fed with myrrh and spicèd wood,
> Each by a sacred tripod held aloft,
> Whose slender feet wide-swerved upon the soft
> Wool-woofèd carpets; fifty wreaths of smoke
> From fifty censers their light voyage took
> To the high roof, still mimicked as they rose
> Along the mirrored walls by twin-clouds odorous.
> Twelve spherèd tables, by silk seats ensphered,
> High as the level of a man's breast reared
> On libbard's paws, upheld the heavy gold
> Of cups and goblets, and the store thrice told
> Of Ceres' horn, and, in huge vessels, wine
> Come from the gloomy tun with merry shine.
> Thus loaded with a feast the tables stood,
> Each shrining in the midst the image of a God.

However, since Keats's poetic style, even over the short space of four years (1816–19), is in many important respects a developing and sometimes changing one, two reservations must be made about this density of his sensory imagery.

First, it is a quality rarely found in his earliest verse, even in 'I stood tip-toe upon a little hill' and *Sleep and Poetry*. It first emerges, unmistakably, in *Endymion*, though even then only sporadically, in passages like the odes to Pan and Bacchus, or in fairly numerous odd lines such as

> your swelling downs, where sweet air stirs
> Blue hare-bells lightly, and where prickly furze
> Buds lavish gold;

or again—

> A shout from the whole multitude arose,
> That lingered in the air like dying rolls
> Of abrupt thunder when Ionian shoals
> Of dolphins bob their noses through the brine.

Secondly, if it is the verse of 1819, poems like *The Eve of St Agnes*, the Odes, and *Lamia*, that displays this loaded density, in the first three hundred lines or so of *The Fall of Hyperion* Keats appears to be moving, perhaps under the unconscious influence of Dante (albeit through translation) towards a more chastened, less lavishly packed kind of expression. It is interesting, for instance, to compare the restrained lines,

> I looked thereon,
> And on the pavèd floor, where nigh were piled
> Faggots of cinnamon and many heaps
> Of other crispèd spice-wood,

with the elaborated description of the fuming censer in Lamia's banquet-room. However, there is no certainty that this change, such as it is, would have become permanent, since the newly written, introductory part of *The Fall of Hyperion* was immediately followed by the ode *To Autumn*, which stands out as a supreme example of sensuous abundance and density.

Another, more complex, answer to the question recently raised is the exceptional immediacy of Keats's sensory imagery—immediacy in the sense of the swiftness, directness, concentration and intensity with which it stimulates and controls the reader's response. This effect is produced partly by the acuteness (not necessarily freshness or originality) of the poet's perception, often of something imaginatively conceived, and partly through his choice of words and phrases (again, not necessarily unusual or surprising, though they may be) that have a maximum power to recreate that perception in the reader's mind.

Though a number of the quotations already given admirably exemplify this immediacy, some demonstration of one or two simple and striking examples may be helpful. For this purpose nothing is more revealing than a line from *The Eve of St Agnes*. As Madeline prepares for bed we are told how she 'Unclasps her warmèd jewels one by one'. Now the sensory qualities we normally associate with jewels are brilliance, colour, and, to some extent perhaps, their tactile properties. Keats might have positively suggested any one of these qualities by some epithet like 'brilliant', 'dazzling', etc., or he might have left the sensory association to our imagination as he does in the preceding line, 'Of all its wreathèd pearls her hair she frees'. In either case (and this is true of the different descriptive reference 'wreathèd') there would probably have been some remoteness of suggestive effect. As it is, the perception communicated through 'warmèd', that the jewels still retain something of the heat of Madeline's body, not only leads us to experience the jewels of this particular episode, instead of precious stones in general, but also brings us into imaginary physical contact with a living woman.

The intense immediacy of this line can be indicated in another way, which has its own special point of interest. In his first draft of the line, as we know from manuscript evidence, Keats wrote 'bosom jewels'. Now obviously 'bosom' would have been a reference of fairly strong sensuous and erotic impact. But how much more impressive in immediacy is Keats's substitution.

Though no absolute division can be made between a poet's perception and the registration of it in his communicating words (for often the two are simultaneous and inseparable), in this line from *The Eve of St Agnes* it is the empathic perception that vitally counts, not the word 'warmèd', an adequate but in itself undistinguished epithet. But on other occasions the immediacy we are discussing

33

does owe a great deal to the force—some would say, the magic—of the language itself and the sensitivity, conscious or not, of its selection. Consider, for one brief example, those lines in the *Ode to a Nightingale* in which Keats describes a wine-beaker as

> Full of the true, the blushful Hippocrene,
> With beaded bubbles winking at the brim.

Here surely, much of the immediacy comes from the peculiar potency of the beautifully chosen words 'blushful' and 'winking', along with the sound effect, the bubbling, that is suggested by the delicately explosive '*b*' alliteration. It was probably something of this kind of verbal artistry and verbal resourcefulness that Arnold had in mind when he spoke of Keats's Shakespearian 'rounded perfection and felicity' of expression.

In this exploitation of language to achieve a maximum immediacy of impression two particular features of Keats's style should be noticed, though admittedly neither of them is pervasively present. The first, sometimes discernible even in the early poems, is his instinctive bent for words of a strong physical impact, in their denotation and often in their sound as well. 'Glut' is a good example of such words, as it occurs in his description of the sea (*On the Sea*, lines 2 and 3), which

> with its mighty swell
> Gluts twice ten thousand caverns,

or in the line from the *Ode on Melancholy*—'Then glut thy sorrow on a morning rose'. 'Flush' (and its cognates) is another example, as in these lines from *Hyperion*:

> And all its curtains of aurorian clouds
> Flushed angerly...

> Flush every thing that hath a vermeil hue.

And there are other words of this type, like 'swell', 'ripe', 'blush', and 'cloy', that an attentive reader may add to the list.

The second feature of style contributing to both immediacy and concentration of effect is the occasional use of what is called synaesthesia. With Keats this usually takes the form of a close fusion of two different sense impressions, as in these lines from *Endymion* (III.798–800):

> Delicious symphonies, like airy flowers,
> Budded and swelled, and full-blown, shed full showers
> Of light, soft, unseen leaves of sounds divine.

This is an unusually sustained example of synaesthesia, but there are many smaller instances to be noticed, as when in *The Fall of Hyperion* he speaks of 'The shadows of melodious utterance' (line 6).

As had already been stated, the singular immediacy of Keats's imagery very rarely, if ever, depends on some highly unusual or startling effect—the effect, for instance, of Browning's description of a lump of lapis lazuli:

> Big as a Jew's head cut off at the nape,
> Blue as a vein o'er the Madonna's breast—

or of Hopkins's lines on Christ:

> And the azurous hung hills are his world-wielding
>   shoulder
> Majestic—as a stallion stalwart, very-violet-sweet!

What, very differently, Keats was aiming at, and constantly achieving from *Endymion* onwards, is perfectly defined in his letter to Taylor, his publisher, of 27 February 1818: 'I think poetry should surprise by a fine excess and not by singularity. It should strike the reader as a wording of his own highest thoughts and appear almost a remembrance'.

One final observation on this exceptionally rich and intense sensibility (perhaps sometimes cloyingly over-profuse and voluptuous) that Keats's poetry communicates. Because of certain marked inclinations—we might almost say, obsessions—it creates its own highly distinctive world of imagination, a specifically Keatsian world, which, once we know his work as a whole, is instantly and vividly recognizable in such a passage as this, from the sonnet 'After dark vapours':

The eyelids with the passing coolness play
Like rose leaves with the drip of summer rains.
The calmest thoughts come round us; as of leaves
    Budding, fruit ripening in stillness, autumn suns
Smiling at eve upon the quiet sheaves,
Sweet Sappho's cheek, a sleeping infant's breath,
    The gradual sand that through an hour-glass runs,
A woodland rivulet, a poet's death.

As detail after detail reveals, these lines could have been written by no other poet but Keats.

The world he creates, predominantly pleasurable, meridional rather than English, is most notably one of luxuriant, fructile vegetation of all kinds, in which we are often smothered or pillowed on grass and flowers. It is a world of dew, root-nourishing moisture, springs, streams and rivers; of bland air and breezes; of rondure and curving lines extending from inanimate objects like shells, pebbles, goblets, urns, and domed or vaulted spaces to curving branches and human shapes; of subdued, delicate, often remote sounds, hush and silence; of softness and coolness in innumerable and frequently most subtle forms; of swooning, dreaming, and sleeping. It is a world, too, that owes something to paintings like Titian's *Bacchus and Ariadne* and Claude's *Enchanted Castle*, which Keats knew directly or had seen in illustration, and also to other works of art.

But these briefly indicated outlines of the Keatsian world would take several pages to fill in, and any sensitive reader can readily trace out its fine and often singular detail for himself. The above quotation from 'After dark vapours' would serve as an excellent beginning.

Auditory Qualities

We have just spoken of sounds—and sometimes the hushing of them—as one of the main constituents of the Keatsian world. But obviously far more important than this for the sensuous richness of his poetry is the incomparable melodic beauty of the verse itself, the enchanting, often highly suggestive word music of controlled vowel and consonant texture that delights us whether the poems are being read aloud or whether we are listening to them with our inner ear.

As always in poetry, this word music is most effective when it is significantly suggestive or meaningful—when, that is to say, it directly contributes to whatever Keats is attempting to communicate. There are countless lines in his poetry, certainly from as early as *Endymion*, that have this compelling aural perfection, such a line for instance as 'Thy hair soft-lifted by the winnowing wind', in which the gentle stirring of wind on something as near weightless as human hair is exactly rendered by an unbroken succession of soft-sounding words and the marked iteration of the light '*i*' vowel in 'lifted' and 'winnowing',

Quite often this reinforcing integral onomatopoeia is sustained through extensive passages of writing. The first stanza of the *Ode to a Nightingale* furnishes an excellent example of such artistry. What, broadly speaking, Keats is attempting to communicate in this stanza is the contrast between his own benumbed, suspended sensation, shot through with some pain, and the serene, unencumbered joyousness of the nightingale and its song. The changing melodic pattern of vowels and consonants perfectly matches this contrast. The sound of the first four lines, dominated by weighty monosyllabic words and by half-rhyming combinations of '*m*' and '*n*' consonants with some other consonant in 'numbness', 'sense', 'hemlock', 'drunk', 'emptied', and 'sunk', produces a dulled, clogged, slightly monotonous effect, momentarily broken by the sharp, stabbing '*a*' vowel of 'aches', 'pains', and 'drains':

> My heart aches, and a drowsy numbness pains
>> My sense, as though of hemlock I had drunk,
> Or emptied some dull opiate to the drains
> One minute past, and Lethe-wards had sunk . . .

Then, through two neutral, modulatory lines, there emerges a strikingly different combination of clean, ringing, often intense sounds (notably in the open '*o*' vowel of 'melodious', 'shadows', and 'throated', and the '*e*' of 'trees', 'beechen green', and 'ease'):

> That thou, light-wingèd Dryad of the trees,

37

In some melodious plot
Of beechen green, and shadows numberless,
Singest of summer in full-throated ease.

Any attempt at descriptive analysis will no doubt fumble;
but there can be no question that the melodic texture of
the first four lines of this stanza admirably suggest the
'drowsy numbness' that Keats is describing, just as that
of the last four suggests, no less impressively, the 'full-
throated ease' of the nightingale's song.

However, there are also many passages in Keats's poetry
where the word music merely adds to the sensuous beauty
and richness of the imagery, with little or no onomatopoeic
effect. The famous 'casement' stanza in *The Eve of St Agnes*
is a good example of such melodic embellishment:

A c[1]asement h[2]igh and triple-arched there was,

All garlanded with carven imageries

Of fruits, and flowers, and bunches of knot-grass,

And d[2]iamonded with p[1]anes of qu[1]aint dev[2]ice

Innumerable of st[1]ains and splendid d[2]yes,

As are the t[2]iger-moth's deep-damasked wings;

And in the midst, 'mong thousand heraldries,

And tw[2]il[2]ight s[1]aints, and dim emblaz[1]onings,

A shielded scutcheon blushed with blood of queens

and kings.

Here the melodic beauty of the writing is chiefly created by
the recurrent, chiming interchange of the '*a*' and '*i*' vowels
marked above; but neither this effect nor the numerous
subsidiary ones, like the repeated sounds in 'arched',
'garlanded', 'carven', 'grass', and in 'scutcheon', 'blushed',

'blood', or the '*m*', '*d*', and '*s*' alliterations, are particularly suggestive in any onomatopoeic way. The ear is delighted by the complex and varied repetitions of sound.

Space will not allow any detailed examination of this verbal music (which would of course include rhythmic effects too) that contributes so much to the sensuous opulence and appeal of Keats's verse. But at least one further point must be made. The kind of melodic pattern that has just been demonstrated in the 'casement' stanza, the combining and interchanging of two or three dominent sounds, is by no means the only one that Keats utilizes. For instance, as an examination of the hymn to Pan in *Endymion* and of the first stanza of the ode *To Autumn* will show, a richness of melodic texture is often achieved by continuous variations, by one prominent sound succeeding upon another to produce numerous local or incidental effects, sometimes onomatopoeic, sometimes merely euphonious. Thus, in the opening lines of *To Autumn*,

> Season of mists and mellow fruitfulness,
> Close bosom friend of the maturing sun,
> Conspiring with him how to load and bless—

there is a marked '*m*' alliteration and the no less strongly echoed 'o' vowel of 'mellow', 'close', and 'load'. But both the alliteration and the assonance are limited to these three lines, and in the continuation of the stanza they are replaced by others.

As no doubt most of this word music is appreciated by the reader subconsciously, so Keats probably created much of it in a subconscious way. At the same time there are strong reasons for believing that the music of his poetry was also, to a considerable extent, a product of what in his sonnet 'If by dull rhymes' he called an 'ear industrious'—industrious with varying degrees of conscious deliberation. There are one or two remarks of his own that reveal an alert awareness of the possibilities of aural suggestion, as when, in a marginal note on *Paradise Lost*, he speaks of 'a cool pleasure in the very sound of *vale*'; and though neither coolness nor pleasure is the effect of his own employment of the word in the first line of *Hyperion*–'Deep in the shady sadness of a vale'–

it certainly produces an appropriate coldness, or chilliness, in the initial setting of the poem. Again, there is the testimony of his friend Bailey, who, in a letter to Monckton Milnes, Keats's first biographer, wrote: 'One of his favourite topics of discourse was the principle of melody in verse, upon which he had his own notions.' Unfortunately Bailey's account of those notions is brief and rather obscure. But there is one other significant sentence in his letter that is worth quoting: 'I remember his telling me that, had he studied music, he had some notions of the combinations of sounds, by which he thought he could have done something as original as his poetry.'

However, the most convincing proof of Keats's 'ear industrious' is to be found in the tentative drafts, alterations, and revisions that so many of the manuscripts of his poems reveal. When we examine these changes, we discover that a high proportion of them involve some sound effect, and that in most instances the final version achieves a definite melodic improvement. Consider, for instance, Keats's first draft of the 'casement' stanza in *The Eve of St Agnes*:

A C̲asement ~~ach'd~~ tripple archd and d̲iamonded

With many coloured glass fronted the moon

       were of
In midst ~~of which~~ a shilded scutcheon shed

High blushing gules; ~~upon she Kneeled saintly down~~

And inly pr̲ayed for gr̲ace and heavenly boon

The blood-red gules fell on her silver cross

And ~~her~~ wh̲itest hands devout.

Obviously there are several reasons to account for the immense superiority of the final version; but among them nothing is more immediately evident than the greater musical beauty that Keats ultimately achieved—after considerable work on the stanza, it should be added.

This continuous striving after verbal perfection, musical and otherwise, that the manuscript evidence so clearly demonstrates, is one outstanding manifestation of the artistry that went to the making of Keats's poetry. Time and time again, as with those flawless, magical lines,

> Charmed magic casements, opening on the foam
> Of perilous seas in fairy lands forlorn,

perfection was attained only after much pondering and revision. But there are other no less convincing demonstrations, which cannot be elaborated here, of the artistry that shapes his work, notably the reflections on poetic style that abound in his letters, and, right from the start, his continual experimentation—with the pentameter couplet and blank verse, with different types of sonnet, with various metrical forms for narrative verse, and so on.

In an often quoted phrase in one of his letters he once urged Shelley to be 'more of an artist', adding a further pointed remark about 'discipline'. Such advice was hardly tactful. But it came from the heart; and no one among the Romantic poets was more entitled to voice it.

Chronology of Keats's Life

1795 Born 31 October at Finsbury, London, the first of four surviving children. His father, Thomas, managed the prosperous horse-hiring business of his father-in-law, John Jennings. (George Keats b.1797; Thomas b.1799; Frances Mary [Fanny] b.1803.)

1803–11 Attends, with George and later Tom, the Rev. John Clarke's school at Enfield.

1804 His father killed in a fall from his horse. His mother remarries.

1804–10 Lives with his grandmother, Mrs Jennings, at Edmonton.

1810 Death of his mother. Mrs Jennings appoints Abbey and Saudell as future guardians for the Keats children.

1811 Apprenticed to Thomas Hammond, a surgeon at Edmonton.

1814 Death of Mrs Jennings.
Writes his first poem, an 'Imitation of Spenser'.

1815 1 October, enters Guy's Hospital as a student.

1816 His first published poem, the sonnet 'O Solitude!', appears in Leigh Hunt's *Examiner*.
25 July qualifies as an apothecary.
On holiday at Margate, August–September. After his return continues for a time to work as a dresser at Guy's Hospital.
October. Writes his sonnet 'On First Looking into Chapman's Homer'.
November. Takes lodgings with George and Tom at 76 Cheapside.
Introduced to Leigh Hunt, Benjamin Haydon, J. H. Reynolds.

1817 3 March publishes his first book, *Poems*.
Moves with George and Tom into new lodgings at 1, Well Walk, Hampstead.
Composition of *Endymion*, April–November.
Visits the Isle of Wight in April, then moves on to

Margate for two or three weeks. In September stays with Benjamin Bailey at Oxford.

1818 Attends Hazlitt's 'Lectures on the English Poets', Jan–March. Composition of *Isabella*, February (or March) to 27 April.

Stays with Tom at Teignmouth, March to early May.

May. *Endymion* published.

June. George and Georgiana, his newly married wife, emigrate to America. With Charles Brown, starts his walking tour through the Lake District and Scotland. Returns in poor physical condition, especially with throat trouble, 18 August.

Composition of the first two Books of *Hyperion*, probably Sept–Oct.

Nurses Tom, who dies with consumption 1 Dec. Probably meets Fanny Brawne for the first time in mid-November.

Accepts Brown's offer to share his half of Wentworth Place, Hampstead.

1819 Visits Chichester and Bedhampton with Brown, January.

Composition of *The Eve of St Agnes*, 18 January to 2 February; of the Odes, late April–May;

Stays with James Rice at Shanklin, Isle of Wight, July. At Winchester (part of the time with Brown), August–October.

Composition of *Lamia*, late June to early September; of *The Fall of Hyperion*, July to 21 September; of the ode '*To Autumn*', on or about 19 September.

October. Living again with Brown at Wentworth Place.

Becomes engaged to Fanny Brawne, November or December.

Serious throat trouble. ,

1820 3 February severe haemorrhage attack.

Publication of *Lamia, Isabella, etc.* (the 1820 *Poems*), July.

Accompanied by Joseph Severn, sails from Gravesend to Italy, 18 September. Reaches Naples 21 October, but detained in quarantine till 31

October.

Writes his last known letter from Rome, 30 November.

1821 23 February dies in Rome. Buried in the English cemetery, 26 February.

Joy and Sorrow

Endymion: a Poetic Romance

from Book IV

There lies a den,
Beyond the seeming confines of the space
Made for the soul to wander in and trace
Its own existence, of remotest glooms.
Dark regions are around it, where the tombs
Of buried griefs the spirit sees, but scarce
One hour doth linger weeping, for the pierce
Of new-born woe it feels more inly smart.
520 And in these regions many a venomed dart
At random flies; they are the proper home
Of every ill; the man is yet to come
Who hath not journeyed in this native hell.
But few have ever felt how calm and well
Sleep may be had in that deep den of all.
There anguish does not sting, nor pleasure pall.
Woe-hurricanes beat ever at the gate,
Yet all is still within and desolate.
Beset with plainful gusts, within ye hear
530 No sound so loud as when on curtained bier
The death-watch tick is stifled. Enter none
Who strive therefore—on the sudden it is won.
Just when the sufferer begins to burn,
Then it is free to him, and from an urn,
Still fed by melting ice, he takes a draught—
Young Semele such richness never quaffed
In her maternal longing! Happy gloom!
Dark paradise! Where pale becomes the bloom
Of health by due; where silence dreariest
540 Is most articulate; where hopes infest;
Where those eyes are the brightest far that keep
Their lids shut longest in a dreamless sleep.
O happy spirit-home! O wondrous soul!
Pregnant with such a den to save the whole
In thine own depth. Hail, gentle Carian!

For never since thy griefs and woes began
Hast thou felt so content. A grievous feud
Hath led thee to this Cave of Quietude.

'In drear-nighted December'

I

In drear-nighted December,
 Too happy, happy tree,
Thy branches ne'er remember
 Their green felicity.
The north cannot undo them
With a sleety whistle through them,
Nor frozen thawings glue them
 From budding at the prime.

II

In drear-nighted December,
 Too happy, happy brook,
Thy bubblings ne'er remember
 Apollo's summer look.
But with a sweet forgetting,
They stay their crystal fretting,
Never, never petting
 About the frozen time.

III

Ah, would 'twere so with many
 A gentle girl and boy!
But were there ever any
 Writhed not of passèd joy?
The feel of not to feel it,
When there is none to heal it,
Nor numbed sense to steel it,
 Was never said in rhyme.

On Sitting Down to Read
King Lear Once Again

O golden-tongued Romance, with serene lute!
    Fair plumèd Siren, Queen of far-away!
    Leave melodizing on this wintry day,
Shut up thine olden pages, and be mute.
Adieu! For, once again, the fierce dispute
    Betwixt damnation and impassioned clay
    Must I burn through, once more humbly assay
The bitter-sweet of this Shakespearian fruit.
Chief Poet, and ye clouds of Albion,
    Begetters of our deep eternal theme!
When through the old oak forest I am gone,
    Let me not wander in a barren dream,
But, when I am consumèd in the fire,
Give me new Phoenix wings to fly at my desire.

'When I have fears...'

When I have fears that I may cease to be
   Before my pen has gleaned my teeming brain,
Before high-pilèd books, in charactery,
   Hold like rich garners the full ripened grain;
When I behold, upon the night's starred face,
   Huge cloudy symbols of a high romance,
And think that I may never live to trace
   Their shadows with the magic hand of chance;
And when I feel, fair creature of an hour,
10   That I shall never look upon thee more,
Never have relish in the fairy power
   Of unreflecting love; then on the shore
Of the wide world I stand alone and think
Till love and fame to nothingness do sink.

To J.H. Reynolds, Esq.

Dear Reynolds, as last night I lay in bed,
There came before my eyes that wonted thread
Of shapes, and shadows, and remembrances,
That every other minute vex and please.
Things all disjointed come from north and south,
Two witch's eyes above a cherub's mouth,
Voltaire with casque and shield and habergeon,
And Alexander with his night-cap on,
Old Socrates a-tying his cravat,
10 And Hazlitt playing with Miss Edgeworth's cat,
And Junius Brutus pretty well so so,
Making the best of his way towards Soho.
    Few are there who escape these visitings—
Perhaps one or two, whose lives have patient wings,
And through whose curtains peeps no hellish nose,
No wild boar tushes, and no mermaid's toes;
But flowers bursting out with lusty pride,
And young Aeolian harps personified;
Some, Titian colours touched into real life.
20 The sacrifice goes on; the pontiff knife
Gleams in the sun, the milk-white heifer lows,
The pipes go shrilly, the libation flows;
A white sail shews above the green-head cliff,
Moves round the point, and throws her anchor stiff.
The mariners join hymn with those on land.
You know the Enchanted Castle—it doth stand
Upon a rock on the border of a lake.
Nested in trees, which all do seem to shake
From some old magic like Urganda's sword.
30 O Phoebus, that I had thy sacred word
To show this castle in fair dreaming wise
Unto my friend, while sick and ill he lies.
    You know it well enough, where it doth seem
A mossy place, a Merlin's Hall, a dream.
You know the clear lake, and the little isles,
The mountains blue, and cold, near-neighbour rills.
All which elsewhere are but half animate

Here do they look alive to love and hate,
To smiles and frowns. They seem a lifted mound
40 Above some giant, pulsing underground.
    Part of the building was a chosen see
Built by a banished Santon of Chaldee;
The other part two thousand years from him
Was built by Cuthbert de Saint Aldebrim;
Then there's a little wing, far from the sun,
Built by a Lapland witch turned maudlin nun—
And many other juts of agèd stone
Founded with many a mason-devil's groan.
    The doors all look as if they oped themselves,
50 The windows as if latched by fays and elves—
And from them comes a silver flash of light
As from the westward of a summer's night;
Or like a beauteous woman's large blue eyes
Gone mad through olden songs and poesies.
    See what is coming from the distance dim!
A golden galley all in silken trim.
Three rows of oars are lightening moment-whiles
Into the verdurous bosoms of those isles.
Towards the shade under the castle wall
60 It comes in silence—now tis hidden all.
The clarion sounds, and from a postern grate
An echo of sweet music doth create
A fear in the poor herdsman who doth bring
His beasts to trouble the enchanted spring.
He tells of the sweet music and the spot
To all his friends—and they believe him not.
    Oh, that our dreamings all of sleep or wake
Would all their colours from the sunset take,
From something of material sublime,
70 Rather than shadow our own soul's daytime
In the dark void of night. For in the world
We jostle . . . but my flag is not unfurled
On the admiral staff—and to philosophize
I dare not yet. Oh, never will the prize,
High reason and the lore of good and ill,
Be my award. Things cannot to the will
Be settled, but they tease us out of thought.
Or is it that imagination brought
Beyond its proper bound, yet still confined,

80 Lost in a sort of Purgatory blind,
    Cannot refer to any standard law
    Of either earth or heaven?
                            It is a flaw
    In happiness to see beyond our bourn –
    It forces us in summer skies to mourn;
    It spoils the singing of the nightingale.
      Dear Reynolds, I have a mysterious tale
    And cannot speak it. The first page I read
    Upon a lampit rock of green sea weed
    Among the breakers. 'Twas a quiet eve;
90 The rocks were silent; the wide sea did weave
    An untumultuous fringe of silver foam
    Along the flat brown sand. I was at home,
    And should have been most happy, but I saw
    Too far into the sea – where every maw
    The greater on the less feeds evermore . . .
    But I saw too distinct into the core
    Of an eternal fierce destruction,
    And so from happiness I far was gone.
    Still am I sick of it; and though today
100 I've gathered young spring-leaves, and flowers gay
    Of periwinkle and wild strawberry,
    Still do I that most fierce destruction see:
    The shark at savage prey, the hawk at pounce,
    The gentle robin, like a pard or ounce,
    Ravening a worm. . . . Away ye horrid moods,
    Moods of one's mind! You know I hate them well,
    You know I'd sooner be a clapping bell
    To some Kamschatkan missionary church,
    Than with these horrid moods be left in lurch.
110 Do you get health – and Tom the same – I'll dance,
    And from detested moods in new romance
    Take refuge. . . . Of bad lines a centaine dose
    Is sure enough, and so 'here follows prose'.

PLATE I   *Claude,*
Landscape with Father of Psyche
"*To what green altar, O mysterious priest,*
Lead'st thou that heifer lowing at the skies?"
(*Grecian Urn*)
A characteristically graceful piece of pictorial
classicism that Keats admired.
(*By courtesy of the British Museum*)

PLATE 2 *Claude*, The Enchanted Castle
"You know the Enchanted Castle—it doth stand
Upon a rock, on the border of a Lake."
(*To J. H. Reynolds*)
*Psyche, frequently cited by Keats, here sits
deserted by Cupid on a rock in the foreground.*
(*By courtesy of the British Museum*)

On Visiting the Tomb of Burns

The town, the churchyard, and the setting sun,
　　The clouds, the trees, the rounded hills all seem,
　　Though beautiful, cold—strange—as in a dream
I dreamèd long ago. Now new begun
The short-lived, paly summer is but won
　　From winter's ague for one hour's gleam.
　　Through sapphire warm their stars do never beam;
All is cold beauty; pain is never done;
For who has mind to relish, Minos-wise,
10　　The real of beauty, free from that dead hue
　　　Sickly imagination and sick pride
　　　　Cast wan upon it? Burns! With honour due
　　　　I have oft honoured thee. Great shadow, hide
Thy face; I sin against thy native skies.

Lines Written in the Highlands
after a Visit to Burns's Country

There is a joy in footing slow across a silent plain
Where patriot battle has been fought, where glory had
    the gain;
There is a pleasure on the heath where Druids old have
    been,
Where mantles grey have rustled by and swept the
    nettles green;
There is a joy in every spot made known by times of old,
New to the feet, although the tale a hundred times be
    told.
There is a deeper joy than all, more solemn in the heart,
More parching to the tongue than all, of more divine a
    smart,
When weary feet forget themselves upon a pleasant turf,
10 Upon hot sand, or flinty road, or sea-shore iron scurf,
Toward the castle or the cot where long ago was born
One who was great through mortal days and died of
    fame unshorn.
Light heatherbells may tremble then, but they are far
    away;
Wood-lark may sing from sandy fern, the sun may hear
    his lay;
Runnels may kiss the grass on shelves and shallows clear,
But their low voices are not heard though come on
    travels drear;
Blood-red the sun may set behind black mountain peaks;
Blue tides may sluice and drench their time in caves and
    weedy creeks;
Eagles may seem to sleep wingwide upon the air;
20 Ring-doves may fly convulsed across to some high-
    cedared lair;
But the forgotten eye is still fast wedded to the ground –
As palmer's that with weariness mid-desert shrine hath
    found.
At such a time the soul's a child, in childhood is the
    brain;

Forgotten is the worldly heart—alone, it beats in vain.
Aye, if a madman could have leave to pass a healthful
    day
To tell his forehead's swoon and faint when first began
    decay,
He might make tremble many a man whose spirit had
    gone forth
To find a bard's low cradle-place about the silent north!
Scanty the hour and few the steps beyond the bourn of
    care,
30 Beyond the sweet and bitter world—beyond it unaware;
Scanty the hour and few the steps, because a longer stay
Would bar return, and make a man forget his mortal
    way.
Oh, horrible to lose the sight of well-remembered face,
Of brother's eyes, of sister's brow, constant to every place,
Filling the air, as on we move, with portraiture intense,
More warm than those heroic tints that fill a painter's
    sense
When shapes of old come striding by and visages of old,
Locks shining black, hair scanty grey, and passions
    manifold.
No, no, that horror cannot be, for at the cable's length
40 Man feels the gentle anchor pull and gladdens in its
    strength—
One hour, half-idiot, he stands by mossy waterfall,
But in the very next he reads his soul's memorial.
He reads it on the mountain's height, where chance he
    may sit down
Upon rough marble diadem, that hill's eternal crown.
Yet be the anchor e'er so fast, room is there for a prayer
That man may never lose his mind on mountains bleak
    and bare;
That he may stray league after league some great
    birthplace to find,
And keep his vision clear from speck, his inward sight
    unblind.

'Welcome joy and welcome sorrow'

Welcome joy and welcome sorrow,
　　Lethe's weed and Hermes' feather;
Come today and come tomorrow,
　　I do love you both together!
　　I love to mark sad faces in fair weather,
And hear a merry laugh amid the thunder.
　　Fair and foul I love together:
Meadows sweet where flames burn under,
And a giggle at a wonder;
10　Visage sage at pantomime;
Funeral and steeple-chime;
Infant playing with a skull;
Morning fair and shipwrecked hull;
Nightshade with the woodbine kissing;
Serpents in red roses hissing;
Cleopatra regal-dressed
With the aspic at her breast;
Dancing music, music sad,
Both together, sane and mad.
20　Muses bright and Muses pale,
Sombre Saturn, Momus hale,
Muses bright and Muses pale,
Bare your faces of the veil!
Laugh and sigh, and laugh again!
Oh, the sweetness of the pain!
Let me see and let me write
Of the day and of the night—
Both together. Let me slake
All my thirst for sweet heart-ache!
30　Let my bower be of yew,
Interwreathed with myrtles new,
Pines and lime-trees full in bloom,
And my couch a low grass tomb.

Hyperion

Book I

Deep in the shady sadness of a vale
Far sunken from the healthy breath of morn,
Far from the fiery noon, and eve's one star,
Sat grey-haired Saturn, quiet as a stone,
Still as the silence round about his lair;
Forest on forest hung about his head
Like cloud on cloud. No stir of air was there,
Not so much life as on a summer's day
Robs not one light seed from the feathered grass,
10   But where the dead leaf fell, there did it rest.
A stream went voiceless by, still deadened more
By reason of his fallen divinity
Spreading a shade; the Naiad 'mid her reeds
Pressed her cold finger closer to her lips.

    Along the margin-sand large foot-marks went,
No further than to where his feet had strayed,
And slept there since. Upon the sodden ground
His old right hand lay nerveless, listless, dead,
Unsceptred; and his realmless eyes were closed,
20   While his bowed head seemed listening to the Earth,
His ancient mother, for some comfort yet.

    It seemed no force could wake him from his place;
But there came one, who with a kindred hand
Touched his wide shoulders, after bending low
With reverence, though to one who knew it not.
She was a Goddess of the infant world;
By her in stature the tall Amazon
Had stood a pigmy's height; she would have ta'en
Achilles by the hair and bent his neck,
30   Or with a finger stayed Ixion's wheel.
Her face was large as that of Memphian sphinx,
Pedestalled haply in a palace court,

When sages looked to Egypt for their lore.
But oh, how unlike marble was that face!
How beautiful, if sorrow had not made
Sorrow more beautiful than Beauty's self.
There was a listening fear in her regard,
As if calamity had but begun;
As if the vanward clouds of evil days
40 Had spent their malice, and the sullen rear
Was with its storèd thunder labouring up.
One hand she pressed upon that aching spot
Where beats the human heart, as if just there,
Though an immortal, she felt cruel pain;
The other upon Saturn's bended neck
She laid, and to the level of his ear
Leaning with parted lips some words she spake
In solemn tenour and deep organ tone—
Some mourning words, which in our feeble tongue
50 Would come in these like accents (O how frail
To that large utterance of the early Gods!):
'Saturn, look up!—though wherefore, poor old King?
I have no comfort for thee, no, not one:
I cannot say, "Oh, wherefore sleepest thou?"
For heaven is parted from thee, and the earth
Knows thee not, thus afflicted, for a God;
And ocean too, with all its solemn noise,
Has from thy sceptre passed; and all the air
Is emptied of thine hoary majesty.
60 Thy thunder, conscious of the new command,
Rumbles reluctant o'er our fallen house;
And thy sharp lightning in unpractised hands
Scorches and burns our once serene domain.
O aching time! O moments big as years!
All as ye pass swell out the monstrous truth,
And press it so upon our weary griefs
That unbelief has not a space to breathe.
Saturn, sleep on! Oh, thoughtless, why did I
Thus violate thy slumbrous solitude?
70 Why should I ope thy melancholy eyes?
Saturn, sleep on, while at thy feet I weep!'

As when, upon a trancèd summer night,
Those green-robed senators of mighty woods,
Tall oaks, branch-charmèd by the earnest stars,
Dream, and so dream all night without a stir,
Save from one gradual solitary gust

Which comes upon the silence, and dies off,
As if the ebbing air had but one wave;
So came these words and went, the while in tears
80 She touched her fair large forehead to the ground,
Just where her falling hair might be outspread
A soft and silken mat for Saturn's feet.
One moon, with alteration slow, had shed
Her silver seasons four upon the night,
And still these two were postured motionless,
Like natural sculpture in cathedral cavern:
The frozen God still couchant on the earth,
And the sad Goddess weeping at his feet;
Until at length old Saturn lifted up
90 His faded eyes, and saw his kingdom gone,
And all the gloom and sorrow of the place,
And that fair kneeling Goddess; and then spake,
As with a palsied tongue, and while his beard
Shook horrid with such aspen malady:
'O tender spouse of gold Hyperion,
Thea, I feel thee ere I see thy face;
Look up, and let me see our doom in it;
Look up, and tell me if this feeble shape
Is Saturn's; tell me, if thou hear'st the voice
100 Of Saturn; tell me, if this wrinkling brow,
Naked and bare of its great diadem,
Peers like the front of Saturn. Who had power
To make me desolate? Whence came the strength?
How was it nurtured to such bursting forth,
While Fate seemed strangled in my nervous grasp?
But it is so; and I am smothered up,
And buried from all godlike exercise
Of influence benign on planets pale,
Of admonitions to the winds and seas,
110 Of peaceful sway above man's harvesting,
And all those acts which Deity supreme
Doth ease its heart of love in.
                                    I am gone
Away from my own bosom; I have left
My strong identity, my real self,
Somewhere between the throne and where I sit
Here on this spot of earth. Search, Thea, search!
Open thine eyes eterne, and sphere them round
Upon all space—space starred, and lorn of light;
Space regioned with life-air, and barren void;
120 Spaces of fire, and all the yawn of hell.

Search, Thea, search! And tell me, if thou seest
A certain shape or shadow, making way
With wings or chariot fierce to repossess
A heaven he lost erewhile: it must—it must
Be of ripe progress: Saturn must be King.
Yes, there must be a golden victory;
There must be Gods thrown down, and trumpets blown
Of triumph calm, and hymns of festival
Upon the gold clouds metropolitan,
130 Voices of soft proclaim, and silver stir
Of strings in hollow shells; and there shall be
Beautiful things made new, for the surprise
Of the sky-children. I will give command:
Thea! Thea! Thea! Where is Saturn?'

This passion lifted him upon his feet,
And made his hands to struggle in the air,
His Druid locks to shake and ooze with sweat,
His eyes to fever out, his voice to cease.
He stood, and heard not Thea's sobbing deep;
140 A little time, and then again he snatched
Utterance thus: 'But cannot I create?
Cannot I form? Cannot I fashion forth
Another world, another universe,
To overbear and crumble this to naught?
Where is another chaos? Where?' That word
Found way unto Olympus, and made quake
The rebel three. Thea was startled up,
And in her bearing was a sort of hope,
As thus she quick-voiced spake, yet full of awe:
150 'This cheers our fallen house. Come to our friends,
O Saturn, come away, and give them heart!
I know the covert, for thence came I hither.'
Thus brief; then with beseeching eyes she went
With backward footing through the shade a space;
He followed, and she turned to lead the way
Through agèd boughs, that yielded like the mist
Which eagles cleave upmounting from their nest.

Meanwhile in other realms big tears were shed,
More sorrow like to this, and such-like woe,
160 Too huge for mortal tongue or pen of scribe.
The Titans fierce, self-hid, or prison-bound,
Groaned for the old allegiance once more,
And listened in sharp pain for Saturn's voice.

But one of the whole mammoth-brood still kept
His sovereignty, and rule, and majesty—
Blazing Hyperion on his orbèd fire
Still sat, still snuffed the incense, teeming up
From man to the sun's God—yet unsecure:
For as among us mortals omens drear
170 Fright and perplex, so also shuddered he—
Not at dog's howl, or gloom-bird's hated screech,
Or the familiar visiting of one
Upon the first toll of his passing-bell,
Or prophesyings of the midnight lamp;
But horrors portioned to a giant nerve
Oft made Hyperion ache. His palace bright,
Bastioned with pyramids of glowing gold,
And touched with shade of bronzèd obelisks,
Glared a blood-red through all its thousand courts,
180 Arches, and domes, and fiery galleries;
And all its curtains of aurorian clouds
Flushed angerly, while sometimes eagle's wings,
Unseen before by Gods or wondering men,
Darkened the place, and neighing steeds were heard,
Not heard before by Gods or wondering men.
Also, when he would taste the spicy wreaths
Of incense, breathed aloft from sacred hills,
Instead of sweets, his ample palate took
Savour of poisonous brass and metal sick.
190 And so, when harboured in the sleepy west,
After the full completion of fair day,
For rest divine upon exalted couch
And slumber in the arms of melody,
He paced away the pleasant hours of ease
With stride colossal, on from hall to hall;
While far within each aisle and deep recess
His wingèd minions in close clusters stood,
Amazed and full of fear; like anxious men
Who on wide plains gather in panting troops,
200 When earthquakes jar their battlements and towers.
Even now, while Saturn, roused from icy trance,
Went step for step with Thea through the woods,
Hyperion, leaving twilight in the rear,
Came slope upon the threshold of the west;
Then, as was wont, his palace-door flew ope
In smoothest silence, save what solemn tubes,
Blown by the serious Zephyrs, gave of sweet

And wandering sounds, slow-breathèd melodies—
And like a rose in vermeil tint and shape,
210   In fragrance soft, and coolness to the eye,
That inlet to severe magnificence
Stood full blown, for the God to enter in.

He entered, but he entered full of wrath;
His flaming robes streamed out beyond his heels,
And gave a roar, as if of earthly fire,
That scared away the meek ethereal Hours
And made their dove-wings tremble. On he flared,
From stately nave to nave, from vault to vault,
Through bowers of fragrant and enwreathèd light,
220   And diamond-pavèd lustrous long arcades,
Until he reached the great main cupola.
There standing fierce beneath he stamped his foot,
And from the basements deep to the high towers
Jarred his own golden region; and before
The quavering thunder thereupon had ceased,
His voice leapt out, despite of godlike curb,
To this result: 'O dreams of day and night!
O monstrous forms! O effigies of pain!
O spectres busy in a cold, cold gloom!
230   O lank-eared phantoms of black-weeded pools!
Why do I know ye? Why have I seen ye? Why
Is my eternal essence thus distraught
To see and to behold these horrors new?
Saturn is fallen, am I too to fall?
Am I to leave this haven of my rest,
This cradle of my glory, this soft clime,
This calm luxuriance of blissful light,
These crystalline pavilions and pure fanes
Of all my lucent empire? It is left
240   Deserted, void, nor any haunt of mine.
The blaze, the splendour and the symmetry
I cannot see–but darkness, death and darkness.
Even here, into my centre of repose,
The shady visions come to domineer,
Insult, and blind, and stifle up my pomp.
Fall? No, by Tellus and her briny robes!
Over the fiery frontier of my realms
I will advance a terrible right arm
Shall scare that infant thunderer, rebel Jove,
250   And bid old Saturn take his throne again.'
He spake, and ceased, the while a heavier threat

Held struggle with his throat but came not forth;
For as in theatres of crowded men
Hubbub increases more they call out 'Hush!',
So at Hyperion's words the phantoms pale
Bestirred themselves, thrice horrible and cold;
And from the mirrored level where he stood
A mist arose, as from a scummy marsh.
At this, through all his bulk an agony
260 Crept gradual, from the feet unto the crown,
Like a lithe serpent vast and muscular
Making slow way, with head and neck convulsed
From over-strainèd might. Released, he fled
To the eastern gates, and full six dewy hours
Before the dawn in season due should blush,
He breathed fierce breath against the sleepy portals,
Cleared them of heavy vapours, burst them wide
Suddenly on the ocean's chilly streams.
The planet orb of fire, whereon he rode
270 Each day from east to west the heavens through,
Spun round in sable curtaining of clouds;
Not therefore veilèd quite, blindfold, and hid,
But ever and anon the glancing spheres,
Circles, and arcs, and broad-belting colure,
Glowed through, and wrought upon the muffling dark
Sweet-shapèd lightnings from the nadir deep
Up to the zenith—hieroglyphics old
Which sages and keen-eyed astrologers
Then living on the earth with labouring thought
280 Won from the gaze of many centuries—
Now lost, save what we find on remnants huge
Of stone, or marble swart, their import gone,
Their wisdom long since fled. Two wings this orb
Possessed for glory, two fair argent wings,
Ever exalted at the God's approach;
And now from forth the gloom their plumes immense
Rose, one by one, till all outspreaded were;
While still the dazzling globe maintained eclipse,
Awaiting for Hyperion's command.
290 Fain would he have commanded, fain took throne
And bid the day begin, if but for change.
He might not. No, though a primeval God,
The sacred seasons might not be disturbed.
Therefore the operations of the dawn
Stayed in their birth, even as here 'tis told.

Those silver wings expanded sisterly,
Eager to sail their orb; the porches wide
Opened upon the dusk demesnes of night;
And the bright Titan, frenzied with new woes,
300   Unused to bend, by hard compulsion bent
His spirit to the sorrow of the time;
And all along a dismal rack of clouds,
Upon the boundaries of day and night,
He stretched himself in grief and radiance faint.
There as he lay, the heaven with its stars
Looked down on him with pity, and the voice
Of Coelus, from the universal space,
Thus whispered low and solemn in his ear:
'O brightest of my children dear, earth-born
310   And sky-engendered, son of mysteries
All unrevealèd even to the powers
Which met at thy creating; at whose joys
And palpitations sweet, and pleasures soft,
I, Coelus, wonder how they came and whence;
And at the fruits thereof what shapes they be,
Distinct, and visible—symbols divine,
Manifestations of that beauteous life
Diffused unseen throughout eternal space.
Of these new-formed art thou, O brightest child!
320   Of these, thy brethren and the Goddesses!
There is sad feud among ye, and rebellion
Of son against his sire. I saw him fall,
I saw my first-born tumbled from his throne!
To me his arms were spread, to me his voice
Found way from forth the thunders round his head!
Pale wox I, and in vapours hid my face.
Art thou, too, near such doom? Vague fear there is:
For I have seen my sons most unlike Gods.
Divine ye were created, and divine
330   In sad demeanour, solemn, undisturbed,
Unruffled, like high Gods, ye lived and ruled.
Now I behold in you fear, hope, and wrath;
Actions of rage and passion—even as
I see them, on the mortal world beneath,
In men who die. This is the grief, O son,
Sad sign of ruin, sudden dismay, and fall!
Yet do thou strive; as thou art capable,
As thou canst move about, an evident God,
And canst oppose to each malignant hour

340 Ethereal presence. I am but a voice;
My life is but the life of winds and tides,
No more than winds and tides can I avail.
But thou canst. Be thou therefore in the van
Of circumstance; yea, seize the arrow's barb
Before the tense string murmur. To the earth!
For there thou wilt find Saturn, and his woes.
Meantime I will keep watch on thy bright sun,
And of thy seasons be a careful nurse.'
Ere half this region-whisper had come down,
350 Hyperion arose, and on the stars
Lifted his curvèd lids, and kept them wide
Until it ceased; and still he kept them wide;
And still they were the same bright, patient stars.
Then with a slow incline of his broad breast,
Like to a diver in the pearly seas,
Forward he stooped over the airy shore,
And plunged all noiseless into the deep night.

Book II

Just at the self-same beat of Time's wide wings
Hyperion slid into the rustled air,
And Saturn gained with Thea that sad place
Where Cybele and the bruisèd Titans mourned.
It was a den where no insulting light
Could glimmer on their tears; where their own groans
They felt, but heard not, for the solid roar
Of thunderous waterfalls and torrents hoarse,
Pouring a constant bulk, uncertain where.
10 Crag jutting forth to crag, and rocks that seemed
Ever as if just rising from a sleep,
Forehead to forehead held their monstrous horns;
And thus in thousand hugest fantasies
Made a fit roofing to this nest of woe.
Instead of thrones, hard flint they sat upon,
Couches of rugged stone, and slaty ridge
Stubborned with iron. All were not assembled,
Some chained in torture, and some wandering.
Coeus, and Gyges, and Briareüs,
20 Typhon, and Dolor, and Porphyrion,
With many more, the brawniest in assault,
Were pent in regions of laborious breath;
Dungeoned in opaque element, to keep

Their clenchèd teeth still clenched, and all their limbs
Locked up like veins of metal, cramped and screwed;
Without a motion, save of their big hearts
Heaving in pain, and horribly convulsed
With sanguine feverous boiling gurge of pulse.
Mnemosyne was straying in the world;
30 Far from her moon had Phoebe wanderèd;
And many else were free to roam abroad,
But for the main, here found they covert drear.
Scarce images of life, one here, one there,
Lay vast and edgeways; like a dismal cirque
Of Druid stones upon a forlorn moor,
When the chill rain begins at shut of eve
In dull November, and their chancel vault,
The heaven itself, is blinded throughout night.
Each one kept shroud, nor to his neighbour gave
40 Or word, or look, or action of despair.
Creüs was one; his ponderous iron mace
Lay by him, and a shattered rib of rock
Told of his rage, ere he thus sank and pined.
Iäpetus another; in his grasp,
A serpent's plashy neck; its barbèd tongue
Squeezed from the gorge, and all its uncurled length
Dead–and because the creature could not spit
Its poison in the eyes of conquering Jove.
Next Cottus; prone he lay, chin uppermost,
50 As though in pain, for still upon the flint
He ground severe his skull, with open mouth
And eyes at horrid working. Nearest him
Asia, born of most enormous Caf,
Who cost her mother Tellus keener pangs,
Though feminine, than any of her sons.
More thought than woe was in her dusky face,
For she was prophesying of her glory;
And in her wide imagination stood
Palm-shaded temples and high rival fanes,
60 By Oxus or in Ganges' sacred isles.
Even as Hope upon her anchor leans,
So leant she, not so fair, upon a tusk
Shed from the broadest of her elephants.
Above her, on a crag's uneasy shelve,
Upon his elbow raised, all prostrate else,
Shadowed Enceladus–once tame and mild
As grazing ox unworried in the meads;

68

Now tiger-passioned, lion-thoughted, wroth,
He meditated, plotted, and even now
70 Was hurling mountains in that second war,
Not long delayed, that scared the younger Gods
To hide themselves in forms of beast and bird.
Not far hence Atlas; and beside him prone
Phorcus, the sire of Gorgons. Neighboured close
Oceanus, and Tethys, in whose lap
Sobbed Clymene among her tangled hair.
In midst of all lay Themis, at the feet
Of Ops the queen all clouded round from sight,
No shape distinguishable, more than when
80 Thick night confounds the pine-tops with the clouds;
And many else whose names may not be told.
For when the Muse's wings are air-ward spread,
Who shall delay her flight? And she must chant
Of Saturn and his guide, who now had climbed
With damp and slippery footing from a depth
More horrid still. Above a sombre cliff
Their heads appeared, and up their stature grew
Till on the level height their steps found ease;
Then Thea spread abroad her trembling arms
90 Upon the precincts of this nest of pain,
And sidelong fixed her eye on Saturn's face.
There saw she direst strife—the supreme God
At war with all the frailty of grief,
Of rage, of fear, anxiety, revenge,
Remorse, spleen, hope, but most of all despair.
Against these plagues he strove in vain; for Fate
Had poured a mortal oil upon his head,
A disanointing poison, so that Thea,
Affrighted, kept her still, and let him pass
100 First onwards in among the fallen tribe.

As with us mortal men, the laden heart
Is persecuted more, and fevered more,
When it is nighing to the mournful house
Where other hearts are sick of the same bruise;
So Saturn, as he walked into the midst,
Felt faint and would have sunk among the rest,
But that he met Enceladus's eye,
Whose mightiness, and awe of him, at once
Came like an inspiration; and he shouted,
110 'Titans, behold your God!' At which some groaned;

Some started on their feet; some also shouted;
Some wept, some wailed, all bowed with reverence.
And Ops, uplifting her black folded veil,
Showed her pale cheeks and all her forehead wan,
Her eye-brows thin and jet, and hollow eyes.
There is a roaring in the bleak-grown pines
When winter lifts his voice; there is a noise
Among immortals when a God gives sign,
With hushing finger, how he means to load
120 His tongue with the full weight of utterless thought,
With thunder, and with music, and with pomp.
Such noise is like the roar of bleak-grown pines,
Which, when it ceases in this mountained world,
No other sound succeeds; but ceasing here,
Among these fallen, Saturn's voice therefrom
Grew up like organ, that begins anew
Its strain, when other harmonies, stopped short,
Leave the dinned air vibrating silverly.
Thus grew it up: 'Not in my own sad breast,
130 Which is its own great judge and searcher-out,
Can I find reason why ye should be thus;
Not in the legends of the first of days,
Studied from that old spirit-leavèd book
Which starry Uranus with finger bright
Saved from the shores of darkness, when the waves
Low-ebbèd still hid it up in shallow gloom—
And the which book ye know I ever kept
For my firm-basèd footstool—ah, infirm!
Not there, nor in sign, symbol, or portent
140 Of element, earth, water, air, and fire—
At war, at peace, or inter-quarrelling
One against one, or two, or three, or all
Each several one against the other three,
As fire with air loud warring when rain-floods
Drown both, and press them both against earth's face,
Where, finding sulphur, a quadruple wrath
Unhinges the poor world; not in that strife,
Wherefrom I take strange lore and read it deep,
Can I find reason why ye should be thus.
150 No, nowhere can unriddle, though I search,
And pore on Nature's universal scroll
Even to swooning, why ye Divinities,
The first-born of all shaped and palpable Gods,
Should cower beneath what, in comparison,

Is untremendous might. Yet ye are here,
O'erwhelm'd, and spurned, and battered, ye are here!
O Titans, shall I say, "Arise!"? Ye groan;
Shall I say "Crouch!"? Ye groan. What can I then?
O Heaven wide! O unseen parent dear!
160 What can I? Tell me, all ye brethren Gods,
How we can war, how engine our great wrath?
Oh, speak your counsel now, for Saturn's ear
Is all a-hungered. Thou, Oceanus,
Ponderest high and deep; and in thy face
I see, astonied, that severe content
Which comes of thought and musing. Give us help!'

So ended Saturn; and the God of the Sea,
Sophist and sage from no Athenian grove
But cogitation in his watery shades,
170 Arose, with locks not oozy, and began,
In murmurs which his first-endeavouring tongue
Caught infant-like from the far-foamed sands:
'O ye, whom wrath consumes, who, passion-stung,
Writhe at defeat, and nurse your agonies!
Shut up your senses, stifle up your ears,
My voice is not a bellows unto ire.
Yet listen, ye who will, whilst I bring proof
How ye, perforce, must be content to stoop;
And in the proof much comfort will I give,
180 If ye will take that comfort in its truth.
We fall by course of Nature's law, not force
Of thunder, or of Jove. Great Saturn, thou
Hast sifted well the atom-universe;
But for this reason, that thou art the King,
And only blind from sheer supremacy,
One avenue was shaded from thine eyes,
Through which I wandered to eternal truth.
And first, as thou wast not the first of powers,
So art thou not the last; it cannot be.
190 Thou art not the beginning nor the end.
From chaos and parental darkness came
Light, the first fruits of that intestine broil,
That sullen ferment, which for wondrous ends
Was ripening in itself. The ripe hour came,
And with it light, and light, engendering
Upon its own producer, forthwith touched
The whole enormous matter into life.
Upon that very hour, our parentage,

The Heavens and the Earth, were manifest;
200   Then thou first-born, and we the giant race,
Found ourselves ruling new and beauteous realms.
Now comes the pain of truth, to whom 'tis pain—
O folly! for to bear all naked truths,
And to envisage circumstance, all calm,
That is the top of sovereignty. Mark well!
As Heaven and Earth are fairer, fairer far
Than chaos and blank darkness, though once chiefs;
And as we show beyond that Heaven and Earth
In form and shape compact and beautiful,
210   In will, in action free, companionship,
And thousand other signs of purer life;
So on our heels a fresh perfection treads,
A power more strong in beauty, born of us
And fated to excel us, as we pass
In glory that old darkness; nor are we
Thereby more conquered than by us the rule
Of shapeless chaos. Say, doth the dull soil
Quarrel with the proud forests it hath fed,
And feedeth still, more comely than itself?
220   Can it deny the chiefdom of green groves?
Or shall the tree be envious of the dove
Because it cooeth, and hath snowy wings
To wander wherewithal and find its joys?
We are such forest-trees, and our fair boughs
Have bred forth, not pale solitary doves,
But eagles golden-feathered, who do tower
Above us in their beauty, and must reign
In right thereof. For 'tis the eternal law
That first in beauty should be first in might;
230   Yea, by that law, another race may drive
Our conquerors to mourn as we do now.
Have ye beheld the young God of the Seas,
My dispossessor? Have ye seen his face?
Have ye beheld his chariot, foamed along
By noble winged creatures he hath made?
I saw him on the calmèd waters scud,
With such a glow of beauty in his eyes,
That it enforced me to bid sad farewell
To all my empire: farewell sad I took,
240   And hither came to see how dolorous fate
Had wrought upon ye, and how I might best
Give consolation in this woe extreme.

Receive the truth, and let it be your balm.'

Whether through posed conviction, or disdain,
They guarded silence when Oceanus
Left murmuring, what deepest thought can tell?
But so it was; none answered for a space,
Save one whom none regarded, Clymene;
And yet she answered not, only complained,
250 With hectic lips, and eyes up-looking mild,
Thus wording timidly among the fierce:
'O Father, I am here the simplest voice,
And all my knowledge is that joy is gone,
And this thing woe crept in among our hearts,
There to remain for ever, as I fear.
I would not bode of evil, if I thought
So weak a creature could turn off the help
Which by just right should come of mighty Gods;
Yet let me tell my sorrow, let me tell
260 Of what I heard, and how it made me weep,
And know that we had parted from all hope.
I stood upon a shore, a pleasant shore,
Where a sweet clime was breathèd from a land
Of fragrance, quietness, and trees, and flowers.
Full of calm joy it was, as I of grief;
Too full of joy and soft delicious warmth;
So that I felt a movement in my heart
To chide, and to reproach that solitude
With songs of misery, music of our woes;
270 And sat me down, and took a mouthèd shell
And murmured into it, and made melody.
Oh, melody no more! For while I sang,
And with poor skill let pass into the breeze
The dull shell's echo, from a bowery strand
Just opposite, an island of the sea,
There came enchantment with the shifting wind,
That did both drown and keep alive my ears.
I threw my shell away upon the sand,
And a wave filled it, as my sense was filled
280 With that new blissful golden melody.
A living death was in each gush of sounds,
Each family of rapturous hurried notes,
That fell, one after one, yet all at once,
Like pearl beads dropping sudden from their string;
And then another, then another strain,
Each like a dove leaving its olive perch,

With music winged instead of silent plumes,
To hover round my head, and make me sick
Of joy and grief at once. Grief overcame,
290   And I was stopping up my frantic ears,
When, past all hindrance of my trembling hands,
A voice came sweeter, sweeter than all tune,
And still it cried, "Apollo! Young Apollo!
The morning-bright Apollo! Young Apollo!"
I fled, it followed me, and cried "Apollo!"
O Father, and O Brethren, had ye felt
Those pains of mine—O Saturn, hadst thou felt,
Ye would not call this too indulgèd tongue
Presumptuous in thus venturing to be heard.'

300   So far her voice flowed on, like timorous brook
That, lingering along a pebbled coast,
Doth fear to meet the sea; but sea it met,
And shuddered. For the overwhelming voice
Of huge Enceladus swallowed it in wrath:
The ponderous syllables, like sullen waves
In the half-glutted hollows of reef-rocks,
Came booming thus, while still upon his arm
He leaned—not rising, from supreme contempt.
'Or shall we listen to the over-wise,
310   Or to the over-foolish, Giant-Gods?
Not thunderbolt on thunderbolt, till all
That rebel Jove's whole armoury were spent,
Not world on world upon these shoulders piled
Could agonize me more than baby-words
In midst of this dethronement horrible.
Speak! Roar! Shout! Yell, ye sleepy Titans all!
Do ye forget the blows, the buffets vile?
Are ye not smitten by a youngling arm?
Dost thou forget, sham Monarch of the Waves,
320   Thy scalding in the seas? What, have I roused
Your spleens with so few simple words as these?
O joy! for now I see ye are not lost:
O joy! for now I see a thousand eyes
Wide-glaring for revenge!' As this he said,
He lifted up his stature vast and stood,
Still without intermission speaking thus:
'Now ye are flames, I'll tell you how to burn,
And purge the ether of our enemies;
How to feed fierce the crooked stings of fire,

330 And singe away the swollen clouds of Jove,
Stifling that puny essence in its tent.
O let him feel the evil he hath done;
For though I scorn Oceanus's lore,
Much pain have I for more than loss of realms.
The days of peace and slumberous calm are fled;
Those days, all innocent of scathing war,
When all the fair Existences of heaven
Came open-eyed to guess what we would speak –
That was before our brows were taught to frown,
340 Before our lips knew else but solemn sounds;
That was before we knew the wingèd thing,
Victory, might be lost, or might be won.
And be ye mindful that Hyperion,
Our brightest brother, still is undisgraced –
Hyperion, lo! his radiance is here!'

All eyes were on Enceladus's face,
And they beheld, while still Hyperion's name
Flew from his lips up to the vaulted rocks,
A pallid gleam across his features stern –
350 Not savage, for he saw full many a God
Wroth as himself. He looked upon them all,
And in each face he saw a gleam of light,
But splendider in Saturn's, whose hoar locks
Shone like the bubbling foam about a keel
When the prow sweeps into a midnight cove.
In pale and silver silence they remained,
Till suddenly a splendour, like the morn,
Pervaded all the beetling gloomy steeps,
All the sad spaces of oblivion,
360 And every gulf, and every chasm old,
And every height, and every sullen depth,
Voiceless, or hoarse with loud tormented streams;
And all the everlasting cataracts,
And all the headlong torrents far and near,
Mantled before in darkness and huge shade,
Now saw the light and made it terrible.
It was Hyperion: a granite peak
His bright feet touched, and there he stayed to view
The misery his brilliance had betrayed
370 To the most hateful seeing of itself.
Golden his hair of short Numidian curl,
Regal his shape majestic, a vast shade
In midst of his own brightness, like the bulk

75

Of Memnon's image at the set of sun
To one who travels from the dusking east;
Sighs, too, as mournful as that Memnon's harp,
He uttered, while his hands contemplative
He pressed together, and in silence stood.
Despondence seized again the fallen Gods
380 At sight of the dejected King of Day,
And many hid their faces from the light.
But fierce Enceladus sent forth his eyes
Among the brotherhood; and, at their glare,
Uprose Iapetus, and Creüs too,
And Phorcus, sea-born, and together strode
To where he towered on his eminence.
There those four shouted forth old Saturn's name;
Hyperion from the peak loud answered, 'Saturn!'
Saturn sat near the mother of the Gods,
390 In whose face was no joy, though all the Gods
Gave from their hollow throats the name of 'Saturn!'

Book III

Thus in alternate uproar and sad peace,
Amazèd were those Titans utterly.
Oh, leave them, Muse! Oh, leave them to their woes;
For thou art weak to sing such tumults dire;
A solitary sorrow best befits
Thy lips, and antheming a lonely grief.
Leave them, O Muse! for thou anon wilt find
Many a fallen old Divinity
Wandering in vain about bewildered shores.
10 Meantime touch piously the Delphic harp,
And not a wind of heaven but will breathe
In aid soft warble from the Dorian flute;
For lo! 'tis for the father of all verse.
Flush every thing that hath a vermeil hue,
Let the rose glow intense and warm the air,
And let the clouds of even and of morn
Float in voluptuous fleeces o'er the hills;
Let the red wine within the goblet boil
Cold as a bubbling well; let faint-lipped shells,
20 On sands, or in great deeps, vermilion turn
Through all their labyrinths; and let the maid
Blush keenly, as with some warm kiss surprised.

Chief isle of the embowered Cyclades,
Rejoice, O Delos, with thine olives green,
And poplars, and lawn-shading palms, and beech
In which the zephyr breathes the loudest song,
And hazels thick, dark-stemmed beneath the shade.
Apollo is once more the golden theme.
Where was he, when the Giant of the Sun
30   Stood bright, amid the sorrow of his peers?
Together had he left his mother fair
And his twin-sister sleeping in their bower,
And in the morning twilight wandered forth
Beside the osiers of a rivulet,
Full ankle-deep in lilies of the vale.
The nightingale had ceased, and a few stars
Were lingering in the heavens, while the thrush
Began calm-throated. Throughout all the isle
There was no covert, no retirèd cave,
40   Unhaunted by the murmurous noise of waves,
Though scarcely heard in many a green recess.
He listened, and he wept, and his bright tears
Went trickling down the golden bow he held.
Thus with half-shut suffusèd eyes he stood,
While from beneath some cumbrous boughs hard by
With solemn step an awful Goddess came,
And there was purport in her looks for him,
Which he with eager guess began to read
Perplexed, the while melodiously he said:
50   'How cam'st thou over the unfooted sea?
Or hath that antique mien and robèd form
Moved in these vales invisible till now?
Sure I have heard those vestments sweeping o'er
The fallen leaves, when I have sat alone
In cool mid-forest; surely I have traced
The rustle of those ample skirts about
These grassy solitudes, and seen the flowers
Lift up their heads, as still the whisper passed.
Goddess! I have beheld those eyes before,
60   And their eternal calm, and all that face,
Or I have dreamed.' 'Yes,' said the supreme shape,
'Thou hast dreamed of me; and awaking up
Didst find a lyre all golden by thy side,
Whose strings touched by thy fingers all the vast
Unwearied ear of the whole universe
Listened in pain and pleasure at the birth

Of such new tuneful wonder. Is't not strange
That thou shouldst weep, so gifted? Tell me, youth,
What sorrow thou canst feel; for I am sad
70 When thou dost shed a tear. Explain thy griefs
To one who in this lonely isle hath been
The watcher of thy sleep and hours of life,
From the young day when first thy infant hand
Plucked witless the weak flowers, till thine arm
Could bend that bow heroic to all times.
Show thy heart's secret to an ancient Power
Who hath forsaken old and sacred thrones
For prophecies of thee, and for the sake
Of loveliness new born.' Apollo then,
80 With sudden scrutiny and gloomless eyes,
Thus answered, while his white melodious throat
Throbbed with the syllables: 'Mnemosyne!
Thy name is on my tongue, I know not how;
Why should I tell thee what thou so well seest?
Why should I strive to show what from thy lips
Would come no mystery? For me, dark, dark,
And painful, vile oblivion seals my eyes.
I strive to search wherefore I am so sad,
Until a melancholy numbs my limbs;
90 And then upon the grass I sit and moan,
Like one who once had wings. Oh, why should I
Feel cursed and thwarted, when the liegeless air
Yields to my step aspirant? Why should I
Spurn the green turf as hateful to my feet?
Goddess benign, point forth some unknown thing.
Are there not other regions than this isle?
What are the stars? There is the sun, the sun!
And the most patient brilliance of the moon!
And stars by thousands! Point me out the way
100 To any one particular beauteous star,
And I will flit into it with my lyre,
And make its silvery splendour pant with bliss.
I have heard the cloudy thunder. Where is power?
Whose hand, whose essence, what Divinity,
Makes this alarum in the elements,
While I here idle listen on the shores
In fearless yet in aching ignorance?
Oh, tell me, lonely Goddess, by thy harp,
That waileth every morn and eventide,
110 Tell me why thus I rave, about these groves.

Mute thou remainest–mute! Yet I can read
A wondrous lesson in thy silent face:
Knowledge enormous makes a God of me.
Names, deeds, grey legends, dire events, rebellions,
Majesties, sovran voices, agonies,
Creations and destroyings, all at once
Pour into the wide hollows of my brain,
And deify me, as if some blithe wine
Or bright elixir peerless I had drunk,
120 And so become immortal.' Thus the God,
While his enkindled eyes, with level glance
Beneath his white soft temples, steadfast kept
Trembling with light upon Mnemosyne.
Soon wild commotions shook him, and made flush
All the immortal fairness of his limbs–
Most like the struggle at the gate of death;
Or liker still to one who should take leave
Of pale immortal death, and with a pang
As hot as death's is chill, with fierce convulse
130 Die into life. So young Apollo anguished;
His very hair, his golden tresses famed,
Kept undulation round his eager neck.
During the pain Mnemosyne upheld
Her arms as one who prophesied. At length
Apollo shrieked–and lo! from all his limbs
Celestial . . .

'Why did I laugh to-night?'

Why did I laugh to-night? No voice will tell;
   No God, no Demon of severe response,
Deigns to reply from Heaven or from Hell.
   Then to my human heart I turn at once—
Heart, thou and I are here sad and alone;
   Say wherefore did I laugh? Oh, mortal pain!
Oh, darkness, darkness! Ever must I moan,
   To question Heaven and Hell and Heart in vain!
Why did I laugh? I know this being's lease
   My fancy to its utmost blisses spreads;
Yet could I on this very midnight cease,
   And the world's gaudy ensigns see in shreds.
Verse, fame, and beauty are intense indeed,
But Death's intenser—Death is Life's high meed.

'How fevered is the man
who cannot look'

How fevered is the man who cannot look
  Upon his mortal days with temperate blood,
Who vexes all the leaves of his life's book,
  And robs his fair name of its maidenhood:
It is as if the rose should pluck herself,
  Or the ripe plum finger its misty bloom,
As if a Naiad, like a meddling elf,
  Should darken her pure grot with muddy gloom;
But the rose leaves herself upon the briar,
  For winds to kiss and grateful bees to feed,
And the ripe plum still wears its dim attire,
    The undisturbèd lake has crystal space.
    Why then should man, teasing the world for grace,
  Spoil his salvation for a fierce miscreed?

Ode to a Nightingale

I

My heart aches, and a drowsy numbness pains
  My sense, as though of hemlock I had drunk,
Or emptied some dull opiate to the drains
  One minute past, and Lethe-wards had sunk.
'Tis not through envy of thy happy lot,
  But being too happy in thine happiness—
    That thou, light-wingèd Dryad of the trees,
      In some melodious plot
  Of beechen green, and shadows numberless,
10   Singest of summer in full-throated ease.

II

Oh, for a draught of vintage that hath been
  Cooled a long age in the deep-delvèd earth,
Tasting of Flora and the country green,
  Dance, and Provençal song, and sunburnt mirth!
Oh, for a beaker full of the warm South,
  Full of the true, the blushful Hippocrene,
    With beaded bubbles winking at the brim,
      And purple-stainèd mouth,
  That I might drink, and leave the world unseen,
20   And with thee fade away into the forest dim—

III

Fade far away, dissolve, and quite forget
  What thou among the leaves hast never known,
The weariness, the fever, and the fret
  Here, where men sit and hear each other groan;
Where palsy shakes a few, sad, last gray hairs,
  Where youth grows pale, and spectre-thin, and dies;
    Where but to think is to be full of sorrow
      And leaden-eyed despairs;
  Where Beauty cannot keep her lustrous eyes,
30   Or new Love pine at them beyond to-morrow.

Away! away! For I will fly to thee,
   Not charioted by Bacchus and his pards,
But on the viewless wings of Poesy,
   Though the dull brain perplexes and retards.
Already with thee! Tender is the night,
    And haply the Queen-Moon is on her throne,
      Clustered around by all her starry fays;
        But here there is no light,
    Save what from heaven is with the breezes blown
40   Through verdurous glooms and winding mossy ways.

V

I cannot see what flowers are at my feet,
   Nor what soft incense hangs upon the boughs,
But, in embalmèd darkness, guess each sweet
   Wherewith the seasonable month endows
The grass, the thicket, and the fruit-tree wild—
    White hawthorn, and the pastoral eglantine;
      Fast-fading violets covered up in leaves;
        And mid-May's eldest child,
    The coming musk-rose, full of dewy wine,
50   The murmurous haunt of flies on summer eves.

VI

Darkling, I listen; and, for many a time
   I have been half in love with easeful Death,
Called him soft names in many a musèd rhyme,
   To take into the air my quiet breath;
Now more than ever seems it rich to die,
    To cease upon the midnight with no pain,
      While thou art pouring forth thy soul abroad
        In such an ecstasy.
    Still wouldst thou sing, and I have ears in vain—
60   To thy high requiem become a sod.

VII

Thou wast not born for death, immortal bird!
   No hungry generations tread thee down;
The voice I hear this passing night was heard
   In ancient days by emperor and clown:
Perhaps the self-same song that found a path
    Through the sad heart of Ruth, when, sick for home,
      She stood in tears amid the alien corn;
        The same that oft-times hath
    Charmed magic casements, opening on the foam
70   Of perilous seas in fairy lands forlorn.

Forlorn! The very word is like a bell
  To toll me back from thee to my sole self!
Adieu! The fancy cannot cheat so well
  As she is famed to do, deceiving elf.
Adieu! adieu! Thy plaintive anthem fades
  Past the near meadows, over the still stream,
    Up the hill-side; and now 'tis buried deep
    In the next valley-glades:
  Was it a vision, or a waking dream?
80   Fled is that music . . . Do I wake or sleep?

Ode on a Grecian Urn

I

Thou still unravished bride of quietness,
   Thou foster-child of silence and slow time,
Silvan historian, who canst thus express
   A flowery tale more sweetly than our rhyme!
What leaf-fringed legend haunts about thy shape
   Of deities or mortals, or of both,
      In Tempe or the dales of Arcady?
   What men or gods are these? What maidens loth?
What mad pursuit? What struggle to escape?
10   What pipes and timbrels? What wild ecstasy?

II

Heard melodies are sweet, but those unheard
   Are sweeter; therefore, ye soft pipes, play on;
Not to the sensual ear, but, more endeared,
   Pipe to the spirit ditties of no tone.
Fair youth beneath the trees, thou canst not leave
   Thy song, nor ever can those trees be bare;
      Bold lover, never, never canst thou kiss,
Though winning near the goal–yet do not grieve:
   She cannot fade, though thou hast not thy bliss,
20   For ever wilt thou love, and she be fair!

III

Ah, happy, happy boughs, that cannot shed
   Your leaves, nor ever bid the spring adieu;
And, happy melodist, unwearièd,
   For ever piping songs for ever new!
More happy love, more happy, happy love!
   For ever warm and still to be enjoyed,
      For ever panting, and for ever young–
All breathing human passion far above,
   That leaves a heart high-sorrowful and cloyed,
30   A burning forehead, and a parching tongue.

IV

Who are these coming to the sacrifice?
  To what green altar, O mysterious priest,
Lead'st thou that heifer lowing at the skies,
  And all her silken flanks with garlands dressed?
What little town by river or sea shore,
  Or mountain-built with peaceful citadel,
    Is emptied of this folk, this pious morn?
And, little town, thy streets for evermore
  Will silent be; and not a soul to tell
40   Why thou art desolate can e'er return.

V

O Attic shape! Fair attitude! With brede
  Of marble men and maidens overwrought,
With forest branches and the trodden weed—
  Thou, silent form, dost tease us out of thought
As doth eternity. Cold pastoral!
  When old age shall this generation waste,
    Thou shalt remain, in midst of other woe
Than ours, a friend to man, to whom thou say'st,
  'Beauty is truth, truth beauty'—that is all
50   Ye know on earth, and all ye need to know.

PLATE 3   *Titian*,
Bacchus and Ariadne
*This scene, set on the isle of
Naxos, underlies "Hymn to Bacchus"
in* Endymion *(p. 208) and, more
central to Keats' imaginative world
in "charioted by Bacchus and his
pards"* (To a Nightingale).
(By courtesy of the National Gallery)

PLATE 4   *C. A. Brown*,
Portrait of Keats
*Charles Brown was a close friend
of Keats, a collector, a writer
and an artist who had travelled quite
widely in search of paintings.
(By courtesy of the National
Portrait Gallery)*

Ode on Melancholy

No, no, go not to Lethe, neither twist
  Wolf's-bane, tight-rooted, for its poisonous wine;
Nor suffer thy pale forehead to be kissed
  By nightshade, ruby grape of Proserpine;
Make not your rosary of yew-berries,
    Nor let the beetle, nor the death-moth be
      Your mournful Psyche, nor the downy owl
A partner in your sorrow's mysteries;
    For shade to shade will come too drowsily,
10   And drown the wakeful anguish of the soul.

II

But when the melancholy fit shall fall
  Sudden from heaven like a weeping cloud,
That fosters the droop-headed flowers all,
  And hides the green hill in an April shroud;
Then glut thy sorrow on a morning rose,
    Or on the rainbow of the salt sand-wave,
      Or on the wealth of globèd peonies;
Or if thy mistress some rich anger shows,
    Imprison her soft hand, and let her rave,
20   And feed deep, deep upon her peerless eyes.

III

She dwells with Beauty—Beauty that must die;
  And Joy, whose hand is ever at his lips
Bidding adieu; and aching Pleasure nigh,
  Turning to poison while the bee-mouth sips.
Aye, in the very temple of Delight
    Veiled Melancholy has her sovran shrine,
      Though seen of none save him whose strenuous
        tongue
Can burst Joy's grape against his palate fine;
His soul shall taste the sadness of her might,
30   And be among her cloudy trophies hung.

Ode on Indolence

I

One morn before me were three figures seen,
  With bowèd necks, and joinèd hands, side-faced;
And one behind the other stepped serene,
  In placid sandals, and in white robes graced;
They passed, like figures on a marble urn,
  When shifted round to see the other side;
    They came again; as when the urn once more
Is shifted round, the first seen shades return;
  And they were strange to me, as may betide
10   With vases, to one deep in Phidian lore.

II

How is it, Shadows, that I knew ye not?
  How came ye muffled in so hush a masque?
Was it a silent deep-disguisèd plot
  To steal away, and leave without a task
My idle days? Ripe was the drowsy hour;
  The blissful cloud of summer indolence
    Benumbed my eyes; my pulse grew less and less;
Pain had no sting, and pleasure's wreath no flower:
  Oh, why did ye not melt, and leave my sense
20   Unhaunted quite of all but—nothingness?

III

A third time passed they by, and, passing, turned
  Each one the face a moment while to me;
Then faded, and to follow them I burned
  And ached for wings because I knew the three;
The first was a fair maid, and Love her name;
  . The second was Ambition, pale of cheek,
    And ever watchful with fatiguèd eye;
The last, whom I love more, the more of blame
  Is heaped upon her, maiden most unmeek,
30   I knew to be my demon Poesy.

They faded, and, forsooth! I wanted wings.
  Oh, folly! What is Love? And where is it?
And, for that poor Ambition—it springs
  From a man's little heart's short fever-fit.
For Poesy! No, she has not a joy—
    At least for me—so sweet as drowsy noons,
      And evenings steeped in honeyed indolence.
Oh, for an age so sheltered from annoy
    That I may never know how change the moons,
40   Or hear the voice of busy common-sense!

V

A third time came they by. Alas, wherefore?
  My sleep had been embroidered with dim dreams;
My soul had been a lawn besprinkled o'er
  With flowers, and stirring shades, and baffled beams.
The morn was clouded, but no shower fell,
    Though in her lids hung the sweet tears of May;
      The open casement pressed a new-leaved vine,
    Let in the budding warmth and throstle's lay;
O Shadows, 'twas a time to bid farewell!
50   Upon your skirts had fallen no tears of mine.

VI

So, ye three Ghosts, adieu! Ye cannot raise
  My head cool-bedded in the flowery grass;
For I would not be dieted with praise,
  A pet-lamb in a sentimental farce!
Fade softly from my eyes, and be once more
  In masque-like figures on the dreamy urn.
    Farewell! I yet have visions for the night,
And for the day faint visions there is store.
    Vanish, ye Phantoms, from my idle sprite
60   Into the clouds, and never more return!

To Autumn

I

Season of mists and mellow fruitfulness,
  Close bosom friend of the maturing sun,
Conspiring with him how to load and bless
  With fruit the vines that round the thatch-eves run:
To bend with apples the mossed cottage-trees,
  And fill all fruit with ripeness to the core;
    To swell the gourd, and plump the hazel shells
  With a sweet kernel; to set budding more,
And still more, later flowers for the bees,
10 Until they think warm days will never cease,
    For summer has o'er-brimmed their clammy cells.

II

Who hath not seen thee oft amid thy store?
  Sometimes whoever seeks abroad may find
Thee sitting careless on a granary floor,
  Thy hair soft-lifted by the winnowing wind;
Or on a half-reaped furrow sound asleep,
  Drowsed with the fume of poppies, while thy hook
    Spares the next swath and all its twinèd flowers;
And sometimes like a gleaner thou dost keep
20 Steady thy laden head across a brook;
  Or by a cyder-press, with patient look,
    Thou watchest the last oozings hours by hours.

III

Where are the songs of spring? Aye, where are they?
  Think not of them, thou hast thy music too—
While barrèd clouds bloom the soft-dying day,
  And touch the stubble-plains with rosy hue.
Then in a wailful choir the small gnats mourn
  Among the river sallows, borne aloft
    Or sinking as the light wind lives or dies;
30 And full-grown lambs loud bleat from hilly bourn;
  Hedge-crickets sing; and now with treble soft
    The red-breast whistles from a garden-croft;
    And gathering swallows twitter in the skies.

The Fall of Hyperion

Canto I

Fanatics have their dreams, wherewith they weave
A paradise for a sect, the savage too
From forth the loftiest fashion of his sleep
Guesses at Heaven; pity these have not
Traced upon vellum or wild Indian leaf
The shadows of melodious utterance.
But bare of laurel they live, dream, and die;
For Poesy alone can tell her dreams,
With the fine spell of words alone can save
10 Imagination from the sable charm
And dumb enchantment. Who alive can say,
'Thou art no poet; may'st not tell thy dreams'?
Since every man whose soul is not a clod
Hath visions, and would speak, if he had loved
And been well nurtured in his mother tongue.
Whether the dream now purposed to rehearse
Be poet's or fanatic's will be known
When this warm scribe my hand is in the grave.

Methought I stood where trees of every clime,
20 Palm, myrtle, oak, and sycamore, and beech,
With plantain, and spice-blossoms, made a screen—
In neighbourhood of fountains, by the noise
Soft-showering in my ears, and, by the touch
Of scent, not far from roses. Turning round,
I saw an arbour with a drooping roof
Of trellis vines, and bells, and larger blooms,
Like floral censers swinging light in air;
Before its wreathèd doorway, on a mound
Of moss, was spread a feast of summer fruits,
30 Which, nearer seen, seemed refuse of a meal
By angel tasted, or our Mother Eve;
For empty shells were scattered on the grass,
And grape-stalks but half bare, and remnants more,

Sweet-smelling, whose pure kinds I could not know.
Still was more plenty than the fabled horn
Thrice emptied could pour forth at banqueting
For Proserpine returned to her own fields,
Where the white heifers low. And appetite
More yearning than on earth I ever felt
40 Growing within, I ate deliciously;
And, after not long, thirsted, for thereby
Stood a cool vessel of transparent juice,
Sipped by the wandered bee, the which I took,
And, pledging all the mortals of the world,
And all the dead whose names are in our lips,
Drank. That full draught is parent of my theme.
No Asian poppy, nor elixir fine
Of the soon-fading jealous Caliphat;
No poison gendered in close monkish cell,
50 To thin the scarlet conclave of old men,
Could so have rapt unwilling life away.
Among the fragrant husks and berries crushed,
Upon the grass I struggled hard against
The domineering potion; but in vain—
The cloudy swoon came on, and down I sunk,
Like a Silenus on an antique vase.
How long I slumbered 'tis a chance to guess.
When sense of life returned, I started up
As if with wings; but the fair trees were gone,
60 The mossy mound and arbour were no more.
I looked around upon the carvèd sides
Of an old sanctuary with roof august,
Builded so high it seemed that filmèd clouds
Might spread beneath, as o'er the stars of heaven.
So old the place was, I remembered none
The like upon the earth: what I had seen
Of grey cathedrals, buttressed walls, rent towers,
The superannuations of sunk realms,
Or nature's rocks toiled hard in waves and winds,
70 Seemed but the faulture of decrepit things
To that eternal domèd monument.
Upon the marble at my feet there lay
Store of strange vessels and large draperies,
Which needs had been of dyed asbestos wove,
Or in that place the moth could not corrupt,
So white the linen; so, in some, distinct
Ran imageries from a sombre loom.
All in a mingled heap confused there lay

Robes, golden tongs, censer and chafing-dish,
80 Girdles, and chains, and holy jewelleries.
Turning from these with awe, once more I raised
My eyes to fathom the space every way—
The embossed roof, the silent massy range
Of columns north and south, ending in mist
Of nothing, then to eastward, where black gates
Were shut against the sunrise evermore.
Then to the west I looked, and saw far off
An image, huge of feature as a cloud,
At level of whose feet an altar slept,
90 To be approached on either side by steps,
And marble balustrade, and patient travail
To count with toil the innumerable degrees.
Towards the altar sober-paced I went,
Repressing haste as too unholy there;
And, coming nearer, saw beside the shrine
One ministering; and there arose a flame.
When in mid-May the sickening east wind
Shifts sudden to the south, the small warm rain
Melts out the frozen incense from all flowers,
100 And fills the air with so much pleasant health
That even the dying man forgets his shroud.
Even so that lofty sacrificial fire,
Sending forth Maian incense, spread around
Forgetfulness of everything but bliss,
And clouded all the altar with soft smoke,
From whose white fragrant curtains thus I heard
Language pronounced: 'If thou canst not ascend
These steps, die on that marble where thou art.
Thy flesh, near cousin to the common dust,
110 Will parch for lack of nutriment—thy bones
Will wither in few years, and vanish so
That not the quickest eye could find a grain
Of what thou now art on that pavement cold.
The sands of thy short life are spent this hour,
And no hand in the universe can turn
Thy hourglass, if these gummed leaves be burnt
Ere thou canst mount up these immortal steps.'
I heard, I looked: two senses both at once,
So fine, so subtle, felt the tyranny
120 Of that fierce threat and the hard task proposed.
Prodigious seemed the toil; the leaves were yet
Burning—when suddenly a palsied chill
Struck from the pavèd level up my limbs,

And was ascending quick to put cold grasp
Upon those streams that pulse beside the throat.
I shrieked; and the sharp anguish of my shriek
Stung my own ears. I strove hard to escape
The numbness, strove to gain the lowest step.
Slow, heavy, deadly was my pace; the cold
130 Grew stifling, suffocating, at the heart;
And when I clasped my hands I felt them not.
One minute before death, my iced foot touched
The lowest stair; and as it touched, life seemed
To pour in at the toes. I mounted up,
As once fair Angels on a ladder flew
From the green turf to Heaven. 'Holy Power,'
Cried I, approaching near the hornèd shrine,
'What am I that should so be saved from death?
What am I that another death come not
140 To choke my utterance sacrilegious here?'
Then said the veilèd shadow: 'Thou hast felt
What 'tis to die and live again before
Thy fated hour. That thou hadst power to do so
Is thy own safety; thou hast dated on
Thy doom.' 'High Prophetess,' said I, 'purge off,
Benign, if so it please thee, my mind's film.'
'None can usurp this height,' returned that shade,
'But those to whom the miseries of the world
Are misery, and will not let them rest.
150 All else who find a haven in the world,
Where they may thoughtless sleep away their days,
If by a chance into this fane they come,
Rot on the pavement where thou rotted'st half.'
'Are there not thousands in the world,' said I,
Encouraged by the sooth voice of the shade,
'Who love their fellows even to the death;
Who feel the giant agony of the world;
And more, like slaves to poor humanity,
Labour for mortal good? I sure should see
160 Other men here: but I am here alone.'
'Those whom thou spak'st of are no visionaries,'
Rejoined that voice. 'They are no dreamers weak,
They seek no wonder but the human face;
No music but a happy-noted voice—
They come not here, they have no thought to come—
And thou art here, for thou art less than they.
What benefit canst thou do, or all thy tribe,
To the great world? Thou art a dreaming thing,

A fever of thyself. Think of the earth;
170   What bliss even in hope is there for thee?
      What haven? Every creature hath its home:
      Every sole man hath days of joy and pain.
      Whether his labours be sublime or low—
      The pain alone; the joy alone; distinct:
      Only the dreamer venoms all his days,
      Bearing more woe than all his sins deserve.
      Therefore, that happiness be somewhat shared,
      Such things as thou are art admitted oft
      Into like gardens thou didst pass erewhile,
180   And suffered in these temples; for that cause
      Thou standest safe beneath this statue's knees.'
      'That I am favoured for unworthiness,
      By such propitious parley medicined
      In sickness not ignoble, I rejoice—
      Aye, and could weep for love of such award.'
      So answered I, continuing: 'If it please,
      Majestic shadow, tell me: sure not all
      Those melodies sung into the world's ear
      Are useless; sure a poet is a sage,
190   A humanist, physician to all men.
      That I am none I feel, as vultures feel
      They are no birds when eagles are abroad.
      What am I then? Thou spakest of my tribe:
      What tribe?' The tall shade veiled in drooping white
      Then spake, so much more earnest, that the breath
      Moved the thin linen folds that drooping hung
      About a golden censer from the hand
      Pendent: 'Art thou not of the dreamer tribe?
      The poet and the dreamer are distinct,
200   Diverse, sheer opposite, antipodes.
      The one pours out a balm upon the world,
      The other vexes it.' Then shouted I
      Spite of myself, and with a Pythia's spleen:
      'Apollo! Faded, far-flown Apollo!
      Where is thy misty pestilence to creep
      Into the dwellings, through the door crannies,
      Of all mock lyrists, large self-worshippers
      And careless hectorers in proud bad verse.
      Though I breathe death with them it will be life
210   To see them sprawl before me into graves.
      Majestic shadow, tell me where I am,
      Whose altar this; for whom this incense curls;
      What image this whose face I cannot see,

For the broad marble knees; and who thou art,
Of accent feminine, so courteous?'

Then the tall shade, in drooping linens veiled,
Spoke out, so much more earnest that her breath
Stirred the thin folds of gauze that drooping hung
About a golden censer from her hand
220 Pendent; and by her voice I knew she shed
Long-treasured tears: 'This temple, sad and lone,
Is all spared from the thunder of a war
Foughten long since by giant hierarchy
Against rebellion; this old image here,
Whose carvèd features wrinkled as he fell,
Is Saturn's; I, Moneta, left supreme,
Sole priestess of his desolation.'
I had no words to answer, for my tongue,
Useless, could find about its roofèd home
230 No syllable of a fit majesty
To make rejoinder to Moneta's mourn.
There was a silence, while the altar's blaze
Was fainting for sweet food. I looked thereon,
And on the pavèd floor, where nigh were piled
Faggots of cinnamon and many heaps
Of other crisped spice-wood—then again
I looked upon the altar, and its horns
Whitened with ashes, and its languorous flame,
And then upon the offerings again;
240 And so by turns—till sad Moneta cried:
'The sacrifice is done, but not the less,
Will I be kind to thee for thy good will.
My power, which to me is still a curse,
Shall be to thee a wonder; for the scenes
Still swooning vivid through my globèd brain,
With an electral changing misery,
Thou shalt with these dull mortal eyes behold,
Free from all pain, if wonder pain thee not.'
As near as an immortal's spherèd words
250 Could to a mother's soften, were these last.
But yet I had a terror of her robes,
And chiefly of the veils, that from her brow
Hung pale, and curtained her in mysteries,
That made my heart too small to hold its blood.
This saw that Goddess, and with sacred hand
Parted the veils. Then saw I a wan face,
Not pined by human sorrows, but bright-blanched

By an immortal sickness which kills not.
It works a constant change, which happy death
260 Can put no end to; deathwards progressing
To no death was that visage; it had passed
The lily and the snow; and beyond these
I must not think now, though I saw that face—
But for her eyes I should have fled away.
They held me back, with a benignant light,
Soft-mitigated by divinest lids
Half-closed, and visionless entire they seemed
Of all external things—they saw me not,
But in blank splendour beamed like the mild moon,
270 Who comforts those she sees not, who knows not
What eyes are upward cast. As I had found
A grain of gold upon a mountain's side,
And twinged with avarice strainèd out my eyes
To search its sullen entrails rich with ore,
So at the view of sad Moneta's brow
I ached to see what things the hollow brain
Behind enwombed; what high tragedy
In the dark secret chambers of her skull
Was acting, that could give so dread a stress
280 To her cold lips, and fill with such a light
Her planetary eyes; and touch her voice
With such a sorrow. 'Shade of Memory!'
Cried I, with act adorant at her feet,
'By all the gloom hung round thy fallen house,
By this last temple, by the golden age,
By great Apollo, thy dear foster child.
And by thyself, forlorn Divinity,
The pale omega of a withered race,
Let me behold, according as thou said'st,
290 What in thy brain so ferments to and fro.'

Extracts from Letters, I

1. To Benjamin Haydon, 11 May 1817

This morning I received a letter from George, by which it appears that money troubles are to follow us up for some time to come, perhaps for always. These vexations are a great hindrance to one. They are not like envy and detraction stimulants to further exertion, as being immediately relative and reflected on at the same time with the prime object, but rather like a nettle leaf or two in your bed. So now I revoke my promise of finishing my poem by the autumn, which I should have done had I gone on as I have done. But I cannot write while my spirit is fevered in a contrary direction, and I am now sure of having plenty of it this summer.

At this moment I am in no enviable situation. I feel that I am not in a mood to write any to-day; and it appears that the loss of it is the beginning of all sorts of irregularities. I am extremely glad that a time must come when everything will 'leave not a wrack behind'. You tell me never to despair— I wish it was as easy for me to observe the saying. Truth is I have a horried morbidity of temperament which has shown itself at intervals. It is, I have no doubt, the greatest enemy and stumbling-block I have to fear—I may even say that it is likely to be the cause of my disappointment. However, every ill has its share of good. This very bane would at any time enable me to look with an obstinate eye on the Devil himself— ay, to be as proud of being the lowest of the human race as Alfred could be in being of the highest. I feel confident I should have been a rebel angel had the opportunity been mine.

2. To Benjamin Bailey, 22 November 1817

O, I wish I was as certain of the end of all your troubles as that of your momentary start about the authenticity of the imagination. I am certain of nothing but of the holiness of the heart's affections and the truth of imagination. What the imagination seizes as beauty must be truth, whether it existed before or not; for I have the same idea of all our passions as of love–they are all in their sublime creative of essential beauty. In a word, you may know my favourite speculation by my first Book and the little song I sent in my last, which is a representation from the fancy of the probable mode of operating in these matters.

The imagination may be compared to Adam's dream–he awoke and found it truth. I am the more zealous in this affair because I have never yet been able to perceive how anything can be known for truth by consequitive [sic] reasoning– and yet it must be. Can it be that even the greatest philosopher ever arrived at his goal without putting aside numerous objections? However it may be, O for a life of sensations rather than of thoughts! It is 'a vision in the form of youth', a shadow of reality to come; and this consideration has further convinced me for it has come as auxiliary to another favourite speculation of mine, that we shall enjoy ourselves hereafter by having what we called happiness on earth repeated in a finer tone and so repeated. And yet such a fate can only befall those who delight in sensation rather than hunger as you do after truth. Adam's dream will do here, and seems to be a conviction that imagination and its empyreal reflection is the same as human life and its spiritual repetition.

But as I was saying, the simple imaginative mind may have its rewards in the repetition of its own silent workings coming continually on the spirit with a fine suddenness. To compare great things with small, have you never, by being surprised with an old melody, in a delicious place, by a delicious voice, felt over again your very speculations and surmises at the time it first operated on your soul? Do you not remember forming to yourself the singer's face more beautiful than it was possible (and yet with the elevation of the moment you did not think so)? Even then you were mounted on the wings of imagination so high–that the prototype must be hereafter– that delicious face you will see. What a time!

I am continually running away from the subject. Sure

this cannot be exactly the case with a complex mind–one that is imaginative and at the same time careful of its fruits, who would exist partly on sensation, partly on thought, to whom it is necessary that years should bring the philosophic mind. . . .

You perhaps at one time thought there was such a thing as worldly happiness to be arrived at, at certain periods of time marked out; you have of necessity from your disposition been thus led away. I scarcely remember counting upon any happiness. I look not for it if it be not in the present hour– nothing startles me beyond the moment. The setting sun will always set me to rights; or if a sparrow come before my window I take part in its existence and pick about the gravel.

The first thing that strikes me on hearing a misfortune having befalled another is this. 'Well, it cannot be helped; he will have the pleasure of trying the resources of his spirit.' And I beg now, my dear Bailey, that hereafter, should you observe anything cold in me, not to put it to the account of heartlessness but abstraction, for I assure you I sometimes feel not the influence of a passion or affection during a whole week. And so long this sometimes continues I begin to suspect myself and the genuineness of my feelings at other times, thinking them a few barren tragedy-tears.

3. To the Same, 23 January 1818

You said: 'Why should woman suffer?' Aye, why should she? 'By heavens I'd coin my very soul and drop my blood for drachmas'! These things are, and he who feels how incompetent the most skyey knight-errantry is to heal this bruised fairness is like a sensitive leaf on the hot hand of thought.

4. To J.H. Reynolds, 19 February 1818

I have an idea that a man might pass a very pleasant life in this manner. Let him on a certain day read a certain page of full poesy or distilled prose, and let him wander with it, and muse upon it, and reflect upon it, and bring home to it, and prophesy upon it, and dream upon it, until it becomes stale.

But when will it do so? Never. When man has arrived at a certain ripeness in intellect any one grand and spiritual passage serves him as a starting-post towards all 'the two-and-thirty palaces'.

How happy is such a 'voyage of conception', what delicious, diligent indolence! A doze upon a sofa does not hinder it, and a nap upon clover engenders ethereal finger-pointings. The prattle of a child gives it wings, and the converse of middle-age a strength to beat them. A strain of music conducts to 'an odd angle of the isle', and when the leaves whisper it puts a 'girdle round the earth'. Nor will this sparing touch of old books be any irreverence to their writers, for perhaps the honours paid by man to man are trifles in comparison to the benefit done by great works to the 'spirit and pulse of good' by their mere passive existence.

Memory should not be called knowledge. Many have original minds who do not think it—they are led away by custom. Now it appears to me that almost any man may like the spider spin from his own inwards his own airy citadel. The points of leaves and twigs on which the spider begins her work are few, and she fills the air with beautiful circuiting. Man should be content with as few points to tip with the fine web of his soul and weave a tapestry empyrean —full of symbols for his spiritual eye, of softness for his spiritual touch, of space for his wandering, of distinctness for his luxury.

But the minds of mortals are so different and bent on such diverse journeys that it may at first appear impossible for any common taste and fellowship to exist between two or three under these suppositions. It is, however, quite the contrary. Minds would leave each other in contrary directions, traverse each other in numberless points, and at last greet each other at the journey's end. An old man and a child would talk together, and the old man be led on his path and the child left thinking.

Man should not dispute or assert but whisper results to his neighbour; and thus, by every germ of spirit sucking the sap from mould ethereal, every human might become great, and humanity, instead of being a wide heath of furze and briars, with here and there a remote oak or pine, would become a grand democracy of forest trees!

It has been an old comparison for our urging on—the beehive. However, it seems to me that we should rather be the flower than the bee, for it is a false notion that more is gained by receiving than giving. No, the receiver and the giver are equal in their benefits. The flower, I doubt not, receives a fair guerdon from the bee—its leaves blush deeper in the next spring; and who shall say between man and woman which is the most delighted? Now it is more noble to sit like Jove than to fly like Mercury. Let us not therefore go hurrying about and collecting honey-bee like, buzzing here and there impatiently from a knowledge of what is to be arrived at; but let us open our leaves like a flower and be passive and receptive, budding patiently under the eye of Apollo and taking hints from every noble insect that favours us with a visit. Sap will be given us for meat and dew for drink....

Now I am sensible all this is a mere sophistication (however it may neighbour to any truths) to excuse my own indolence, so I will not deceive myself that man should be equal with Jove, but think himself very well off as a sort of scullion-Mercury, or even a humble bee. It is no matter whether I am right or wrong, either one way or the other, if there is sufficient to lift a little time from your shoulders.

5. To John Taylor, 24 April 1818

I think I did very wrong to leave you all the trouble of *Endymion*, but I could not help it then. Another time I shall be more bent to all sorts of troubles and disagreeables. Young men for some time have an idea that such a thing as happiness is to be had, and therefore are extremely impatient under any unpleasant restraining. In time however, of such stuff is the world about them, they know better, and instead of striving from uneasiness, greet it as an habitual sensation, a pannier which is to weigh upon them through life....

I was purposing to travel over the north this summer. There is but one thing to prevent me—I know nothing, I have read nothing; and I mean to follow Solomon's directions of 'get wisdom—get understanding'. I find cavalier days are gone by. I find that I can have no enjoyment in

the world but continual drinking of knowledge. I find there
is no worthy pursuit but the idea of doing some good for
the world. Some do it with their society, some with their
wit, some with their benevolence, some with a sort of power
of conferring pleasure and good humour on all they meet,
and in a thousand ways all equally dutiful to the command
of great Nature. There is but one way for me–the road lies
lies through application, study, and thought. I will pursue
it, and to that end purpose retiring for some years. I have
been hovering for some time between an exquisite sense of
the luxurious and a love for philosophy. Were I calculated
for the former I should be glad, but as I am not I shall
turn all my soul to the latter.

6. To J.H. Reynolds, 3 May 1818

An extensive knowledge is needful to thinking people. It
takes away the heat and fever, and helps, by widening
speculation, to ease the 'burden of the mystery'–a thing I
begin to understand a little, and which weighed upon you
in the most gloomy and true sentence in your letter. The
difference of high sensations with and without knowledge
appears to me this. In the latter case we are falling continually ten thousand fathoms deep and being blown up
again without wings and with all the horror of a bare-
shouldered creature. In the former case our shoulders are
fledge, and we go through the same air and space without
fear.

This is running one's rigs on the score of abstracted benefit.
When we come to human life and the affections it is impossible to know how a parallel of breast and head can be
drawn. You will forgive me for thus privately treading out
of my depth, and take it for treading as schoolboys tread
the water. It is impossible to know how far knowledge will
console us for the death of a friend and the ill 'that flesh is
heir to'....

I compare human life to a large mansion of many apart-
ments, two of which I can only describe, the doors of the
rest being as yet shut upon me. The first we step into we
call the infant or thoughtless chamber, in which we remain

as long as we do not think. We remain there a long while, and nothwithstanding the doors of the second chamber remain wide open, showing a bright appearance, we care not to hasten to it; but are at length imperceptibly impelled by the awakening of this thinking principle within us.

30   We no sooner get into the second chamber, which I shall call the chamber of maiden-thought, than we become intoxicated with the light and the atmosphere. We see nothing but pleasant wonders, and think of delaying there for ever in delight. However, among the effects this breathing is father of is that tremendous one of sharpening one's vision into the heart and nature of man–of convincing one's nerves that the world is full of misery and heartbreak, pain, sickness, and oppression, whereby this chamber of maiden-thought becomes gradually darkened, and at the same time

40 on all sides of it many doors are set open, but all dark, all leading to dark passages. We see not the balance of good and evil. We are in a mist. *We* are now in that state–we feel the 'burden of the mystery'. To this point was Wordsworth come, as far as I can conceive, when he wrote 'Tintern Abbey', and it seems to me that his genius is explorative of those dark passages. Now if we live and go on thinking, we too shall explore them.

7. To Benjamin Bailey, 10 June 1818

I was in hopes some little time back to be able to relieve your dullness by my spirits–to point out things in the world worth your enjoyment; and now I am never alone without rejoicing that there is such a thing as death, without placing my ultimate in the glory of dying for a great human purpose. Perhaps if my affairs were in a different state, I should not have written the above. You shall judge. I have two brothers –one is driven by the 'burden of society' to America, the other, with an exquisite love of life, is in a lingering state.

10 My love for my brothers, from the early loss of our parents and even for earlier misfortunes, has grown into an affection 'passing the love of women'. I have been ill-tempered with them, I have vexed them; but the thought of them has always stifled the impression that any woman might other-

wise have made upon me. I have a sister too and may not follow them, either to America or to the grave. Life must be undergone, and I certainly derive a consolation from the thought of writing one or two more poems before it ceases.

8. To Mrs Wylie, 6 August 1818

My brother George has ever been more than a brother to me. He has been my greatest friend, and I can never forget the sacrifice you have made for his happiness. As I walk along the mountains here I am full of these things, and lay in wait, as it were, for the pleasure of seeing you, immediately on my return to town. I wish above all things to say a word of comfort to you, but I know not how. It is impossible to prove that black is white. It is impossible to make out that sorrow is joy or joy is sorrow.

9. To George and Georgiana Keats, 19 March and 21 April 1819

This morning I am in a sort of temper indolent and supremely careless. I long after a stanza or two of Thomson's *Castle of Indolence*. My passions are all asleep from my having slumbered till nearly eleven and weakened the animal fibre all over me to a delightful sensation about three degrees on this side of faintness. If I had teeth of pearl and the breath of lilies, I should call it langour, but as I am* I must call it laziness. In this state of effeminacy the fibres of the brain are relaxed in common with the rest of the body, and to such a happy degree that pleasure has no show of enticement and pain no unbearable frown. Neither poetry nor ambition nor love have any alertness of countenance as they pass by me. They seem rather like three figures on a Greek vase–a man and two women whom no one but myself could distinguish in their disguisement. This is the only happiness, and is a rare instance of advantage in the body overpowering the mind.

I have this moment received a note from Haslam in which

he expects the death of his father, who has been for some
time in a state of insensibility. His mother bears up, he says,
very well. I shall go to town tomorrow to see him. This is
the world—thus we cannot expect to give way many hours
to pleasure. Circumstances are like clouds continually
gathering and bursting. While we are laughing the seed of
some trouble is put into the wide arable land of events.
While we are laughing it sprouts, it grows, and suddenly
bears a poison fruit which we must pluck. (*19 March 1819*)

I have been reading lately two very different books, Robertson's *America* and Voltaire's *Siècle de Louis XIV*. It is like
walking arm-in-arm between Pizarro and the great-little
Monarch. In how lamentable a case do we see the great
body of people in both instances. In the first, where men
might seem to inherit quiet of mind from unsophisticated
senses, from uncontamination of civilization, and especially
from their being, as it were, estranged from the mutual helps
of society and its mutual injuries (and thereby more immediately under the protection of Providence), even there
they had mortal pains to bear as bad or even worse than
bailiffs, debts, and poverties of civilized life.

The whole appears to resolve into this—that man is
originally 'a poor forked creature', subject to the same
mischances as the beasts of the forest, destined to hardships
and disquietude of some kind or other. If he improves by
degrees his bodily accommodations and comforts, at each
stage, at each ascent, there are waiting for him a fresh set
of annoyances. He is mortal, and there is still a heaven with
its stars above his head. The most interesting question that
can come before us is how far, by the persevering endeavours
of a seldom-appearing Socrates, mankind may be made
happy. I can imagine such happiness carried to an extreme,
but what must it end in?—death. And who could in such a
case bear with death? The whole troubles of life, which are
now frittered away in a series of years, would then be
accumulated for the last days of a being who, instead of
hailing its approach, would leave this world as Eve left
Paradise.

But in truth I do not at all believe in this sort of perfec-
tibility. The nature of the world will not admit of it; the
inhabitants of the world will correspond to itself. Let the

fish philosophize the ice away from the rivers in winter time
and they shall be at continual play in the tepid delight of
summer. Look at the Poles and the sands of Africa, whirl-
pools and volcanoes. Let men exterminate them, and I will
say that they may arrive at earthly happiness. The point at
which man may arrive is as far as the parallel state in inanimate nature and no further. For instance, suppose a rose
to have sensation. It blooms on a beautiful morning, it
enjoys itself; but there comes a cold wind, a hot sun—it
cannot escape it, it cannot destroy its annoyances—they are
as native to the world as itself. No more can man be happy
in spite; the worldly elements will prey upon his nature.

The common cognomen of this world among the mis-
guided and superstitious is 'a vale of tears', from which we
are to be redeemed by a certain arbitrary interposition of
God and taken to Heaven. What a little, circumscribed,
straightened notion! Call the world, if you please, 'the vale
of soul-making'; then you will find out the use of the world.
(I am speaking now in the highest terms for human nature,
admitting it to be immortal, which I will here take for
granted for the purpose of showing a thought which has
struck me concerning it.) I say '*soul*-making'—soul as distinguished from an intelligence. There may be intelligences
or sparks of the divinity in millions, but they are not souls
till they acquire identities, till each one is personally itself.
Intelligences are atoms of perception—they know and they
see and they are pure; in short they are God. How then are
souls to be made? How then are these sparks which are God
to have identity given them, so as ever to possess a bliss
peculiar to each one's individual existence? How but by the
medium of a world like this?

This point I sincerely wish to consider because I think it
is a grander system of salvation than the Christian religion;
or rather it is a system of spirit-creation. This is effected by
three grand materials acting the one upon the other for a
series of years. These three materials are the intelligence,
the human heart (as distinguished from intelligence or
mind), and the world or elemental space suited for the
proper action of mind and heart on each other for the purpose of forming the soul or intelligence destined to possess
the sense of identity.

I can scarcely express what I but dimly perceive; and yet I think I perceive it. That you may judge the more clearly I will put it in the most homely form possible. I will call the world a school instituted for the purpose of teaching little children to read; I will call the human heart the horn-book used in that school; and I will call the child able to read the soul made from that school and its horn-book. Do you not see how necessary a world of pains and troubles is to school an intelligence and make it a soul?–a place where the heart must feel and suffer in a thousand diverse ways? Not *110* merely is the heart a horn-book. It is the mind's Bible, it is the mind's experience; it is the teat from which the mind or intelligence sucks its identity. As various as the lives of men are, so various become their souls; and thus does God make individual beings, souls, identical souls, of the sparks of his own essence. This appears to me a faint sketch of a system of salvation which does not affront our reason and humanity. I am convinced that many difficulties which Christians labour under would vanish before it. (*21 April 1819*)

10. To James Rice, 14 February 1820

I am sorry to bear of your relapse and hypochondriac symptoms attending it. Let us hope for the best, as you say. I shall follow your example in looking to the future good rather than brooding upon present ill. I have not been so worn with lengthened illnesses as you have, therefore cannot answer you on your own ground with respect to those haunting and deformed thoughts and feelings you speak of. When I have been or supposed myself in health, I have had my share of them, especially within this last year. I may say *10* that for sixth months before I was taken ill I had not passed a tranquil day–either that gloom overspread me or I was suffering under some passionate feeling; or, if I turned to versify, that acerbated the poison of either sensation. The beauties of Nature had lost their power over me. How astonishingly (here I must premise that illness, as far as I can judge in so short a time, has relieved my mind of a load of deceptive thoughts and images and makes me per-ceive things in a truer light) how astonishingly does the chance of leaving the world impress a sense of its natural beauties on us. Like poor Falstaff, though I do not babble, I think of green fields. I muse with the greatest affection on every flower I have known from my infancy. Their shapes and colours are as new to me as if I had just created them with a superhuman fancy. It is because they are connected with the most thoughtless and happiest moments of our lives. I have seen foreign flowers in hothouses of the most beautiful nature, but I do not care a straw for them. The simple flowers of our spring are what I want to see again.

La Belle Dame Sans Merci

'Happy is England!'

Happy is England! I could be content
　To see no other verdure than its own,
　To feel no other breezes than are blown
Through its tall woods with high romances blent.
Yet do I sometimes feel a languishment
　For skies Italian, and an inward groan
　To sit upon an Alp as on a throne,
And half forget what world or worldling meant.
Happy is England, sweet her artless daughters,
10　　Enough their simple loveliness for me,
　　Enough their whitest arms in silence clinging.
　Yet do I often warmly burn to see
　　Beauties of deeper glance, and hear their singing,
And float with them about the summer waters.

On a Leander Gem which Miss Reynolds, my Kind Friend, Gave Me

Come hither all sweet maidens soberly,
Down-looking ay, and with a chastened light
  Hid in the fringes of your eyelids white,
And meekly let your fair hands joinèd be.
Are ye so gentle that ye could not see,
    Untouched, a victim of your beauty bright
    Sinking away to his young spirit's night,
Sinking bewildered 'mid the dreary sea?
'Tis young Leander toiling to his death.
    Nigh swooning, he doth purse his weary lips
      For Hero's cheek and smiles against her smile.
    Oh, horrid dream! See how his body dips
      Dead-heavy; arms and shoulders gleam awhile;
He's gone; up bubbles all his amorous breath!

Endymion: a Poetic Romance

from Book I

Wherein lies happiness? In that which becks
Our ready minds to fellowship divine,
A fellowship with essence, till we shine
780 Full alchemized, and free of space. Behold
The clear religion of heaven! Fold
A rose leaf round thy finger's taperness
And soothe thy lips; hist, when the airy stress
Of music's kiss impregnates the free winds,
And with a sympathetic touch unbinds
Aeolian magic from their lucid wombs—
Then old songs waken from enclouded tombs,
Old ditties sigh above their father's grave,
Ghosts of melodious prophesyings rave
790 Round every spot where trod Apollo's foot;
Bronze clarions awake and faintly bruit
Where long ago a giant battle was;
And, from the turf, a lullaby doth pass
In every place where infant Orpheus slept.
Feel we these things? That moment have we stepped
Into a sort of oneness, and our state
Is like a floating spirit's. But there are
Richer entanglements, enthralments far
More self-destroying, leading, by degrees,
800 To the chief intensity: the crown of these
Is made of love and friendship, and sits high
Upon the forehead of humanity.
All its more ponderous and bulky worth
Is friendship, whence there ever issues forth
A steady splendour; but at the tip-top
There hangs by unseen film an orbèd drop
Of light, and that is love. Its influence,
Thrown in our eyes, genders a novel sense,
At which we start and fret, till in the end,
810 Melting into its radiance, we blend,

Mingle, and so become a part of it—
Nor with aught else can our souls interknit
So wingedly. When we combine therewith,
Life's self is nourished by its proper pith,
And we are nurtured like a pelican brood.
Aye, so delicious is the unsating food
That men, who might have towered in the van
Of all the congregated world, to fan
And winnow from the coming step of time
820   All chaff of custom, wipe away all slime
Left by men-slugs and human serpentry,
Have been content to let occasion die,
Whilst they did sleep in love's elysium.
And, truly, I would rather be struck dumb
Than speak against this ardent listlessness,
For I have ever thought that it might bless
The world with benefits unknowingly,
As does the nightingale, up-perchèd high,
And cloistered among cool and bunchèd leaves—
830   She sings but to her love, nor e'er conceives
How tiptoe night holds back her dark-grey hood.
Just so may love, although 'tis understood
The mere commingling of passionate breath,
Produce more than our searching witnesseth—
What I know not, but who, of men, can tell
That flowers would bloom, or that green fruit would
      swell
To melting pulp, that fish would have bright mail,
The earth its dower of river, wood, and vale,
The meadows runnels, runnels pebble-stones,
840   The seed its harvest, or the lute its tones,
Tones ravishment, or ravishment its sweet,
If human souls did never kiss and greet?

Time's Sea

Time's sea hath been five years at its slow ebb,
   Long hours have to and fro let creep the sand,
Since I was tangled in thy beauty's web,
   And snared by the ungloving of thine hand.
And yet I never look on midnight sky,
   But I behold thine eyes' well-memoried light.
I cannot look upon the rose's dye,
   But to thy cheek my soul doth take its flight.
I cannot look on any budding flower,
   But my fond ear, in fancy at thy lips
And hearkening for a love-sound, doth devour
   Its sweets in the wrong sense. Thou dost eclipse
Every delight with sweet remembering,
And grief unto my darling joys dost bring.

Isabella; or, The Pot of Basil

Fair Isabel, poor simple Isabel!
  Lorenzo, a young palmer in Love's eye!
They could not in the self-same mansion dwell
  Without some stir of heart, some malady;
They could not sit at meals but feel how well
  It soothèd each to be the other by;
They could not, sure, beneath the same roof sleep
But to each other dream, and nightly weep.

II

With every morn their love grew tenderer,
10   With every eve deeper and tenderer still;
He might not in house, field, or garden stir,
  But her full shape would all his seeing fill;
And his continual voice was pleasanter
  To her than noise of trees or hidden rill;
Her lute-string gave an echo of his name,
She spoilt her half-done broidery with the same.

He knew whose gentle hand was at the latch
  Before the door had given her to his eyes;
And from her chamber-window he would catch
20   Her beauty farther than the falcon spies;
And constant as her vespers would he watch,
  Because her face was turned to the same skies;
And with sick longing all the night outwear,
To hear her morning-step upon the stair.

IV

A whole long month of May in this sad plight
  Made their cheeks paler by the break of June:
'Tomorrow will I bow to my delight,
  Tomorrow will I ask my lady's boon.'
'Oh, may I never see another night,
30   Lorenzo, if thy lips breathe not love's tune.'
So spake they to their pillows; but, alas,

Honeyless days and days did he let pass—

V

Until sweet Isabella's untouched cheek
   Fell sick within the rose's just domain,
Fell thin as a young mother's, who doth seek
   By every lull to cool her infant's pain.
'How ill she is,' said he, 'I may not speak,
   And yet I will, and tell my love all plain.
If looks speak love-laws, I will drink her tears,
40 And at the least 'twill startle off her cares.'

VI

So said he one fair morning, and all day
   His heart beat awfully against his side;
And to his heart he inwardly did pray
   For power to speak; but still the ruddy tide
Stifled his voice and pulsed resolve away—
   Fevered his high conceit of such a bride,
Yet brought him to the meekness of a child.
Alas! when passion is both meek and wild!

VII

So once more he had waked and anguishèd
50 A dreary night of love and misery,
If Isabel's quick eye had not been wed
   To every symbol on his forehead high.
She saw it waxing very pale and dead,
   And straight all flushed; so lispèd tenderly,
'Lorenzo!'—here she ceased her timid quest,
But in her tone and look he read the rest.

VIII

'O Isabella, I can half perceive
   .That I may speak my grief into thine ear.
If thou didst ever anything believe,
60 Believe how I love thee, believe how near
My soul is to its doom. I would not grieve
   Thy hand by unwelcome pressing, would not fear
Thine eyes by gazing, but I cannot live
Another night and not my passion shrive.

IX

Love, thou art leading me from wintry cold,
   Lady, thou leadest me to summer clime,
And I must taste the blossoms that unfold

119

In its ripe warmth this gracious morning time.'
So said, his erewhile timid lips grew bold,
70   And poesied with hers in dewy rhyme.
Great bliss was with them, and great happiness
Grew like a lusty flower in June's caress.

X

Parting they seemed to tread upon the air,
    Twin roses by the zephyr blown apart
Only to meet again more close, and share
    The inward fragrance of each other's heart.
She, to her chamber gone, a ditty fair
    Sang, of delicious love and honeyed dart;
He with light steps went up a western hill,
80   And bade the sun farewell, and joyed his fill.

XI

All close they met again, before the dusk
    Had taken from the stars its pleasant veil,
All close they met, all eves, before the dusk
    Had taken from the stars its pleasant veil,
Close in a bower of hyacinth and musk,
    Unknown of any, free from whispering tale.
Ah, better had it been for ever so,
Than idle ears should pleasure in their woe.

XII

Were they unhappy then? It cannot be.
90   Too many tears for lovers have been shed,
Too many sighs give we to them in fee,
    Too much of pity after they are dead,
Too many doleful stories do we see,
    Whose matter in bright gold were best be read,
Except in such a page where Theseus' spouse
Over the pathless waves towards him bows.

XIII

But, for the general award of love,
    The little sweet doth kill much bitterness.
Though Dido silent is in under-grove,
100   And Isabella's was a great distress,
Though young Lorenzo in warm Indian clove
    Was not embalmed, this truth is not the less—
Even bees, the little almsmen of spring-bowers,
Know there is richest juice in poison-flowers.

With her two brothers this fair lady dwelt,
    Enrichèd from ancestral merchandise,
And for them many a weary hand did swelt
    In torchèd mines and noisy factories,
And many once proud-quivered loins did melt
110   In blood from stinging whip. With hollow eyes
Many all day in dazzling river stood,
To take the rich-ored driftings of the flood.

XV

For them the Ceylon diver held his breath,
    And went all naked to the hungry shark;
For them his ears gushed blood; for them in death
    The seal on the cold ice with piteous bark
Lay full of darts; for them alone did seethe
    A thousand men in troubles wide and dark.
Half-ignorant, they turned an easy wheel
120 That set sharp racks at work to pinch and peel.

XVI

Why were they proud? Because their marble founts
    Gushed with more pride than do a wretch's tears?
Why were they proud? Because fair orange-mounts
    Were of more soft ascent than lazar stairs?
Why were they proud? Because red-lined accounts
    Were richer than the songs of Grecian years?
Why were they proud? Again we ask aloud,
Why in the name of glory were they proud?

XVII

Yet were these Florentines as self-retired
130   In hungry pride and gainful cowardice,
As two close Hebrews in that land inspired,
    Paled in and vineyarded from beggar-spies.
The hawks of ship-mast forests, the untired
    And panniered mules for ducats and old lies,
Quick cat's-paws on the generous stray-away,
Great wits in Spanish, Tuscan, and Malay.

XVIII

How was it these same ledger-men could spy
    Fair Isabella in her downy nest?
How could they find out in Lorenzo's eye
140   A straying from his toil? Hot Egypt's pest
Into their vision covetous and sly!

How could these money-bags see east and west?
Yet so they did—and every dealer fair
Must see behind, as doth the hunted hare.

XIX

O eloquent and famed Boccaccio!
Of thee we now should ask forgiving boon,
And of thy spicy myrtles as they blow,
And of thy roses amorous of the moon,
And of thy lilies, that do paler grow
150   Now they can no more hear thy ghittern's tune,
For venturing syllables that ill beseem
The quiet glooms of such a piteous theme.

XX

Grant thou a pardon here, and then the tale
Shall move on soberly, as it is meet;
There is no other crime, no mad assail
To make old prose in modern rhyme more sweet.
But it is done—succeed the verse or fail—
To honour thee, and thy gone spirit greet,
To stead thee as a verse in English tongue,
160   An echo of thee in the north wind sung.

XXI

These brethren having found by many signs
What love Lorenzo for their sister had,
And how she loved him too, each unconfines
His bitter thoughts to other, well nigh mad
That he, the servant of their trade designs,
Should in their sister's love be blithe and glad,
When 'twas their plan to coax her by degrees
To some high noble and his olive-trees.

XXII

And many a jealous conference had they,
170   And many times they bit their lips alone,
Before they fixed upon a surest way
To make the youngster for his crime atone.
And at the last, these men of cruel clay
Cut Mercy with a sharp knife to the bone,
For they resolvèd in some forest dim
To kill Lorenzo, and there bury him.

XXIII

So on a pleasant morning, as he leant

Into the sunrise, o'er the balustrade
Of the garden-terrace, towards him they bent
180   Their footing through the dews, and to him said,
'You seem there in the quiet of content,
   Lorenzo, and we are most loth to invade
Calm speculation, but if you are wise,
Bestride your steed while cold is in the skies.

XXIV

Today we purpose, aye, this hour we mount,
   To spur three leagues towards the Apennine.
Come down, we pray thee, ere the hot sun count
   His dewy rosary on the eglantine.'
Lorenzo, courteously as he was wont,
190   Bowed a fair greeting to these serpents' whine,
And went in haste, to get in readiness,
With belt and spur and bracing huntsman's dress.

XXV

And as he to the court-yard passed along,
   Each third step did he pause, and listened oft
If he could hear his lady's matin-song,
   Or the light whisper of her footstep soft.
And as he thus over his passion hung,
   He heard a laugh full musical aloft,
When, looking up, he saw her features bright
200 Smile through an indoor lattice, all delight.

XXVI

'Love, Isabel!' said he, 'I was in pain
   Lest I should miss to bid thee a good morrow.
Ah, what if I should lose thee, when so fain
   I am to stifle all the heavy sorrow
Of a poor three hours' absence? But we'll gain
   Out of the amorous dark what day doth borrow.
Good bye! I'll soon be back.' 'Good bye!' said she,
And as he went she chanted merrily.

XXVII

So the two brothers and their murdered man
210   Rode past fair Florence, to where Arno's stream
Gurgles through straitened banks, and still doth fan
   Itself with dancing bulrush, and the bream
Keeps head against the freshets. Sick and wan
   The brothers' faces in the ford did seem,
Lorenzo's flush with love. They passed the water

Into a forest quiet for the slaughter.

XXVIII

There was Lorenzo slain and buried in,
   There in that forest did his great love cease.
Ah, when a soul doth thus its freedom win,
220   It aches in loneliness—is ill at peace
As the break-covert blood-hounds of such sin.
   They dipped their swords in the water, and did tease
Their horses homeward with convulsèd spur,
Each richer by his being a murderer.

XXIX

They told their sister how, with sudden speed,
   Lorenzo had ta'en ship for foreign lands,
Because of some great urgency and need
   In their affairs, requiring trusty hands.
Poor girl! Put on thy stifling widow's weed,
230   And 'scape at once from Hope's accursèd bands.
To-day thou wilt not see him, nor to-morrow,
And the next day will be a day of sorrow.

XXX

She weeps alone for pleasures not to be,
   Sorely she wept until the night came on,
And then, instead of love, O misery!
   She brooded o'er the luxury alone.
His image in the dusk she seemed to see,
   And to the silence made a gentle moan,
Spreading her perfect arms upon the air,
240 And on her couch low murmuring, 'Where? Oh, where?'

XXXI

But Selfishness, Love's cousin, held not long
   Its fiery vigil in her single breast.
She fretted for the golden hour, and hung
   Upon the time with feverish unrest—
Not long, for soon into her heart a throng
   Of higher occupants, a richer zest,
Came tragic—passion not to be subdued,
And sorrow for her love in travels rude.

XXXII

In the mid days of autumn, on their eves,
250   The breath of winter comes from far away

And the sick west continually bereaves
　　Of some bold tinge, and plays a roundelay
Of death among the bushes and the leaves,
　　To make all bare before he dares to stray
From his north cavern. So sweet Isabel
By gradual decay from beauty fell,

XXXIII

Because Lorenzo came not. Oftentimes
　　She asked her brothers, with an eye all pale,
Striving to be itself, what dungeon climes
260　　Could keep him off so long? They spake a tale
Time after time, to quiet her. Their crimes
　　Came on them, like a smoke from Hinnom's vale,
And every night in dreams they groaned aloud
To see their sister in her snowy shroud.

XXXIV

And she had died in drowsy ignorance,
　　But for a thing more deadly dark than all.
It came like a fierce potion, drunk by chance,
　　Which saves a sick man from the feathered pall
For some few gasping moments; like a lance,
270　　Waking an Indian from his cloudy hall
With cruel pierce, and bringing him again
Sense of the gnawing fire at heart and brain.

XXXV

It was a vision. In the drowsy gloom,
　　The dull of midnight, at her couch's foot
Lorenzo stood, and wept. The forest tomb
　　Had marred his glossy hair which once could shoot
Lustre into the sun, and put cold doom
　　Upon his lips, and taken the soft lute
From his lorn voice, and past his loamèd ears
280　　Had made a miry channel for his tears.

XXXVI

Strange sound it was, when the pale shadow spake,
　　For there was striving, in its piteous tongue,
To speak as when on earth it was awake,
　　And Isabella on its music hung.
Languor there was in it, and tremulous shake,
　　As in a palsied Druid's harp unstrung.
And through it moaned a ghostly under-song,
Like hoarse night-gusts sepulchral briars among.

125

XXXVII

Its eyes, though wild, were still all dewy bright
290　　With love, and kept all phantom fear aloof
From the poor girl by magic of their light,
　　The while it did unthread the horrid woof
Of the late darkened time—the murderous spite
　　Of pride and avarice, the dark pine roof
In the forest, and the sodden turfèd dell,
Where, without any word, from stabs he fell.

Saying moreover, 'Isabel, my sweet!
　　Red whortle-berries droop above my head,
And a large flint-stone weighs upon my feet;
300　　Around me beeches and high chestnuts shed
Their leaves and prickly nuts; a sheep-fold bleat
　　Comes from beyond the river to my bed.
Go, shed one tear upon my heather-bloom,
And it shall comfort me within the tomb.

XXXIX

I am a shadow now, alas! alas!
　　Upon the skirts of human-nature dwelling
Alone. I chant alone the holy mass,
　　While little sounds of life are round me knelling,
And glossy bees at noon do fieldward pass,
310　　And many a chapel bell the hour is telling,
Paining me through. Those sounds grow strange to me,
And thou art distant in humanity.

I know what was, I feel full well what is,
　　And I should rage, if spirits could go mad.
Though I forget the taste of earthly bliss,
　　That paleness warms my grave, as though I had
A seraph chosen from the bright abyss
　　To be my spouse. Thy paleness makes me glad;
Thy beauty grows upon me, and I feel
320　　A greater love through all my essence steal.'

XLI

The spirit mourned 'Adieu!'—dissolved and left
　　The atom darkness in a slow turmoil,
As when of healthful midnight sleep bereft,
　　Thinking on rugged hours and fruitless toil
We put our eyes into a pillowy cleft,
　　And see the spangly gloom froth up and boil.

It made sad Isabella's eyelids ache,
And in the dawn she started up awake—

XLII

'Ha! ha!' said she, 'I knew not this hard life,
330   I thought the worst was simple misery.
I thought some Fate with pleasure or with strife
    Portioned us—happy days, or else to die.
But there is crime—a brother's bloody knife!
    Sweet spirit, thou hast schooled my infancy.
I'll visit thee for this, and kiss thine eyes,
And greet thee morn and even in the skies.'

XLIII

When the full morning came, she had devised
    How she might secret to the forest hie;
How she might find the clay, so dearly prized,
340   And sing to it one latest lullaby;
How her short absence might be unsurmised,
    While she the inmost of the dream would try.
Resolved, she took with her an agèd nurse,
And went into that dismal forest-hearse.

XLIV

See, as they creep along the river side,
    How she doth whisper to that agèd dame,
And, after looking round the champaign wide,
    Shows her a knife. 'What feverous hectic flame
Burns in thee, child? What good can thee betide,
350   That thou should'st smile again?' The evening came,
And they had found Lorenzo's earthy bed—
The flint was there, the berries at his head.

XLV

Who hath not loitered in a green church-yard,
    And let his spirit, like a demon-mole,
Work through the clayey soil and gravel hard,
    To see skull, coffined bones, and funeral stole,
Pitying each form that hungry Death hath marred,
    And filling it once more with human soul?
Ah, this is holiday to what was felt
360   When Isabella by Lorenzo knelt.

XLVI

She gazed into the fresh-thrown mould, as though
    One glance did fully all its secrets tell.

127

Clearly she saw, as other eyes would know
    Pale limbs at bottom of a crystal well.
Upon the murderous spot she seemed to grow,
    Like to a native lily of the dell—
Then with her knife, all sudden, she began
To dig more fervently than misers can.

XLVII

Soon she turned up a soilèd glove, whereon
370   Her silk had played in purple phantasies,
She kissed it with a lip more chill than stone,
    And put in in her bosom, where it dries
And freezes utterly unto the bone
    Those dainties made to still an infant's cries.
Then 'gan she work again, nor stayed her care,
But to throw back at times her veiling hair.

XLVIII

That old nurse stood beside her wondering,
    Until her heart felt pity to the core
At sight of such a dismal labouring,
380   And so she kneelèd, with her locks all hoar,
And put her lean hands to the horrid thing—
    Three hours they laboured at this travail sore.
At last they felt the kernel of the grave,
And Isabella did not stamp and rave.

XLIX

Ah, wherefore all this wormy circumstance?
    Why linger at the yawning tomb so long?
Oh, for the gentleness of old romance,
    The simple plaining of a minstrel's song!
Fair reader, at the old tale take a glance,
390   For here, in truth, it doth not well belong
To speak—Oh, turn thee to the very tale,
And taste the music of that vision pale.

L

With duller steel than the Persean sword
    They cut away no formless monster's head,
But one, whose gentleness did well accord
    With death, as life. The ancient harps have said,
Love never dies, but lives, immortal Lord.
    If Love impersonate was ever dead,
Pale Isabella kissed it, and low moaned.
400 'Twas Love—cold, dead indeed, but not dethroned.

LI

In anxious secrecy they took it home,
   And then the prize was all for Isabel.
She calmed its wild hair with a golden comb,
   And all around each eye's sepulchral cell
Pointed each fringèd lash. The smearèd loam
   With tears, as chilly as a dripping well,
She drenched away—and still she combed, and kept
Sighing all day—and still she kissed, and wept.

Then in a silken scarf—sweet with the dews
410   Of precious flowers plucked in Araby,
And divine liquids come with odorous ooze
   Through the cold serpent-pipe refreshfully—
She wrapped it up, and for its tomb did choose
   A garden-pot, wherein she laid it by,
And covered it with mould, and o'er it set
Sweet basil, which her tears kept ever wet.

LIII

And she forgot the stars, the moon, and sun,
   And she forgot the blue above the trees,
And she forgot the dells where waters run,
420   And she forgot the chilly autumn breeze.
She had no knowledge when the day was done,
   And the new morn she saw not, but in peace
Hung over her sweet basil evermore,
And moistened it with tears unto the core.

And so she ever fed it with thin tears,
   Whence thick and green and beautiful it grew,
So that it smelt more balmy than its peers
   Of basil-tufts in Florence, for it drew
Nurture besides, and life, from human fears,
430   From the fast mouldering head there shut from view.
So that the jewel, safely casketed,
Came forth, and in perfumèd leafits spread.

LV

O Melancholy, linger here awhile!
   O Music, Music, breathe despondingly!
O Echo, Echo, from some sombre isle,
   Unknown, Lethean, sigh to us—Oh, sigh!
Spirits in grief, lift up your heads, and smile.
   Lift up your heads, sweet spirits, heavily,

And make a pale light in your cypress glooms,
440　Tinting with silver wan your marble tombs.

LVI

Moan higher, all ye syllables of woe,
　　From the deep throat of sad Melpomene!
Through bronzèd lyre in tragic order go,
　　And touch the strings into a mystery.
Sound mournfully upon the winds and low,
　　For simple Isabel is soon to be
Among the dead. She withers, like a palm
Cut by an Indian for its juicy balm.

LVII

Oh, leave the palm to wither by itself,
450　　Let not quick winter chill its dying hour!
It may not be—those Baälites of pelf,
　　Her brethren, noted the continual shower
From her dead eyes, and many a curious elf,
　　Among her kindred, wondered that such dower
Of youth and beauty should be thrown aside
By one marked out to be a noble's bride.

LVIII

And, furthermore, her brethren wondered much
　　Why she sat drooping by the basil green,
And why it flourished, as by magic touch.
460　　Greatly they wondered what the thing might mean.
They could not surely give belief that such
　　A very nothing would have power to wean
Her from her own fair youth, and pleasures gay,
And even remembrance of her love's delay.

LIX

Therefore they watched a time when they might sift
　　This hidden whim, and long they watched in vain.
For seldom did she go to chapel-shrift,
　　And seldom felt she any hunger-pain.
And when she left, she hurried back, as swift
470　　As bird on wing to breast its eggs again,
And, patient as a hen-bird, sat her there
Beside her basil, weeping through her hair.

LX

Yet they contrived to steal the basil-pot,
　　And to examine it in secret place.

The thing was vile with green and livid spot,
　　And yet they knew it was Lorenzo's face.
The guerdon of their murder they had got,
　　And so left Florence in a moment's space,
Never to turn again. Away they went,
With blood upon their heads, to banishment.

LXI

O Melancholy, turn thine eyes away!
　　O Music, Music, breathe despondingly!
O Echo, Echo, on some other day,
　　From isles Lethean, sigh to us—Oh, sigh!
Spirits of grief, sing not your 'Well-a-way!'
　　For Isabel, sweet Isabel, will die—
Will die a death too lone and incomplete,
Now they have ta'en away her basil sweet.

LXII

Piteous she looked on dead and senseless things,
　　Asking for her lost basil amorously.
And with melodious chuckle in the strings
　　Of her lorn voice, she oftentimes would cry
After the pilgrim in his wanderings,
　　To ask him where her basil was, and why
'Twas hid from her: 'For cruel 'tis,' said she,
'To steal my basil-pot away from me.'

LXIII

And so she pined, and so she died forlorn,
　　Imploring for her basil to the last.
No heart was there in Florence but did mourn
　　In pity of her love, so overcast.
And a sad ditty of this story born
　　From mouth to mouth through all the country
　　　　passed.
Still is the burthen sung: 'Oh, cruelty,
To steal my basil-pot away from me!'

The Eve of St Agnes

I

St. Agnes' Eve—ah, bitter chill it was!
The owl, for all his feathers, was a-cold;
The hare limped trembling through the frozen grass,
And silent was the flock in woolly fold.
Numb were the Beadsman's fingers, while he told
His rosary, and while his frosted breath,
Like pious incense from a censer old,
Seemed taking flight for heaven, without a death,
Past the sweet Virgin's picture, while his prayer he saith.

II

His prayer he saith, this patient, holy man;
Then takes his lamp, and riseth from his knees,
And back returneth, meagre, barefoot, wan,
Along the chapel aisle by slow degrees.
The sculptured dead, on each side, seem to freeze,
Imprisoned in black, purgatorial rails.
Knights, ladies, praying in dumb orat'ries,
He passeth by; and his weak spirit fails
To think how they may ache in icy hoods and mails.

III

Northward he turneth through a little door,
And scarce three steps, ere music's golden tongue
Flattered to tears this agèd man and poor;
But no—already had his deathbell rung,
The joys of all his life were said and sung;
His was harsh penance on St. Agnes' Eve.
Another way he went, and soon among
Rough ashes sat he for his soul's reprieve,
And all night kept awake for sinners' sake to grieve.

IV

That ancient Beadsman heard the prelude soft,
And so it chanced for many a door was wide
From hurry to and fro. Soon, up aloft,
The silver, snarling trumpets 'gan to chide;

The level chambers, ready with their pride,
Were glowing to receive a thousand guests;
The carvèd angels, ever eager-eyed,
Stared, where upon their heads the cornice rests,
With hair blown back, and wings put cross-wise on
     their breasts.

V

At length burst in the argent revelry,
With plume, tiara, and all rich array,
Numerous as shadows haunting fairily
40   The brain, new stuffed in youth, with triumphs gay
Of old romance. These let us wish away,
And turn, sole-thoughted, to one Lady there,
Whose heart had brooded, all that wintry day,
On love, and winged St. Agnes' saintly care,
As she had heard old dames full many times declare.

VI

They told her how, upon St. Agnes' Eve,
Young virgins might have visions of delight,
And soft adorings from their loves receive
Upon the honeyed middle of the night,
50   If ceremonies due they did aright;
As, supperless to bed they must retire,
And couch supine their beauties, lily white,
Nor look behind, nor sideways, but require
Of Heaven with upward eyes for all that they desire.

VII

Full of this whim was thoughtful Madeline.
The music, yearning like a God in pain,
She scarcely heard; her maiden eyes divine,
Fixed on the floor, saw many a sweeping train
Pass by—she heeded not at all; in vain
60   Came many a tiptoe, amorous cavalier,
And back retired—not cooled by high disdain,
But she saw not; her heart was otherwhere.
She sighed for Agnes' dreams, the sweetest of the year.

VIII

She danced along with vague, regardless eyes,
Anxious her lips, her breathing quick and short.
The hallowed hour was near at hand. She sighs
Amid the timbrels and the thronged resort
Of whisperers in anger, or in sport;

'Mid looks of love, defiance, hate, and scorn,
70   Hoodwinked with fairy fancy–all amort,
Save to St. Agnes and her lambs unshorn,
And all the bliss to be before to-morrow morn.

IX

So, purposing each moment to retire,
She lingered still. Meantime, across the moors,
Had come young Porphyro, with heart on fire
For Madeline. Beside the portal doors,
Buttressed from moonlight, stands he and implores
All saints to give him sight of Madeline
But for one moment in the tedious hours,
80   That he might gaze and worship all unseen;
Perchance speak, kneel, touch, kiss–in sooth such things
        have been.

X

He ventures in—let no buzzed whisper tell,
All eyes be muffled, or a hundred swords
Will storm his heart, love's feverous citadel.
For him, those chambers held barbarian hordes,
Hyena foemen, and hot-blooded lords,
Whose very dogs would execrations howl
Against his lineage; not one breast affords
Him any mercy, in that mansion foul,
90   Save one old beldame, weak in body and in soul.

XI

Ah, happy chance! The agèd creature came,
Shuffling along with ivory-headed wand,
To where he stood, hid from the torch's flame,
Behind a broad hall-pillar, far beyond
The sound of merriment and chorus bland.
He startled her; but soon she knew his face,
And grasped his fingers in her palsied hand,
Saying, 'Mercy, Porphyro! Hie thee from this place;
They are all here to-night, the whole blood-thirsty race!

XII

100   Get hence! Get hence! There's dwarfish Hildebrand—
He had a fever late, and in the fit
He cursèd thee and thine, both house and land;
Then there's that old Lord Maurice, not a whit
More tame for his gray hairs. Alas me! Flit,
Flit like a ghost away!' 'Ah, gossip dear,

We're safe enough; here in this arm-chair sit,
And tell me how—' 'Good Saints! Not here, not here;
Follow me, child, or else these stones will be thy bier.'

XIII

He followed through a lowly archèd way,
Brushing the cobwebs with his lofty plume,
And as she muttered, 'Well-a—well-a-day!'
He found him in a little moonlight room,
Pale, latticed, chill, and silent as a tomb.
'Now tell me where is Madeline,' said he,
'Oh, tell me, Angela, by the holy loom
Which none but secret sisterhood may see,
When they St. Agnes' wool are weaving piously.'

XIV

'St. Agnes? Ah! It is St. Agnes' Eve—
Yet men will murder upon holy days:
Thou must hold water in a witch's sieve,
And be liege-lord of all the elves and fays,
To venture so; it fills me with amaze
To see thee, Porphyro!—St. Agnes' Eve!
God's help! My lady fair the conjuror plays
This very night. Good angels her deceive!
But let me laugh awhile, I've mickle time to grieve.'

XV

Feebly she laugheth in the languid moon,
While Porphyro upon her face doth look,
Like puzzled urchin on an agèd crone
Who keepeth closed a wondrous riddle-book,
As spectacled she sits in chimney nook.
But soon his eyes grew brilliant, when she told
His lady's purpose, and he scarce could brook
Tears at the thought of those enchantments cold,
And Madeline asleep in lap of legends old.

XVI

Sudden a thought came like a full-blown rose,
Flushing his brow, and in his painèd heart
Made purple riot; then doth he propose
A stratagem that makes the beldame start:
'A cruel man and impious thou art—
Sweet lady, let her pray, and sleep, and dream
Alone with her good angels, far apart

135

From wicked men like thee. Go, go! I deem
Thou canst not surely be the same that thou didst seem.'

XVII

'I will not harm her, by all saints I swear,'
Quoth Porphyro: 'Oh, may I ne'er find grace
When my weak voice shall whisper its last prayer,
If one of her soft ringlets I displace,
Or look with ruffian passion in her face—
150   Good Angela, believe me by these tears,
Or I will, even in a moment's space,
Awake with horrid shout my foemen's ears,
And beard them, though they be more fanged than
    wolves and bears.'

XVIII

'Ah, why wilt thou affright a feeble soul?
A poor, weak, palsy-stricken, churchyard thing,
Whose passing-bell may ere the midnight toll!
Whose prayers for thee, each morn and evening,
Were never missed.' Thus plaining doth she bring
A gentler speech from burning Porphyro,
160   So woeful, and of such deep sorrowing,
That Angela gives promise she will do
Whatever he shall wish, betide her weal or woe.

XIX

Which was to lead him, in close secrecy,
Even to Madeline's chamber, and there hide
Him in a closet, of such privacy
That he might see her beauty unespied,
And win perhaps that night a peerless bride,
While legioned fairies paced the coverlet
And pale enchantment held her sleepy-eyed.
170   Never on such a night have lovers met
Since Merlin paid his Demon all the monstrous debt.

XX

'It shall be as thou wishest,' said the Dame,
'All cates and dainties shall be storèd there
Quickly on this feast-night; by the tambour frame
Her own lute thou wilt see. No time to spare,
For I am slow and feeble, and scarce dare
On such a catering trust my dizzy head.
Wait here, my child, with patience; kneel in prayer

136

The while. Ah! Thou must needs the lady wed,
180 Or may I never leave my grave among the dead.'

XXI

So saying, she hobbled off with busy fear.
The lover's endless minutes slowly passed;
The dame returned, and whispered in his ear
To follow her; with agèd eyes aghast
From fright of dim espial. Safe at last,
Through many a dusky gallery, they gain
The maiden's chamber, silken, hushed, and chaste,
Where Porphyro took covert, pleased amain.
His poor guide hurried back with agues in her brain.

XXII

190 Her faltering hand upon the balustrade,
Old Angela was feeling for the stair,
When Madeline, St. Agnes' charmèd maid,
Rose, like a missioned spirit, unaware.
With silver taper's light, and pious care,
She turned, and down the agèd gossip led
To a safe level matting. Now prepare,
Young Porphyro, for gazing on that bed—
She comes, she comes again, like ring-dove frayed and
fled.

XXIII

Out went the taper as she hurried in;
200 Its little smoke, in pallid moonshine, died.
She closed the door, she panted, all akin
To spirits of the air, and visions wide—
No uttered syllable, or woe betide!
But to her heart, her heart was voluble,
Paining with eloquence her balmy side,
As though a tongueless nightingale should swell
Her throat in vain, and die, heart-stifled, in her dell.

XXIV

A casement high and triple-arched there was,
All garlanded with carven imageries
210 Of fruits, and flowers, and bunches of knot-grass,
And diamonded with panes of quaint device
Innumerable of stains and splendid dyes,
As are the tiger-moth's deep-damasked wings;
And in the midst, 'mong thousand heraldries,

And twilight saints, and dim emblazonings,
A shielded scutcheon blushed with blood of queens and
    kings.

XXV

Full on this casement shone the wintry moon,
  And threw warm gules on Madeline's fair breast
  As down she knelt for heaven's grace and boon;
220   Rose-bloom fell on her hands, together pressed,
  And on her silver cross soft amethyst,
  And on her hair a glory, like a saint.
She seemed a splendid angel, newly dressed,
  Save wings, for Heaven. Porphyro grew faint;
She knelt, so pure a thing, so free from mortal taint.

XXVI

Anon his heart revives; her vespers done,
  Of all its wreathèd pearls her hair she frees;
  Unclasps her warmèd jewels one by one;
  Loosens her fragrant bodice; by degrees
230   Her rich attire creeps rustling to her knees.
  Half-hidden, like a mermaid in sea-weed,
  Pensive awhile she dreams awake, and sees,
  In fancy, fair St. Agnes in her bed,
But dares not look behind, or all the charm is fled.

XXVII

Soon, trembling in her soft and chilly nest,
  In sort of wakeful swoon, perplexed she lay,
  Until the poppied warmth of sleep oppressed
  Her soothèd limbs, and soul fatigued—away
240   Flown, like a thought, until the morrow-day;
  Blissfully havened both from joy and pain;
  Clasped like a missal where swart Paynims pray;
  Blinded alike from sunshine and from rain,
As though a rose should shut, and be a bud again.

XXVIII

Stol'n to this paradise, and so entranced,
  Porphyro gazed upon her empty dress,
  And listened to her breathing, if it chanced
  To wake into a slumbrous tenderness;
  Which when he heard, that minute did he bless,
  And breathed himself, then from the closet crept,
250   Noiseless as fear in a wide wilderness—

And over the hushed carpet, silent, stepped,
And 'tween the curtains peeped, where, lo!—how fast
   she slept.

XXIX

Then by the bed-side, where the faded moon
Made a dim, silver twilight, soft he set
A table and, half anguished, threw thereon
A cloth of woven crimson, gold, and jet.
Oh, for some drowsy Morphean amulet!
The boisterous, midnight, festive clarion,
The kettle-drum and far-heard clarionet,
Affray his ears, though but in dying tone;—
The hall door shuts again, and all the noise is gone.

XXX

And still she slept an azure-lidded sleep,
In blanchèd linen, smooth and lavendered,
While he from forth the closet brought a heap
Of candied apple, quince, and plum, and gourd,
With jellies soother than the creamy curd,
And lucent syrops, tinct with cinnamon;
Manna and dates, in argosy transferred
From Fez; and spicèd dainties, every one,
From silken Samarcand to cedared Lebanon.

XXXI

These delicates he heaped with glowing hand
On golden dishes and in baskets bright
Of wreathèd silver; sumptuous they stand
In the retired quiet of the night,
Filling the chilly room with perfume light.
'And now, my love, my seraph fair, awake!
Thou art my heaven, and I thine eremite.
Open thine eyes, for meek St. Agnes' sake,
Or I shall drowse beside thee, so my soul doth ache.'

XXXII

Thus whispering, his warm, unnervèd arm
Sank in her pillow. Shaded was her dream
By the dusk curtains; 'twas a midnight charm
Impossible to melt as icèd stream.
The lustrous salvers in the moonlight gleam,
Broad golden fringe upon the carpet lies.
It seemed he never, never could redeem

139

From such a steadfast spell his lady's eyes;
So mused awhile, entoiled in woofèd phantasies.

XXXIII

Awakening up, he took her hollow lute,
290   Tumultuous, and, in chords that tenderest be,
He played an ancient ditty, long since mute,
In Provence called, 'La belle dame sans mercy',
Close to her ear touching the melody—
Wherewith disturbed, she uttered a soft moan.
He ceased—she panted quick—and suddenly
Her blue affrayèd eyes wide open shone;
Upon his knees he sank, pale as smooth-sculptured stone.

XXXIV

Her eyes were open, but she still beheld,
Now wide awake, the vision of her sleep—
300   There was a painful change, that nigh expelled
The blisses of her dream so pure and deep.
At which fair Madeline began to weep,
And moan forth witless words with many a sigh,
While still her gaze on Porphyro would keep;
Who knelt, with joinèd hands and piteous eye,
Fearing to move or speak, she looked so dreamingly.

XXXV

'Ah, Porphyro!' said she, 'but even now
Thy voice was at sweet tremble in mine ear,
Made tuneable with every sweetest vow,
310   And those sad eyes were spiritual and clear.
How changed thou art! How pallid, chill, and drear!
Give me that voice again, my Porphyro,
Those looks immortal, those complainings dear!
Oh, leave me not in this eternal woe,
For if thou diest, my love, I know not where to go.'

XXXVI

Beyond a mortal man impassioned far
At these voluptuous accents, he arose,
Ethereal, flushed, and like a throbbing star
Seen mid the sapphire heaven's deep repose;
320   Into her dream he melted, as the rose
Blendeth its odour with the violet,
Solution sweet—meantime the frost-wind blows
Like Love's alarum pattering the sharp sleet

Against the window-panes; St. Agnes' moon hath set.

XXXVII

'Tis dark; quick pattereth the flaw-blown sleet.
'This is no dream, my bride, my Madeline!'
'Tis dark; the icèd gusts still rave and beat.
'No dream, alas! alas! and woe is mine!
Porphyro will leave me here to fade and pine.
330   Cruel! What traitor could thee hither bring?
I curse not, for my heart is lost in thine,
Though thou forsakest a deceivèd thing—
A dove forlorn and lost with sick, unprunèd wing.'

XXXVIII

'My Madeline! Sweet dreamer! Lovely bride!
Say, may I be for ay thy vassal blest?
Thy beauty's shield, heart-shaped and vermeil dyed?
Ah, silver shrine, here will I take my rest
After so many hours of toil and quest,
A famished pilgrim—saved by miracle.
340   Though I have found, I will not rob thy nest
Saving of thy sweet self; if thou think'st well
To trust, fair Madeline, to no rude infidel.

XXXIX

Hark! 'Tis an elfin-storm from fairy land,
Of haggard seeming, but a boon indeed.
Arise—arise! The morning is at hand;
The bloated wassailers will never heed.
Let us away, my love, with happy speed—
There are no ears to hear, or eyes to see,
Drowned all in Rhenish and the sleepy mead.
350   Awake! Arise, my love, and fearless be!
For o'er the southern moors I have a home for thee.'

XL

She hurried at his words, beset with fears,
For there were sleeping dragons all around,
At glaring watch, perhaps, with ready spears;
Down the wide stairs a darkling way they found.
In all the house was heard no human sound;
A chain-drooped lamp was flickering by each door;
The arras, rich with horseman, hawk, and hound,
Fluttered in the besieging wind's uproar;
360 And the long carpets rose along the gusty floor.

141

XLI

They glide, like phantoms, into the wide hall;
Like phantoms, to the iron porch they glide;
Where lay the Porter, in uneasy sprawl,
With a huge empty flagon by his side.
The wakeful bloodhound rose and shook his hide,
But his sagacious eye an inmate owns.
By one, and one, the bolts full easy slide;
The chains lie silent on the footworn stones;
The key turns, and the door upon its hinges groans.

370   And they are gone—aye, ages long ago
These lovers fled away into the storm.
That night the Baron dreamt of many a woe,
And all his warrior-guests, with shade and form
Of witch and demon, and large coffin-worm,
Were long be-nightmared. Angela the old
Died palsy-twitched, with meagre face deform;
The Beadsman, after thousand aves told,
For ay unsought for slept among his ashes cold.

'As Hermes once took to his feathers light'

As Hermes once took to his feathers light,
   When lullèd Argus, baffled, swooned and slept,
So on a Delphic reed, my idle sprite
   So played, so charmed, so conquered, so bereft
The dragon-world of all its hundred eyes;
   And, seeing it asleep, so fled away—
Not to pure Ida with its snow-cold skies,
   Nor unto Tempe where Jove grieved that day;
But to that second circle of sad hell,
   Where in the gust, the whirlwind, and the flaw
Of rain and hail-stones, lovers need not tell
   Their sorrows. Pale were the sweet lips I saw,
Pale were the lips I kissed, and fair the form
I floated with, about that melancholy storm.

La Belle Dame Sans Merci

I

Oh, what can ail thee, knight-at-arms,
  Alone and palely loitering?
The sedge has withered from the lake,
  And no birds sing!

II

Oh, what can ail thee, knight-at-arms,
  So haggard and so woe-begone?
The squirrel's granary is full,
  And the harvest's done.

III

I see a lily on thy brow,
10   With anguish moist and fever-dew,
And on thy cheek a fading rose
  Fast withereth too.

IV

I met a lady in the meads
  Full beautiful, a fairy's child,
Her hair was long, her foot was light,
  And her eyes were wild.

V

I made a garland for her head,
  And bracelets too, and fragrant zone;
She looked at me as she did love,
20   And made sweet moan.

VI

I set her on my pacing steed,
  And nothing else saw all day long;
For sidelong would she bend, and sing
  A fairy's song.

VII

She found me roots of relish sweet,
  And honey wild, and manna dew;

And sure in language strange she said,
  'I love thee true'.

VIII

She took me to her elfin grot,
30 And there she wept, and sighed full sore,
And there I shut her wild wild eyes
  With kisses four.

IX

And there she lullèd me asleep,
  And there I dreamed–Ah! woe betide!—
The latest dream I ever dreamed
  On the cold hill side.

X

I saw pale kings, and princes too,
  Pale warriors, death-pale were they all;
They cried–'La belle Dame sans merci
40 Hath thee in thrall!'

XI

I saw their starved lips in the gloam
  With horrid warning gapèd wide,
And I awoke, and found me here
  On the cold hill side.

XII

And this is why I sojourn here,
  Alone and palely loitering,
Though the sedge is withered from the lake,
  And no birds sing.

Otho the Great

Act V: Scene 5

Ludolph.   There should be three more here:
For two of them, they stay away perhaps,
Being gloomy-minded, haters of fair revels—
They know their own thoughts best.

                                As for the third,
Deep blue eyes, semi-shaded in white lids,
60   Finished with lashes fine for more soft shade,
Completed by her twin-arched ebon brows;
White temples of exactest elegance,
Of even mould, felicitous and smooth;
Cheeks fashioned tenderly on either side,
So perfect, so divine that our poor eyes
Are dazzled with the sweet proportioning,
And wonder that 'tis so—the magic chance!
Her nostrils, small, fragrant, fairy-delicate;
Her lips—I swear no human bones e'er wore
70   So taking a disguise. You shall behold her!
We'll have her presently; aye, you shall see her,
And wonder at her, friends, she is so fair—
She is the world's chief jewel, and by heaven
She's mine by right of marriage! She is mine!
Patience, good people, in fit time I send
A summoner. She will obey my call,
Being a wife most mild and dutiful.
First I would hear what music is prepared
To herald and receive her—let me hear!
80   *Sigifred.* Bid the musicians soothe him tenderly.
                              [*A soft strain of music.*
Ludolph. Ye have none better? No—I am content;
'Tis a rich sobbing melody, with reliefs
Full and majestic; it is well enough,
And will be sweeter when ye see her pace
Sweeping into this presence, glistened o'er
With emptied caskets, and her train upheld
By ladies, habited in robes of lawn

Sprinkled with golden crescents, others bright
In silks, with spangles showered, and bowed to
90 By Duchesses and pearlèd Margravines!
Sad, that the fairest creature of the earth—
I pray you mind me not—'tis sad, I say,
That the extremest beauty of the world
Should so entrench herself away from me,
Behind a barrier of engendered guilt!
Second Lady. Ah! what a moan!
First Knight.   Most piteous indeed!
Ludolph. She shall be brought before this company,
And then—then—
First Lady.   He muses.
Gersa.   O, Fortune, where will this
    end?
Sigifred. I guess his purpose! Indeed he must not have
100 That pestilence brought in—that cannot be,
There we must stop him.
Gersa.   I am lost! Hush, hush!
He is about to rave again.
Ludolph. A barrier of guilt! I was the fool,
She was the cheater! Who's the cheater now,
And who the fool? The entrapped, the cagèd fool,
The bird-limed raven? She shall croak to death
Secure! Methinks I have her in my fist,
To crush her with my heel! Wait, wait! I marvel
My father keeps away: good friend—ah! Sigifred!
110 Do bring him to me—and Erminia
I fain would see before I sleep—and Ethelbert,
That he may bless me, as I know he will
Though I have cursed him.
Sigifred.   Rather suffer me
To lead you to them—
Ludolph.   No, excuse me, no!
The day is not quite done. Go bring them hither.
                              [*Exit* Sigifred.
Certes, a father's smile should, like sunlight,
Slant on my sheafèd harvest of ripe bliss—
Besides, I thirst to pledge my lovely bride
In a deep goblet: let me see—what wine?
120 The strong Iberian juice, or mellow Greek?
Or pale Calabrian? Or the Tuscan grape?
Or of old Aetna's pulpy wine presses,
Black stained with the fat vintage, as it were

147

The purple slaughter-house, where Bacchus' self
Pricked his own swollen veins? Where is my Page?
Page.   Here, here!
Ludolph. Be ready to obey me; anon thou shalt
Bear a soft message for me; for the hour
Draws near when I must make a winding up
Of bridal mysteries. A fine-spun vengeance!
130 Carve it on my tomb, that when I rest beneath
Men shall confess—This Prince was gulled and cheated,
But from the ashes of disgrace he rose
More than a fiery dragon, and did burn
His ignominy up in purging fires!
Did I not send, sir, but a moment past,
For my father?
Gersa.   You did.
Ludolph.   Perhaps 'twould be
Much better he came not.
Gersa.   He enters now!

Enter Otho, Erminia, Ethelbert, Sigifred, *and Physician.*

Ludolph. O thou good man, against whose sacred head
I was a mad conspirator, chiefly too
140 For the sake of my fair newly wedded wife,
Now to be punished, do not look so sad!
Those charitable eyes will thaw my heart,
Those tears will wash away a just resolve,
A verdict ten times sworn! Awake, awake!
Put on a judge's brow, and use a tongue
Made iron-stern by habit! Thou shalt see
A deed to be applauded, 'scribed in gold!
Join a loud voice to mine, and so denounce
What I alone will execute!
Otho.   Dear son,
150 What is it? By your father's love, I sue
That it be nothing merciless!
Ludolph.   To that demon?
Not so! No! She is in temple-stall
Being garnished for the sacrifice, and I,
The Priest of Justice, will immolate her
Upon the altar of wrath! She stings me through!
Even as the worm doth feed upon the nut,
So she, a scorpion, preys upon my brain!
I feel her gnawing here! Let her but vanish,
Then, father, I will lead your legions forth,

160 Compact in steelèd squares, and spearèd files,
And bid our trumpets speak a fell rebuke
To nations drowsed in peace!
Otho.   To-morrow, son,
Be your word law; forget to-day—
Ludolph.   I will
When I have finished it! Now! now! I'm pight
Tight-footed for the deed!
Erminia.   Alas! Alas!
Ludolph. What Angel's voice is that? Erminia!
Ah! gentlest creature, whose sweet innocence
Was almost murdered; I am penitent,
Wilt thou forgive me? And thou, holy man,
170 Good Ethelbert, shall I die in peace with you?
Erminia. Die, my lord!
Ludolph.   I feel it possible.
Otho.   Physician?
Physician. I fear me he is past my skill.
Otho.   Not so!
Ludolph. I see it—I see it—I have been wandering!
Half-mad—not right here—I forget my purpose.
Bestir, bestir, Auranthe! Ha! Ha! Ha!
Youngster! Page! Go bid them drag her to me!
Obey! This shall finish it!   [*Draws a dagger.*
Otho.   O my son! my son!
Sigifred. This must not be—stop there!
Ludolph.   Am I obeyed?
A little talk with her—no harm—haste! haste!
                                    [*Exit Page.*
180 Set her before me—never fear I can strike.
Several Voices. My Lord! My Lord!
Gersa.   Good Prince!
Ludolph. Why do ye trouble me? Out—out—out away!
There she is! Take that! And that! No, no—
That's not well done. Where is she?
            [*The doors open. Enter Page. Several women are seen
            grouped about Auranthe in the inner room.*
Page. Alas! My Lord, my Lord! They cannot move her!
Her arms are stiff—her fingers clenched and cold!
Ludolph. She's dead!
                    [*Staggers and falls into their arms.*
Ethelbert.   Take away the dagger.
Gersa.   Softly; so!
Otho. Thank God for that!
Sigifred.   It could not harm him now.

 Gersa. No!—brief be his anguish!

190 *Ludolph.* She's gone—I am content. Nobles, good night!
 Where is your hand, father? What sultry air!
 We are all weary—faint—set ope the doors—
 I will to bed!—To-morrow—   *[Dies.*

THE CURTAIN FALLS

Lamia

Part I

Upon a time, before the fairy broods
Drove Nymph and Satyr from the prosperous woods,
Before king Oberon's bright diadem,
Sceptre, and mantle clasped with dewy gem,
Frighted away the Dryads and the Fauns
From rushes green, and brakes, and cowslipped lawns,
The ever-smitten Hermes empty left
His golden throne, bent warm on amorous theft.
From high Olympus had he stolen light,
10 On this side of Jove's clouds, to escape the sight
Of his great summoner, and made retreat
Into a forest on the shores of Crete.
For somewhere in that sacred island dwelt
A nymph to whom all hoofèd Satyrs knelt,
At whose white feet the languid Tritons poured
Pearls, while on land they withered and adored.
Fast by the springs where she to bathe was wont,
And in those meads where sometime she might haunt,
Were strewn rich gifts, unknown to any Muse,
20 Though Fancy's casket were unlocked to choose.
Ah, what a world of love was at her feet!
So Hermes thought, and a celestial heat
Burnt from his wingèd heels to either ear,
That from a whiteness, as the lily clear,
Blushed into roses 'mid his golden hair,
Fallen in jealous curls about his shoulders bare.

From vale to vale, from wood to wood, he flew,
Breathing upon the flowers his passion new,
And wound with many a river to its head
30 To find where this sweet nymph prepared her secret
         bed.
In vain; the sweet nymph might nowhere be found,
And so he rested on the lonely ground,
Pensive, and full of painful jealousies
Of the Wood-Gods and even the very trees.

There as he stood, he heard a mournful voice,
Such as, once heard, in gentle heart destroys
All pain but pity; thus the lone voice spake:
'When from this wreathèd tomb shall I awake!
When move in a sweet body fit for life,
40 And love, and pleasure, and the ruddy strife
Of hearts and lips! Ah, miserable me!'
The God, dove-footed, glided silently
Round bush and tree, soft-brushing in his speed
The taller grasses and full-flowering weed,
Until he found a palpitating snake,
Bright, and cirque-couchant in a dusky brake.

She was a gordian shape of dazzling hue,
Vermilion-spotted, golden, green and blue;
Striped like a zebra, freckled like a pard,
50 Eyed like a peacock, and all crimson barred;
And full of silver moons, that, as she breathed,
Dissolved, or brighter shone, or interwreathed
Their lustres with the gloomier tapestries--
So rainbow-sided, touched with miseries,
She seemed, at once, some penanced lady elf,
Some demon's mistress, or the demon's self.
Upon her crest she wore a wannish fire
Sprinkled with stars, like Ariadne's tiar;
Her head was serpent, but ah, bitter-sweet!
60 She had a woman's mouth with all its pearls complete;
And for her eyes--what could such eyes do there
But weep, and weep, that they were born so fair,
As Proserpine still weeps for her Sicilian air?
Her throat was serpent, but the words she spake
Came, as through bubbling honey, for love's sake,
And thus--while Hermes on his pinions lay,
Like a stooped falcon ere he takes his prey:

'Fair Hermes, crowned with feathers, fluttering light,
I had a splendid dream of thee last night:
70 I saw thee sitting, on a throne of gold,
Among the Gods, upon Olympus old,
The only sad one; for thou didst not hear
The soft, lute-fingered Muses chanting clear,
Nor even Apollo when he sang alone,
Deaf to his throbbing throat's long, long melodious
    moan.
I dreamt I saw thee, robed in purple flakes,
Break amorous through the clouds, as morning breaks,

And, swiftly as a bright Phoebean dart,
Strike for the Cretan isle; and here thou art!
80   Too gentle Hermes, hast thou found the maid?'
Whereat the star of Lethe not delayed
His rosy eloquence, and thus inquired:
'Thou smooth-lipped serpent, surely high inspired!
Thou beauteous wreath, with melancholy eyes,
Possess whatever bliss thou canst devise,
Telling me only where my nymph is fled—
Where she doth breathe!' 'Bright planet, thou hast
    said,'
Returned the snake, 'but seal with oaths, fair God!'
'I swear,' said Hermes, 'by my serpent rod,
90   And by thine eyes, and by thy starry crown!'
Light flew his earnest words, among the blossoms blown.
Then thus again the brilliance feminine:
'Too frail of heart! For this lost nymph of thine,
Free as the air, invisibly, she strays
About these thornless wilds; her pleasant days
She tastes unseen; unseen her nimble feet
Leave traces in the grass and flowers sweet;
From weary tendrils, and bowed branches green,
She plucks the fruit unseen, she bathes unseen;
100   And by my power is her beauty veiled
To keep it unaffronted, unassailed
By the love-glances of unlovely eyes
Of Satyrs, Fauns, and bleared Silenus' sighs.
Pale grew her immortality, for woe
Of all these lovers, and she grievèd so
I took compassion on her, bade her steep
Her hair in weird syrups, that would keep
Her loveliness invisible, yet free
To wander as she loves, in liberty.
110   Thou shalt behold her, Hermes, thou alone,
If thou wilt, as thou swearest, grant my boon!'
Then, once again, the charmèd God began
An oath, and through the serpent's ears it ran
Warm, tremulous, devout, psalterian.
Ravished, she lifted her Circean head,
Blushed a live damask, and swift-lisping said,
'I was a woman, let me have once more
A woman's shape, and charming as before.
I love a youth of Corinth—Oh, the bliss!
120   Give me my woman's form, and place me where he is.
Stoop, Hermes, let me breathe upon thy brow,

And thou shalt see thy sweet nymph even now.'
The God on half-shut feathers sank serene,
She breathed upon his eyes, and swift was seen
Of both the guarded nymph near-smiling on the green.
It was no dream; or say a dream it was,
Real are the dreams of Gods, and smoothly pass
Their pleasures in a long immortal dream.
One warm, flushed moment, hovering, it might seem
130 Dashed by the wood-nymph's beauty, so he burned;
Then, lighting on the printless verdure, turned
To the swooned serpent, and with languid arm,
Delicate, put to proof the lithe Caducean charm.
So done, upon the nymph his eyes he bent
Full of adoring tears and blandishment,
And towards her stepped: she, like a moon in wane,
Faded before him, cowered, nor could restrain
Her fearful sobs, self-folding like a flower
That faints into itself at evening hour.
140 But the God fostering her chillèd hand,
She felt the warmth, her eyelids opened bland,
And, like new flowers at morning song of bees,
Bloomed, and gave up her honey to the lees.
Into the green-recessèd woods they flew;
Nor grew they pale, as mortal lovers do.

   Left to herself, the serpent now began
To change; her elfin blood in madness ran,
Her mouth foamed, and the grass, therewith besprent,
Withered at dew so sweet and virulent;
150 Her eyes in torture fixed and anguish drear,
Hot, glazed, and wide, with lid-lashes all sear,
Flashed phosphor and sharp sparks, without one cooling
    tear.
The colours all inflamed throughout her train,
She writhed about, convulsed with scarlet pain.
A deep volcanian yellow took the place
Of all her milder-moonèd body's grace;
And, as the lava ravishes the mead,
Spoilt all her silver mail, and golden brede;
Made gloom of all her frecklings, streaks and bars,
160 Eclipsed her crescents, and licked up her stars,
So that, in moments few, she was undressed
Of all her sapphires, greens, and amethyst,
And rubious-argent; of all these bereft,
Nothing but pain and ugliness were left.

Still shone her crown; that vanished, also she
Melted and disappeared as suddenly;
And in the air, her new voice luting soft,
Cried, 'Lycius! Gentle Lycius!' Borne aloft
With the bright mists about the mountains hoar
170   These words dissolved; Crete's forests heard no more.

Whither fled Lamia, now a lady bright,
A full-born beauty new and exquisite?
She fled into that valley they pass o'er
Who go to Corinth from Cenchreas' shore;
And rested at the foot of those wild hills,
The rugged founts of the Peraean rills,
And of that other ridge whose barren back
Stretches, with all its mist and cloudy rack,
South-westward to Cleone. There she stood
180   About a young bird's flutter from a wood,
Fair, on a sloping green of mossy tread,
By a clear pool, wherein she passionèd
To see herself escaped from so sore ills,
While her robes flaunted with the daffodils.
  Ah, happy Lycius!—for she was a maid
More beautiful than ever twisted braid,
Or sighed, or blushed, or on spring-flowered lea
Spread a green kirtle to the minstrelsy;
A virgin purest lipped, yet in the lore
190   Of love deep learnèd to the red heart's core;
Not one hour old, yet of sciential brain
To unperplex bliss from its neighbour pain,
Define their pettish limits, and estrange
Their points of contact and swift counterchange;
Intrigue with the specious chaos, and dispart
Its most ambiguous atoms with sure art;
As though in Cupid's college she had spent
Sweet days a lovely graduate, still unshent,
And kept his rosy terms in idle languishment.

200   Why this fair creature chose so fairily
By the wayside to linger, we shall see;
But first 'tis fit to tell how she could muse
And dream, when in the serpent prison-house,
Of all she list, strange or magnificent:
How, ever, where she willed, her spirit went;
Whether to faint Elysium, or where
Down through tress-lifting waves the Nereids fair
Wind into Thetis' bower by many a pearly stair;

Or where God Bacchus drains his cups divine,
210 Stretched out, at ease, beneath a glutinous pine;
Or where in Pluto's gardens palatine
Mulciber's columns gleam in far piazzian line.
And sometimes into cities she would send
Her dream, with feast and rioting to blend;
And once, while among mortals dreaming thus,
She saw the young Corinthian Lycius
Charioting foremost in the envious race,
Like a young Jove with calm uneager face,
And fell into a swooning love of him.
220 Now on the moth-time of that evening dim
He would return that way, as well she knew,
To Corinth from the shore; for freshly blew
The eastern soft wind, and his galley now
Grated the quaystones with her brazen prow
In port Cenchreas, from Egina isle
Fresh anchored; whither he had been awhile
To sacrifice to Jove, whose temple there
Waits with high marble doors for blood and incense
        rare.
Jove heard his vows, and bettered his desire;
230 For by some freakful chance he made retire
From his companions, and set forth to walk,
Perhaps grown wearied of their Corinth talk.
Over the solitary hills he fared,
Thoughtless at first, but ere eve's star appeared
His fantasy was lost, where reason fades,
In the calmed twilight of Platonic shades.
Lamia beheld him coming, near, more near—
Close to her passing, in indifference drear,
His silent sandals swept the mossy green;
240 So neighboured to him, and yet so unseen
She stood. He passed, shut up in mysteries,
His mind wrapped like his mantle, while her eyes
Followed his steps, and her neck regal white
Turned—syllabling thus, 'Ah, Lycius bright,
And will you leave me on the hills alone?
Lycius, look back, and be some pity shown!'
He did—not with cold wonder fearingly,
But Orpheus-like at an Eurydice;
For so delicious were the words she sung,
250 It seemed he had loved them a whole summer long.
And soon his eyes had drunk her beauty up,
Leaving no drop in the bewildering cup,

And still the cup was full—while he, afraid
Lest she should vanish ere his lip had paid
Due adoration, thus began to adore
(Her soft look growing coy, she saw his chain so sure):
'Leave thee alone! Look back! Ah, Goddess, see
Whether my eyes can ever turn from thee!
For pity do not this sad heart belie—
260   Even as thou vanishest so shall I die.
Stay! Though a naiad of the rivers, stay!
To thy far wishes will thy streams obey.
Stay! Though the greenest woods be thy domain,
Alone they can drink up the morning rain.
Though a descended Pleiad, will not one
Of thine harmonious sisters keep in tune
Thy spheres, and as thy silver proxy shine?
So sweetly to these ravished ears of mine
Came thy sweet greeting, that if thou shouldst fade
270   Thy memory will waste me to a shade—
For pity do not melt!' 'If I should stay,'
Said Lamia, 'here, upon this floor of clay,
And pain my steps upon these flowers too rough,
What canst thou say or do of charm enough
To dull the nice remembrance of my home?
Thou canst not ask me with thee here to roam
Over these hills and vales, where no joy is—
Empty of immortality and bliss!
Thou art a scholar, Lycius, and must know
280   That finer spirits cannot breathe below
In human climes, and live. Alas, poor youth,
What taste of purer air hast thou to soothe
My essence? What serener palaces,
Where I may all my many senses please,
And by mysterious sleights a hundred thirsts appease?
It cannot be. Adieu!' So said, she rose
Tiptoe with white arms spread. He, sick to lose
The amorous promise of her lone complain,
Swooned, murmuring of love, and pale with pain.
290   The cruel lady, without any show
Of sorrow for her tender favourite's woe,
But rather, if her eyes could brighter be,
With brighter eyes and slow amenity,
Put her new lips to his, and gave afresh
The life she had so tangled in her mesh;
And as he from one trance was wakening
Into another, she began to sing,

Happy in beauty, life, and love, and everything,
A song of love, too sweet for earthly lyres,
300   While, like held breath, the stars drew in their panting
          fires.
And then she whispered in such trembling tone,
As those who, safe together met alone
For the first time through many anguished days,
Use other speech than looks; bidding him raise
His drooping head, and clear his soul of doubt,
For that she was a woman, and without
Any more subtle fluid in her veins
Than throbbing blood, and that the self-same pains
Inhabited her frail-strung heart as his.
310   And next she wondered how his eyes could miss
Her face so long in Corinth, where, she said,
She dwelt but half retired, and there had led
Days happy as the gold coin could invent
Without the aid of love; yet in content
Till she saw him, as once she passed him by,
Where 'gainst a column he leant thoughtfully
At Venus' temple porch, 'mid baskets heaped
Of amorous herbs and flowers, newly reaped
Late on that eve, as 'twas the night before
320   The Adonian feast; whereof she saw no more,
But wept alone those days, for why should she adore?
Lycius from death awoke into amaze,
To see her still, and singing so sweet lays;
Then from amaze into delight he fell
To hear her whisper woman's lore so well;
And every word she spake enticed him on
To unperplexed delight and pleasure known.
Let the mad poets say whate'er they please
Of the sweet Fairies, Peris, Goddesses,
330   There is not such a treat among them all,
Haunters of cavern, lake, and waterfall,
As a real woman, lineal indeed
From Pyrrha's pebbles or old Adam's seed.
Thus gentle Lamia judged, and judged aright,
That Lycius could not love in half a fright,
So threw the goddess off, and won his heart
More pleasantly by playing woman's part,
With no more awe than what her beauty gave,
That, while it smote, still guaranteed to save.
340   Lycius to all made eloquent reply,
Marrying to every word a twinborn sigh;

And last, pointing to Corinth, asked her sweet,
If 'twas too far that night for her soft feet.
The way was short, for Lamia's eagerness
Made, by a spell, the triple league decrease
To a few paces; not at all surmised
By blinded Lycius, so in her comprised.
They passed the city gates, he knew not how,
So noiseless, and he never thought to know.

350   As men talk in a dream, so Corinth all,
Throughout her palaces imperial
And all her populous streets and temples lewd,
Muttered, like tempest in the distance brewed,
To the wide-spreaded night above her towers.
Men, women, rich and poor, in the cool hours
Shuffled their sandals o'er the pavement white,
Companioned or alone; while many a light
Flared, here and there, from wealthy festivals,
And threw their moving shadows on the walls,
360   Or found them clustered in the corniced shade
Of some arched temple door or dusky colonnade.

Muffling his face, of greeting friends in fear,
Her fingers he pressed hard, as one came near
With curled gray beard, sharp eyes, and smooth bald
      crown,
Slow-stepped, and robed in philosophic gown.
Lycius shrank closer, as they met and passed,
Into his mantle, adding wings to haste,
While hurried Lamia trembled: 'Ah,' said he,
'Why do you shudder, love, so ruefully?
370   Why does your tender palm dissolve in dew?'—
'I'm wearied,' said fair Lamia, 'tell me who
Is that old man? I cannot bring to mind
His features. Lycius! Wherefore did you blind
Yourself from his quick eyes?' Lycius replied,
''Tis Apollonius sage, my trusty guide
And good instructor; but to-night he seems
The ghost of folly haunting my sweet dreams.'

While yet he spake they had arrived before
A pillared porch, with lofty portal door,
380   Where hung a silver lamp, whose phosphor glow
Reflected in the slabbèd steps below,
Mild as a star in water; for so new,
And so unsullied was the marble hue,

So through the crystal polish, liquid fine,
Ran the dark veins, that none but feet divine
Could e'er have touched there. Sounds Aeolian
Breathed from the hinges, as the ample span
Of the wide doors disclosed a place unknown
Some time to any, but those two alone,
390 And a few Persian mutes, who that same year
Were seen about the markets. None knew where
They could inhabit; the most curious
Were foiled, who watched to trace them to their house.
And but the flitter-wingèd verse must tell,
For truth's sake, what woe afterwards befell,
'Twould humour many a heart to leave them thus,
Shut from the busy world, of more incredulous.

Part II

Love in a hut, with water and a crust,
Is—Love, forgive us!—cinders, ashes, dust;
Love in a palace is perhaps at last
More grievous torment than a hermit's fast.
That is a doubtful tale from fairy land,
Hard for the non-elect to understand.
Had Lycius lived to hand his story down,
He might have given the moral a fresh frown,
Or clenched it quite; but too short was their bliss
10 To breed distrust and hate, that make the soft voice hiss.
Beside, there, nightly, with terrific glare,
Love, jealous grown of so complete a pair,
Hovered and buzzed his wings, with fearful roar,
Above the lintel of their chamber door,
And down the passage cast a glow upon the floor.

For all this, came a ruin: side by side
They were enthronèd, in the even tide,
Upon a couch, near to a curtaining
Whose airy texture, from a golden string,
20 Floated into the room and let appear
Unveiled the summer heaven, blue and clear,
Betwixt two marble shafts. There they reposed,
Where use had made it sweet, with eyelids closed,
Saving a tithe which love still open kept,
That they might see each other while they almost slept;
When from the slope side of a suburb hill,

Deafening the swallow's twitter, came a thrill
Of trumpets – Lycius started – the sounds fled,
But left a thought a-buzzing in his head.
30 For the first time, since first he harboured in
That purple-linèd palace of sweet sin,
His spirit passed beyond its golden bourn
Into the noisy world almost forsworn.
The lady, ever watchful, penetrant,
Saw this with pain, so arguing a want
Of something more, more than her empery
Of joys; and she began to moan and sigh
Because he mused beyond her, knowing well
That but a moment's thought is passion's passing-bell.
40 'Why do you sigh, fair creature?' whispered he;
'Why do you think?' returned she tenderly,
'You have deserted me – where am I now?
Not in your heart while care weighs on your brow –
No, no, you have dismissed me; and I go
From your breast houseless; aye, it must be so.'
He answered, bending to her open eyes,
Where he was mirrored small in paradise,
'My silver planet, both of eve and morn!
Why will you plead yourself so sad forlorn,
50 While I am striving how to fill my heart
With deeper crimson, and a double smart?
How to entangle, trammel up and snare
Your soul in mine, and labyrinth you there
Like the hid scent in an unbudded rose?
Aye, a sweet kiss – you see your mighty woes.
My thoughts! Shall I unveil them? Listen then!
What mortal hath a prize, that other men
May be confounded and abashed withal,
But lets it sometimes pace abroad majestical,
60 And triumph, as in thee I should rejoice
Amid the hoarse alarm of Corinth's voice.
Let my foes choke, and my friends shout afar,
While through the throngèd streets your bridal car
Wheels round its dazzling spokes.' The lady's cheek
Trembled; she nothing said, but, pale and meek,
Arose and knelt before him, wept a rain
Of sorrows at his words; at last with pain
Beseeching him, the while his hand she wrung,
To change his purpose. He thereat was stung,
70 Perverse, with stronger fancy to reclaim
Her wild and timid nature to his aim.

Besides, for all his love, in self-despite,
Against his better self, he took delight
Luxurious in her sorrows, soft and new.
His passion, cruel grown, took on a hue
Fierce and sanguineous as 'twas possible
In one whose brow had no dark veins to swell.
Fine was the mitigated fury, like
Apollo's presence when in act to strike
80 The serpent–ha, the serpent! Certes, she
Was none. She burnt, she loved the tyranny,
And, all subdued, consented to the hour
When to the bridal he should lead his paramour.
Whispering in midnight silence, said the youth,
'Sure some sweet name thou hast, though, by my truth,
I have not asked it, ever thinking thee
Not mortal, but of heavenly progeny,
As still I do. Hast any mortal name,
Fit appellation for this dazzling frame?
90 Or friends or kinsfolk on the citied earth,
To share our marriage feast and nuptial mirth?'
'I have no friends,' said Lamia, 'no, not one;
My presence in wide Corinth hardly known:
My parents' bones are in their dusty urns
Sepulchred, where no kindled incense burns,
Seeing all their luckless race are dead, save me,
And I neglect the holy rite for thee.
Even as you list invite your many guests;
But if, as now it seems, your vision rests
100 With any pleasure on me, do not bid
Old Apollonius–from him keep me hid.'
Lycius, perplexed at words so blind and blank,
Made close inquiry; from whose touch she shrank,
Feigning a sleep; and he to the dull shade
Of deep sleep in a moment was betrayed.
    It was the custom then to bring away
The bride from home at blushing shut of day,
Veiled, in a chariot, heralded along
By strewn flowers, torches, and a marriage song,
110 With other pageants; but this fair unknown
Had not a friend. So being left alone
(Lycius was gone to summon all his kin)
And knowing surely she could never win
His foolish heart from its mad pompousness,
She set herself, high-thoughted, how to dress
The misery in fit magnificence.

She did so, but 'tis doubtful how and whence
Came, and who were her subtle servitors.
About the halls, and to and from the doors,
120 There was a noise of wings, till in short space
The glowing banquet-room shone with wide-archèd
    grace.
A haunting music, sole perhaps and lone
Supportress of the fairy-roof, made moan
Throughout, as fearful the whole charm might fade.
Fresh carvèd cedar, mimicking a glade
Of palm and plantain, met from either side,
High in the midst, in honour of the bride;
Two palms and then two plantains, and so on,
From either side their stems branched one to one
130 All down the aislèd place; and beneath all
There ran a stream of lamps straight on from wall to
    wall.
So canopied lay an untasted feast
Teeming with odours. Lamia, regal dressed,
Silently paced about, and as she went,
In pale contented sort of discontent,
Missioned her viewless servants to enrich
The fretted splendour of each nook and niche.
Between the tree-stems, marbled plain at first,
Came jasper panels; then, anon, there burst
140 Forth creeping imagery of slighter trees,
And with the larger wove in small intricacies.
Approving all, she faded at self-will,
And shut the chamber up, close, hushed and still,
Complete and ready for the revels rude,
When dreadful guests would come to spoil her solitude.

The day appeared, and all the gossip rout.
O senseless Lycius! Madman! Wherefore flout
The silent-blessing fate, warm cloistered hours,
And show to common eyes these secret bowers?
150 The herd approached; each guest, with busy brain,
Arriving at the portal, gazed amain,
And entered marvelling—for they knew the street,
Remembered it from childhood all complete
Without a gap, yet ne'er before had seen
That royal porch, that high-built fair demesne.
So in they hurried all, mazed, curious and keen—
Save one, who looked thereon with eye severe,
And with calm-planted steps walked in austere.

'Twas Apollonius: something too he laughed,
160 As though some knotty problem that had daffed
His patient thought had now begun to thaw,
And solve and melt–'twas just as he foresaw.

He met within the murmurous vestibule
His young disciple. ''Tis no common rule,
Lycius,' said he, 'for uninvited guest
To force himself upon you, and infest
With an unbidden presence the bright throng
Of younger friends; yet must I do this wrong,
And you forgive me.' Lycius blushed, and led
170 The old man through the inner doors broad-spread;
With reconciling words and courteous mien
Turning into sweet milk the sophist's spleen.

Of wealthy lustre was the banquet-room,
Filled with pervading brilliance and perfume:
Before each lucid panel fuming stood
A censer fed with myrrh and spicèd wood,
Each by a sacred tripod held aloft,
Whose slender feet wide-swerved upon the soft
Wool-woofèd carpets; fifty wreaths of smoke
180 From fifty censers their light voyage took
To the high roof, still mimicked as they rose
Along the mirrored walls by twin-clouds odorous.
Twelve spherèd tables, by silk seats ensphered,
High as the level of a man's breast reared
On libbard's paws, upheld the heavy gold
Of cups and goblets, and the store thrice told
Of Ceres' horn, and, in huge vessels, wine
Come from the gloomy tun with merry shine.
Thus loaded with a feast the tables stood,
190 Each shrining in the midst the image of a God.

When in an antichamber every guest
Had felt the cold full sponge to pleasure pressed,
By ministering slaves, upon his hands and feet,
And fragrant oils with ceremony meet
Poured on his hair, they all moved to the feast
In white robes, and themselves in order placed
Around the silken couches, wondering
Whence all this mighty cost and blaze of wealth could
        spring.

Soft went the music the soft air along,

200 While fluent Greek a vowelled undersong
Kept up among the guests, discoursing low
At first, for scarcely was the wine at flow;
But when the happy vintage touched their brains,
Louder they talk, and louder come the strains
Of powerful instruments. The gorgeous dyes,
The space, the splendour of the draperies,
The roof of awful richness, nectarous cheer,
Beautiful slaves, and Lamia's self, appear,
Now, when the wine has done its rosy deed,
210 And every soul from human trammels freed,
No more so strange; for merry wine, sweet wine,
Will make Elysian shades not too fair, too divine.
Soon was God Bacchus at meridian height;
Flushed were their cheeks, and bright eyes double
    bright.
Garlands of every green, and every scent
From vales deflowered, or forest-trees branch-rent,
In baskets of bright osiered gold were brought
High as the handles heaped, to suit the thought
Of every guest—that each, as he did please,
220 Might fancy-fit his brows, silk-pillowed at his ease.
    What wreath for Lamia? What for Lycius?
What for the sage, old Apollonius?
Upon her aching forehead be there hung
The leaves of willow and of adder's tongue;
And for the youth, quick, let us strip for him
The thyrsus, that his watching eyes may swim
Into forgetfulness; and, for the sage,
Let spear-grass and the spiteful thistle wage
War on his temples. Do not all charms fly
230 At the mere touch of cold philosophy?
There was an awful rainbow once in heaven:
We know her woof, her texture; she is given
In the dull catalogue of common things.
Philosophy will clip an Angel's wings,
Conquer all mysteries by rule and line,
Empty the haunted air and gnomed mine—
Unweave a rainbow, as it erewhile made
The tender-personed Lamia melt into a shade.

By her glad Lycius sitting, in chief place,
240 Scarce saw in all the room another face,
Till, checking his love trance, a cup he took
Full brimmed, and opposite sent forth a look

From his old teacher's wrinkled countenance,
And pledge him. The bald-head philosopher
Had fixed his eye, without a twinkle or stir
Full on the alarmèd beauty of the bride,
Brow-beating her fair form, and troubling her sweet
    pride.
Lycius then pressed her hand, with devout touch,
250 As pale it lay upon the rosy couch:
'Twas icy, and the cold ran through his veins;
Then sudden it grew hot, and all the pains
Of an unnatural heat shot to his heart.
'Lamia, what means this? Wherefore dost thou start?
Know'st thou that man?' Poor Lamia answered not.
He gazed into her eyes, and not a jot
Owned they the lovelorn piteous appeal;
More, more he gazed; his human senses reel;
Some hungry spell that loveliness absorbs;
260 There was no recognition in those orbs.
'Lamia!' he cried—and no soft-toned reply.
The many heard, and the loud revelry
Grew hush; the stately music no more breathes;
The myrtle sickened in a thousand wreaths.
By faint degrees, voice, lute, and pleasure ceased;
A deadly silence step by step increased,
Until it seemed a horrid presence there,
And not a man but felt the terror in his hair.
'Lamia!' he shrieked; and nothing but the shriek
270 With its sad echo did the silence break.
'Begone, foul dream!' he cried, gazing again
In the bride's face, where now no azure vein
Wandered on fair-spaced temples; no soft bloom
Misted the cheek; no passion to illume
The deep-recessèd vision. All was blight;
Lamia, no longer fair, there sat a deadly white.
'Shut, shut those juggling eyes, thou ruthless man!
Turn them aside, wretch! Or the righteous ban
Of all the Gods, whose dreadful images
280 Here represent their shadowy presences,
May pierce them on the sudden with the thorn
Of painful blindness; leaving thee forlorn,
In trembling dotage to the feeblest fright
Of conscience, for their long offended might,
For all thine impious proud-heart sophistries,
Unlawful magic, and enticing lies.
Corinthians! Look upon that gray-beard wretch!

Mark how, possessed, his lashless eyelids stretch
Around his demon eyes! Corinthians, see!
290   My sweet bride withers at their potency.'
'Fool!' said the sophist, in an under-tone
Gruff with contempt; which a death-nighing moan
From Lycius answered, as heart-struck and lost,
He sank supine beside the aching ghost.
'Fool! Fool!' repeated he, while his eyes still
Relented not, nor moved: 'From every ill
Of life have I preserved thee to this day,
And shall I see thee made a serpent's prey?'
Then Lamia breathed death-breath; the sophist's eye,
300   Like a sharp spear, went through her utterly,
Keen, cruel, perceant, stinging. She, as well
As her weak hand could any meaning tell,
Motioned him to be silent; vainly so,
He looked and looked again a level *No*!
'A serpent!' echoed he; no sooner said,
Than with a frightful scream she vanishèd:
And Lycius' arms were empty of delight,
As were his limbs of life, from that same night.
On the high couch he lay—his friends came round—
310   Supported him—no pulse, or breath they found,
And, in its marriage robe, the heavy body wound.

'The day is gone and all its sweets are gone'

The day is gone, and all its sweets are gone!
  Sweet voice, sweet lips, soft hand, and softer breast,
Warm breath, light whisper, tender semi-tone,
  Bright eyes, accomplished shape, and languorous waist!
Faded the flower and all its budded charms,
  Faded the sight of beauty from my eyes,
Faded the shape of beauty from my arms,
  Faded the voice, warmth, whiteness, paradise.
Vanished unseasonably at shut of eve,
  When the dusk holiday, or holinight,
Of fragrant-curtained love begins to weave
  The woof of darkness thick, for hid delight;
But, as I've read love's missal through to-day,
He'll let me sleep, seeing I fast and pray.

To [Fanny]

What can I do to drive away
Remembrance from my eyes? For they have seen,
Aye, an hour ago, my brilliant Queen!
Touch has a memory. Oh, say, love, say,
What can I do to kill it and be free
In my old liberty?
When every fair one that I saw was fair,
Enough to catch me in but half a snare,
Not keep me there;
10   When, howe'er poor or particoloured things,
My muse had wings,
And ever ready was to take her course
Whither I bent her force,
Unintellectual, yet divine to me.
Divine, I say! What sea-bird o'er the sea
Is a philosopher the while he goes
Winging along where the great water throes?

   How shall I do
   To get anew
20 Those moulted feathers, and so mount once more
   Above, above
   The reach of fluttering Love,
And make him cower lowly while I soar?
Shall I gulp wine? No, that is vulgarism,
A heresy and schism,
   Foisted into the canon law of love;
No—wine is only sweet to happy men;
   More dismal cares
   Seize on me unawares—
30 Where shall I learn to get my peace again?
To banish thoughts of that most hateful land,
Dungeoner of my friends, that wicked strand
Where they were wrecked and live a wretched life;
That monstrous region, whose dull rivers pour
Ever from their sordid urns unto the shore,
Unowned of any weedy-hairèd gods;
Whose winds, all zephyrless, hold scourging rods,

Iced in the great lakes, to afflict mankind;
Whose rank-grown forests, frosted, black, and blind,
40 Would fright a Dryad; whose harsh-herbaged meads.
Make lean and lank the starved ox while he feeds.
There bud flowers have no scent, birds no sweet song,
And great unerring Nature once seems wrong.
Oh, for some sunny spell
To dissipate the shadows of this hell!
Say they are gone–with the new dawning light
Steps forth my lady bright!
Oh, let me once more rest
My soul upon that dazzling breast!
50 Let once again these aching arms be placed,
The tender gaolers of thy waist!
And let me feel that warm breath here and there
To spread a rapture in my very hair–
Oh, the sweetness of the pain!
Give me those lips again!
Enough! Enough! It is enough for me
To dream of thee!

'I cry your mercy, pity, love'

I cry your mercy, pity, love—aye love!
    Merciful love that tantalizes not,
One-thoughted, never-wandering, guileless love,
    Unmasked, and being seen—without a blot!
Oh, let me have thee whole—all, all, be mine!
    That shape, that fairness, that sweet minor zest
Of love, your kiss—those hands, those eyes divine,
    That warm, white, lucent, million-pleasured breast;
Yourself—your soul—in pity give me all,
    Withhold no atom's atom or I die;
Or living on perhaps, your wretched thrall,
    Forget, in the mist of idle misery,
Life's purposes—the palate of my mind
Losing its gust, and my ambition blind!

'Bright star!'

Bright star! Would I were steadfast as thou art—
  Not in lone splendour hung aloft the night
And watching, with eternal lids apart,
  Like nature's patient, sleepless eremite,
The moving waters at their priestlike task
  Of pure ablution round earth's human shores,
Or gazing on the new soft-fallen mask
  Of snow upon the mountains and the moors;
No—yet still steadfast, still unchangeable,
  Pillowed upon my fair love's ripening breast,
To feel for ever its soft fall and swell,
  Awake for ever in a sweet unrest,
Still, still to hear her tender-taken breath,
And so live ever—or else swoon to death.

Extracts from Letters, II

11. To Benjamin Bailey, 18 July 1818

I am certain I have not a right feeling towards women. At this moment I am striving to be just to them, but I cannot. Is it because they fall so far beneath my boyish imagination? When I was a schoolboy I thought a fair woman a pure goddess. My mind was a soft nest in which some one of them slept, though she knew it not. I have no right to expect more than their reality. I thought them etherial above men; I find them perhaps equal–great by comparison is very small.

Insult may be inflicted in more ways than by word or action. One who is tender of being insulted does not like to think an insult against another; I do not like to think insults in a lady's company. I commit a crime with her which absence would not have known. Is it not extraordinary? When among men I have no evil thoughts, no malice, no spleen. I feel free to speak or to be silent. I can listen and from every one I can learn. My hands are in my pockets; I am free from all suspicion, and comfortable. When I am among women I have evil thoughts, malice, spleen. I cannot speak or be silent. I am full of suspicions and therefore listen to nothing; I am in a hurry to be gone. You must be charitable and put all this perversity to my being disappointed since boyhood. Yet, with such feelings, I am happier alone among crowds of men, by myself, or with a friend or two.

With all this, trust me, Bailey, I have not the least idea that men of different feelings and inclinations are more short-sighted than myself. I never rejoiced more than at my brother's marriage and shall do so at that of any of my friends. I must absolutely get over this–but how? The only way is to find the root of evil and so cure it 'with backward

mutters of dissevering power'. That is a difficult thing, for
an obstinate prejudice can seldom be produced but from a
gordian complication of feelings, which must take time to
unravel and care to keep unravelled. I could say a good
deal about this, but I will leave it in hopes of better and more
worthy dispositions–and also content that I am wronging
no one, for after all I do think better of womankind than to
suppose they care whether Mister John Keats, five feet
40   high, likes them or not.

12. To George and Georgiana Keats, 14 and 24 October 1818

She is not a Cleopatra, but she is at least a Charmian. She
has a rich eastern look; she has fine eyes and fine manners.
When she comes into a room she makes an impression the
same as the beauty of a leopardess. She is too fine and too
conscious of herself to repulse any man who may address
her–from habit she thinks that nothing *particular*.

I always find myself more at ease with such a woman.
The picture before me always gives me a life and animation
which I cannot possibly feel with anything inferior. I am at
10   such times too much occupied in admiring to be awkward
or on a tremble. I forget myself entirely because I live in her.
You will by this time think I am in love with her; so before
I go any further I will tell you I am not. She kept me awake
one night as a tune of Mozart's might do. I speak of the
thing as a pastime and an amusement, than which I can
feel none deeper than a conversation with an imperial
woman, the very 'yes' and and 'no' of whose lips is to me a
banquet. I don't cry to take the moon home with me in
my pocket; nor do I fret to leave her behind me. I like her
20   and her like because one has no *sensations*–what we both are
is taken for granted.

You will suppose I have by this had much talk with her.
No such thing–there are the Miss Reynoldses on the look-
out. They think I don't admire her because I did not stare
at her; they call her a flirt to me. What a want of knowledge!
She walks across a room in such a manner that a man is

drawn to her with a magnetic power. This they call flirting! They do not know things; they do not know what a woman is. I believe, though, she has faults—the same as Charmian and Cleopatra might have had. Yet she is a fine thing, speaking in a worldly way; for there are two distinct tempers of mind in which we judge of things—the worldly, theatrical, and pantomimical, and the unearthly, spiritual, and etherial. In the former Buonaparte, Lord Byron, and this Charmian hold the first place in our minds; in the latter John Howard, Bishop Hooker rocking his child's cradle, and you, my dear sister, are the conquering feelings. As a man in the world I love the rich talk of a Charmian; as an eternal being I love the thought of you. I should like her to ruin me, and I should like you to save me. (*14 October 1818*)

Since I wrote thus far I have met with that same lady again whom I saw at Hastings, and whom I met when we were going to the English Opera. It was in a street that goes from Bedford Row to Lamb's Conduit Street. I passed her and turned back. She seemed glad of it—glad to see me and not offended at my passing her before. We walked on towards Islington, where we called on a friend of hers who keeps a boarding school . . .

Our walk ended in 34 Gloucester Street, Queen Square —not exactly so, for we went upstairs into her sitting room, a very tasty sort of place with books, pictures, a bronze statue of Buonaparte, music, aeolian harp, a parrot, a linnet, a case of choice liqueurs, etc., etc. She behaved in the kindest manner—made me take home a grouse for Tom's dinner, asked for my address for the purpose of sending more game.

As I had warmed with her before and kissed her, I thought it would be living backwards not to do so again. She had better taste; she perceived how much a thing of course it was and shrunk from it—not in a prudish way, but in, as I say, a good taste. She contrived to disappoint me in a way which made me feel more pleasure than a simple kiss could do. She said I should please her much more if I would only press her hand and go away.

Whether she was in a different disposition when I saw her before or whether I have in fancy wronged her I cannot tell. I expect to pass some pleasant hours with her now and

then, in which I feel I shall be of service to her in matters
of knowledge and taste. If I can, I will. I have no libidinous
70 thoughts about her—she and your George are the only women
a peu près de mon age whom I would be content to know for
their mind and friendship alone.

I shall in a short time write you as far as I know how I
intend to pass my life. I cannot think of those things now
Tom is so unwell and weak. Notwithstanding your happiness and your recommendation I hope I shall never
marry. Though the most beautiful creature were waiting
for me at the end of a journey or a walk, though the carpet
were of silk, the curtains of morning clouds, the chairs and
80 sofa stuffed with cygnet's down, the food manna, the wine
beyond claret, the window opening on Winander mere,
I should not feel—or rather my happiness would not be so
fine, as my solitude is sublime. Then, instead of what I
have described, there is a sublimity to welcome me home.
The roaring of the wind is my wife, and the stars through
the window pane are my children. The mighty abstract
idea I have of beauty in all things stifles the more divided
and minute domestic happiness. An amiable wife and sweet
children I contemplate as a part of that beauty, but I must
90 have a thousand of those beautiful particles to fill up my
heart. I feel more and more every day, as my imagination
strengthens, that I do not live in this world alone but in a
thousand worlds. (*24 October 1818*)

13. To the Same, 18 December 1818

Shall I give you Miss Brawne? She is about my height, with
a fine style of countenance of the lengthened sort. She wants
sentiment in every feature. She manages to make her hair
look well. Her nostrils are fine, though a little painful, her
mouth is bad and good, her profile is better than her full
face, which indeed is not full but pale and thin without
showing any bone. Her shape is very graceful and so are
her movements. Her arms are good, her hands badish, her
feet tolerable. She is not seventeen. But she is ignorant,
10 monstrous in her behaviour—flying out in all directions,
calling people such names that I was forced lately to make

use of the term *Minx*. This is, I think, not from any innate vice but from a penchant she has for acting stylishly. I am however tired of such style and shall decline any more of it.

14. To Fanny Brawne, 1 July 1819

I am glad I had not an opportunity of sending off a letter which I wrote for you on Tuesday night–'twas too much like one out of Rousseau's *Héloïse*. I am more reasonable this morning. The morning is the only proper time for me to write to a beautiful girl whom I love so much, for at night, when the lonely day has closed and the lonely, silent, unmusical chamber is waiting to receive me as into a sepulchre, then, believe me, my passion gets entirely the sway; then I would not have you see those rhapsodies which I
10   once thought it impossible I should ever give way to, and which I have often laughed at in another, for fear you should think me either too unhappy or perhaps a little mad.

I am now at a very pleasant cottage window, looking on to a beautiful hilly country, with a glimpse of the sea. The morning is very fine. I do not know how elastic my spirit might be, what pleasure I might have in living here and breathing and wandering as free as a stag about this beautiful coast, if the remembrance of you did not weigh so upon me. I have never known any unalloyed happiness for many
20   days together–the death or sickness of someone has always spoilt my hours. And now, when none such troubles oppress me, it is, you must confess, very hard that another sort of pain should haunt me. Ask yourself, my love, whether you are not very cruel to have so entrammeled me, so destroyed my freedom.

Will you confess this in the letter?–You must write immediately and do all you can to console me in it. Make it rich as a draught of poppies to intoxicate me; write the softest words and kiss them that I may at least touch my
30   lips where yours have been.

For myself I know not how to express my devotion to so fair a form. I want a brighter word than bright, a fairer word than fair. I almost wish we were butterflies and lived but three summer days–three such days with you I could fill with more delight than fifty common years could ever contain. But however selfish I may feel, I am sure I could never act selfishly. As I told you a day or two before I left Hampstead, I will never return to London if my Fate does not turn up Pam or at least a court card. Though I could centre my happiness in you, I cannot expect to engross your heart so entirely. Indeed, if I thought you felt as much for me as I do for you at this moment, I do not think I could restrain myself from seeing you again tomorrow for the delight of one embrace. But no–I must live upon hope and chance. In case of the worst that can happen, I shall still love you; but what hatred shall I have for another! Some lines I read the other day are continually ringing a peal in my ears:

> To see those eyes I prize above mine own
> Dart favours on another–
> And those sweet lips, yielding immortal nectar,
> Be gently pressed by any but myself–
> Think, think, Francesca, what a cursed thing
> It were beyond expression!

15. To the Same, 25 July 1819

You cannot conceive how I ache to be with you, how I would die for one hour–for what is in the world? I say you cannot conceive–it is impossible you should look with such eyes upon me as I have upon you; it cannot be. Forgive me if I wander a little this evening, for I have been all day employed in a very abstract poem, and I am in deep love with you–two things which must excuse me. I have, believe me, not been an age in letting you take possession of me. The very first week I knew you I wrote myself your vassal, but burnt the letter, as the very next time I saw you I thought you manifested some dislike to me. If you should ever feel for man at the first sight what I did for you, I am lost. Yet I should not quarrel with you, but hate myself if such a thing were to happen–only I should burst if the thing were not as fine a man as you are as a woman.

Perhaps I am too vehement. Then fancy me on my knees,

especially when I mention a part of your letter which hurt
me. You say. speaking of Mr Severn, 'but you must be
satisfied in knowing that I admired you much more than
20   your friend'. My dear love, I cannot believe there ever was
or ever could be anything to admire in me, especially as
far as sight goes. I cannot be admired; I am not a thing
to be admired. You are, I love you; all I can bring you is
a swooning admiration of your beauty. I hold that place
among men that snub-nosed brunettes with meeting eye-
brows do among women–they are trash to me unless I find
one among them with a fire in her heart like the one that
burns in mine. You absorb me in spite of myself–you alone,
for I look not forward with any pleasure to what is called
30   being settled in the world. I tremble at domestic cares, yet
for you I would meet them, though if it would leave you
the happier I would rather die than do so.

I have two luxuries to brood over in my walks, your
loveliness and the hour of my death. O that I could have
possession of them both in the same minute. I hate the
world: it batters too much the wings of my self-will, and
would I could take a sweet poison from your lips to send
me out of it. From no others would I take it. I am indeed
astonished to find myself so careless of all charms but yours,
40   remembering as I do the time when even a bit of ribband
was a matter of interest with me. What softer words can I
find for you after this? What it is I will not read. Nor will
I say more here, but in a postscript answer anything else
you may have mentioned in your letter in so many words,
for I am distracted with a thousand thoughts. I will imagine
you Venus tonight and pray, pray, pray to your star like
a heathen.

16. To the Same, 16 August 1819

What shall I say for myself? I have been here four days and
have not yet written you. 'Tis true I have had many teasing
letters of business to dismiss, and I have been in the claws, like
a serpent in an eagle's, of the last act of our tragedy. This is no
excuse. I know it; I do not presume to offer it. I have no
right either to ask a speedy answer to let me know how lenient

you are. I must remain some days in a mist–I see you through a mist, as I dare say you do me by this time.

Believe in the first letters I wrote you. I assure you I felt as I wrote–I could not write so now. The thousand images I have had pass through my brain, my uneasy spirits, my unguessed fate, all spread as a veil between me and you. Remember I have had no idle leisure to brood over you; 'tis well perhaps I have not. I could not have endured the throng of jealousies that used to haunt me before I had plunged so deeply into imaginary interests. I would fain, as my sails are set, sail on without interruption for a brace of months longer. I am in complete cue–in the fever, and shall in these four months do an immense deal.

This page, as my eye skims over it, I see is excessively unloverlike and ungallant. I cannot help it–I am no officer in yawning quarters, no parson-Romeo. My mind is heaped to the full, stuffed like a cricket ball. If I strive to fill it more, it would burst. I know the generality of women would hate me for this–that I should have so unsoftened, so hard a mind as to forget them–forget the brightest realities for the dull imaginations of my own brain. But I conjure you to give it a fair thinking and ask yourself whether 'tis not better to to explain my feelings to you than write artificial passion. Besides, you would see through it; it would be vain to strive to deceive you.

'Tis harsh, harsh–I know it. My heart seems now made of iron; I could not write a proper answer to an invitation to Idalia. You are my judge; my forehead is on the ground. You seem offended at a little, simple, innocent, childish playfulness in my last. I did not seriously mean to say that you were endeavouring to make me keep my promise. I beg your pardon for it. 'Tis but *just* your pride should take the alarm–*seriously*. You say I may do as I please. I do not think with any conscience I can. My cash resources are for the present stopped–I fear for some time. I spend no money, but it increases my debts.

I have all my life thought very little of these matters–they seem not to belong to me. It may be a proud sentence, but, by heaven, I am as entirely above all matters of interest as the sun is above the earth; and though of my own money I should be careless, of my friends I must be spare. You see how

I go on—like so many strokes of a hammer. I cannot help it—
I am impelled, driven to it. I am not happy enough for
silken phrases and silver sentences. I can no more use
soothing words to you than if I were at this moment engaged
in a charge of cavalry....
Forgive me for this flint-worded letter, and believe and see
that I cannot think of you without some sort of energy,
though *mal à propos*. Even as I leave off it seems to me that a
few more moments' thought of you would uncrystallize
and dissolve me. I must not give way to it but turn to my
writing again. If I fail, I shall die hard. O my love, your lips
are growing sweet again to my fancy—I must forget them.

17. To John Taylor, 23 August 1819

I equally dislike the favour of the public with the love of a
woman—they are both a cloying treacle to the wings of
independence.

18. To Fanny Brawne, 13 September 1819

I have been hurried to town by a letter from my brother
George; it is not of the brightest intelligence. Am I mad or
not? I came by the Friday night coach and have not yet
been to Hampstead. Upon my soul it is not my fault. I
cannot resolve to mix any pleasure with my days: they go
one like another undistinguishable. If I were to see you today,
it would destroy the half comfortable sullenness I enjoy at
present into downright perplexities. I love you too much to
venture to Hampstead. I feel it is not paying a visit but
venturing into a fire. *Que ferai-je*, as the French novel
writers say in fun, and I in earnest. Really, what can I do?
Knowing well that my life must be passed in fatigue and
trouble, I have been endeavouring to wean myself from you,
for, to myself alone, what can be much of a misery? As far as
they regard myself, I can despise all events, but I cannot
cease to love you. This morning I scarcely know what I am
doing. I am going to Walthamstow. I shall return to Winchester tomorrow, whence you shall hear from me in a few

days. I am a coward–I cannot bear the pain of being happy.
'Tis out of the question; I must admit no thought of it.

19. To George and Georgiana Keats, 17 September 1819

I saw Haslam. He is very much occupied with love and
business, being one of Mr Saunders' executors and lover to a
young woman. He showed me her picture by Severn. I think
she is, though not very cunning, too cunning for him.
Nothing strikes me so forcibly with a sense of the ridiculous as
love. A man in love, I do think, cuts the sorriest figure in the
world. Even when I know a poor fool to be really in pain
about it, I could burst out laughing in his face. His pathetic
visage becomes irresistible. Not that I take Haslam as a
10 pattern for lovers–he is a very worthy man and a good
friend. His love is very amusing.

20. To Fanny Brawne, 13 October 1819

This moment I have set myself to copy some verses out fair.
I cannot proceed with any degree of content. I must write
you a line or two and see if that will assist in dismissing you
from my mind for ever so short a time. Upon my soul I can
think of nothing else. The time is passed when I had power to
advise and warn you against the unpromising morning of my
life. My love has made me selfish. I cannot exist without you.
I am forgetful of everything but seeing you again. My life
seems to stop there–I see no further. You have absorbed me.
10 I have a sensation at the present moment as though I was
dissolving. I should be exquisitely miserable without the
hope of soon seeing you; I should be afraid to separate myself
far from you. My sweet Fanny, will your heart never change?
My love, will it? I have no limit now to my love. Your note
came in just here–I cannot be happier away from you. 'Tis
richer than an argosy of pearls. Do not threat me even in jest.
I have been astonished that men could die martyrs for
religion–I have shuddered at it. I shudder no more–I could
be martyred for my religion. Love is my religion–I could die

for that. I could die for you. My creed is love, and you are its only tenet. You have ravished me away by a power I cannot resist; and yet I could resist till I saw you; and even since I have seen you I have endeavoured often 'to reason against the reasons of my love'. I can do that no more–the pain would be too great. My love is selfish. I cannot breathe without you.

21. To the Same, March 1820

You fear sometimes I do not love you so much as you wish? My dear girl, I love you ever and ever and without reserve. The more I have known you the more have I loved–in every way. Even my jealousies have been agonies of love; in the hottest fit I ever had I would have died for you. I have vexed you too much–but for love! Can I help it? You are always new. The last of your kisses was ever the sweetest; the last smile the brightest; the last movement the gracefullest. When you passed my window home yesterday, I was filled with as
10 much admiration as if I had then seen you for the first time.

You uttered a half complaint once that I only loved your beauty. Have I nothing else then to love in you but that? Do not I see a heart naturally furnished with wings imprison itself with me? No ill prospect has been able to turn your thoughts a moment from me. This perhaps should be as much a subject of sorrow as joy; but I will not talk of that. Even if you did not love me, I could not help an entire devotion to you. How much more deeply then must I feel for you knowing you love me. My mind has been the most
20 discontented and restless one that ever was put into a body too small for it. I never felt my mind repose upon anything with complete and undistracted enjoyment–upon no person but you. When you are in the room, my thoughts never fly out of the window–you always concentrate my whole senses. The anxiety shown about our loves in your last note is an immense pleasure to me. However, you must not suffer such speculations to molest you any more; nor will I any more believe you can have the least pique against me. Brown is gone out, but here is Mrs Wylie. When she is gone I shall be
30 awake for you. Remembrances to your mother.

Poems Various

To My Brother George

Full many a dreary hour have I passed,
My brain bewildered and my mind o'ercast
With heaviness, in seasons when I've thought
No sphery strains by me could e'er be caught
From the blue dome, though I to dimness gaze
On the far depth where sheeted lightning plays,
Or, on the wavy grass outstretched supinely,
Pry 'mong the stars, to strive to think divinely;
That I should never hear Apollo's song,
Though feathery clouds were floating all along
The purple west and, two bright streaks between,
The golden lyre itself were dimly seen;
That the still murmur of the honey bee
Would never teach a rural song to me;
That the bright glance from beauty's eyelids slanting
Would never make a lay of mine enchanting,
Or warm my breast with ardour to unfold
Some tale of love and arms in time of old.

But there are times when those that love the bay
Fly from all sorrowing far, far away.
A sudden glow comes on them, naught they see
In water, earth, or air, but poesy.
It has been said, dear George, and true I hold it
(For knightly Spenser to Libertas told it),
That when a poet is in such a trance,
In air he sees white coursers paw and prance,
Bestridden of gay knights in gay apparel,
Who at each other tilt in playful quarrel,
And what we, ignorantly, sheet-lightning call,
Is the swift opening of their wide portal,
When the bright warder blows his trumpet clear,
Whose tones reach naught on earth but poet's ear.
When these enchanted portals open wide,
And through the light the horsemen swiftly glide,
The poet's eye can reach those golden halls
And view the glory of their festivals:
Their ladies fair, that in the distance seem

Fit for the silvering of a seraph's dream;
Their rich brimmed goblets, that incessant run
40 Like the bright spots that move about the sun;
And, when upheld, the wine from each bright jar
Pours with the lustre of a falling star.
Yet further off are dimly seen their bowers,
Of which no mortal eye can reach the flowers—
And 'tis right just, for well Apollo knows
'Twould make the poet quarrel with the rose.
All that's revealed from that far seat of blisses
Is the clear fountains' interchanging kisses,
As gracefully descending, light and thin,
50 Like silver streaks across a dolphin's fin
When he upswimmeth from the coral caves,
And sports with half his tail above the waves.

These wonders strange he sees, and many more,
Whose head is pregnant with poetic lore.
Should he upon an evening ramble fare
With forehead to the soothing breezes bare,
Would he naught see but the dark, silent blue
With all its diamonds trembling through and through?
Or the coy moon, when in the waviness
60 Of whitest clouds she does her beauty dress,
And staidly paces higher up, and higher,
Like a sweet nun in holy-day attire?
Ah, yes, much more would start into his sight—
The revelries and mysteries of night.
And should I ever see them, I will tell you
Such tales as needs must with amazement spell you.

These are the living pleasures of the bard,
But richer far posterity's award.
What does he murmur with his latest breath,
70 While his proud eye looks through the film of death?
'What though I leave this dull and earthly mould,
Yet shall my spirit lofty converse hold
With after times. The patriot shall feel
My stern alarum, and unsheathe his steel,
Or in the senate thunder out my numbers
To startle princes from their easy slumbers.
The sage will mingle with each moral theme
My happy thoughts sententious; he will teem
With lofty periods when my verses fire him,
80 And then I'll stoop from heaven to inspire him.
Lays have I left of such a dear delight

That maids will sing them on their bridal night.
Gay villagers, upon a morn of May,
When they have tired their gentle limbs with play,
And formed a snowy circle on the grass,
And placed in midst of all that lovely lass
Who chosen is their queen—with her fine head
Crowned with flowers purple, white, and red,
For there the lily and the musk-rose, sighing,
90   Are emblems true of hapless lovers dying;
Between her breasts, that never yet felt trouble,
A bunch of violets, full-blown and double,
Serenely sleep. She from a casket takes
A little book—and then a joy awakes
About each youthful heart, with stifled cries,
And rubbing of white hands, and sparkling eyes,
For she's to read a tale of hopes, and fears,
One that I fostered in my youthful years.
The pearls, that on each glistening circlet sleep,
100   Gush ever and anon with silent creep,
Lured by the innocent dimples. To sweet rest
Shall the dear babe, upon its mother's breast,
Be lulled with songs of mine. Fair world, adieu!
Thy dales and hills are fading from my view.
Swiftly I mount, upon wide spreading pinions,
Far from the narrow bounds of thy dominions.
Full joy I feel, while thus I cleave the air,
That my soft verse will charm thy daughters fair
And warm thy sons!' Ah, my dear friend and brother,
110   Could I, at once, my mad ambition smother
For tasting joys like these, sure I should be
Happier, and dearer to society.
At times, 'tis true, I've felt relief from pain
When some bright thought has darted through my brain;
Through all that day I've felt a greater pleasure
Than if I'd brought to light a hidden treasure.
As to my sonnets, though none else should heed them,
I feel delighted, still, that you should read them.
Of late, too, I have had much calm enjoyment,
120   Stretched on the grass at my best loved employment
Of scribbling lines for you. These things I thought
While, in my face, the freshest breeze I caught.
E'en now I'm pillowed on a bed of flowers
That crowns a lofty clift, which proudly towers
Above the ocean-waves. The stalks and blades
Chequer my tablet with their quivering shades.

On one side is a field of drooping oats
Through which the poppies show their scarlet coats,
So pert and useless that they bring to mind
130 The scarlet coats that pester human-kind.
And on the other side, outspread, is seen
Ocean's blue mantle streaked with purple and green.
Now 'tis I see a canvassed ship, and now
Mark the bright silver curling round her prow.
I see the lark down-dropping to his nest,
And the broad winged sea-gull never at rest,
For when no more he spreads his feathers free
His breast is dancing on the restless sea.
Now I direct my eyes into the west,
140 Which at this moment is in sunbeams dressed—
Why westward turn? 'Twas but to say adieu!
'Twas but to kiss my hand, dear George, to you!

'How many bards gild the lapses of time'

How many bards gild the lapses of time!
  A few of them have ever been the food
  Of my delighted fancy – I could brood
Over their beauties, earthly, or sublime;
And often, when I sit me down to rhyme,
    These will in throngs before my mind intrude:
    But no confusion, no disturbance rude
Do they occasion; 'tis a pleasing chime.
So the unnumbered sounds that evening store:
    The songs of birds, the whispering of the leaves,
The voice of waters, the great bell that heaves
    With solemn sound, and thousand others more
That distance of recognizance bereaves,
    Make pleasing music, and not wild uproar.

On First Looking into Chapman's Homer

Much have I travelled in the realms of gold,
 And many goodly states and kingdoms seen;
 Round many western islands have I been
Which bards in fealty to Apollo hold.
Oft of one wide expanse had I been told
 That deep-browed Homer ruled as his demesne;
 Yet did I never breathe its pure serene
Till I heard Chapman speak out loud and bold.
Then felt I like some watcher of the skies
 When a new planet swims into his ken;
Or like stout Cortez when with eagle eyes
 He stared at the Pacific, and all his men
Looked at each other with a wild surmise—
 Silent, upon a peak in Darien.

To My Brothers

Small, busy flames play through the fresh-laid coals,
  And their faint cracklings o'er our silence creep
  Like whispers of the household gods that keep
A gentle empire o'er fraternal souls.
And while for rhymes I search around the poles,
  Your eyes are fixed, as in poetic sleep,
  Upon the lore so voluble and deep
That ay at fall of night our care condoles.
This is your birth-day, Tom, and I rejoice
  That thus it passes smoothly, quietly.
Many such eves of gently whispering noise
  May we together pass, and calmly try
What are this world's true joys, ere the great voice
  From its fair face shall bid our spirits fly.

'Great spirits now on earth are sojourning'

Great spirits now on earth are sojourning:
   He of the cloud, the cataract, the lake,
   Who on Helvellyn's summit, wide awake,
Catches his freshness from Archangel's wing;
He of the rose, the violet, the spring,
   The social smile, the chain for freedom's sake;
   And lo!—whose stedfastness would never take
A meaner sound than Raphael's whispering.
And other spirits there are standing apart
   Upon the forehead of the age to come.
These, these will give the world another heart
   And other pulses. Hear ye not the hum
Of mighty workings?——
   Listen awhile ye nations, and be dumb.

Sleep and Poetry

[Extract]

O Poesy! For thee I hold my pen
That am not yet a glorious denizen
Of thy wide heaven. Should I rather kneel
50 Upon some mountain-top until I feel
A glowing splendour around about me hung,
And echo back the voice of thine own tongue?
O Poesy! For thee I grasp my pen
That am not yet a glorious denizen
Of thy wide heaven. Yet, to my ardent prayer,
Yield from thy sanctuary some clear air,
Smoothed for intoxication by the breath
Of flowering bays, that I may die a death
Of luxury and my young spirit follow
60 The morning sunbeams to the great Apollo
Like a fresh sacrifice; or, if I can bear
The o'erwhelming sweets, 'twill bring to me the fair
Visions of all places. A bowery nook
Will be elysium—an eternal book
Whence I may copy many a lovely saying
About the leaves and flowers, about the playing
Of nymphs in woods and fountains, and the shade
Keeping a silence round a sleeping maid,
And many a verse from so strange influence
70 That we must ever wonder how and whence
It came. Also imaginings will hover
Round my fire-side, and haply there discover
Vistas of solemn beauty, where I'd wander
In happy silence, like the clear Meander
Through its lone vales, and where I found a spot
Of awfuller shade, or an enchanted grot,
Or a green hill o'erspread with chequered dress
Of flowers and, fearful from its loveliness,
Write on my tablets all that was permitted,
80 All that was for our human senses fitted.

Then the events of this wide world I'd seize
Like a strong giant, and my spirit tease
Till at its shoulders it should proudly see
Wings to find out an immortality.
Stop and consider! Life is but a day;
A fragile dew-drop on its perilous way
From a tree's summit; a poor Indian's sleep
While his boat hastens to the monstrous steep
Of Montmorenci. Why so sad a moan?
90　Life is the rose's hope while yet unblown;
The reading of an ever-changing tale;
The light uplifting of a maiden's veil;
A pigeon tumbling in clear summer air;
A laughing school-boy, without grief or care,
Riding the springy branches of an elm.

Oh, for ten years, that I may overwhelm
Myself in poesy; so I may do the deed
That my own soul has to itself decreed.
Then will I pass the countries that I see
100　In long perspective, and continually
Taste their pure fountains. First the realm I'll pass
Of Flora and old Pan: sleep in the grass,
Feed upon apples red and strawberries,
And choose each pleasure that my fancy sees;
Catch the white-handed nymphs in shady places
To woo sweet kisses from averted faces,
Play with their fingers, touch their shoulders white
Into a pretty shrinking with a bite
As hard as lips can make it, till, agreed,
110　A lovely tale of human life we'll read.
And one will teach a tame dove how it best
May fan the cool air gently o'er my rest;
Another, bending o'er her nimble tread,
Will set a green robe floating round her head,
And still will dance with ever varied ease,
Smiling upon the flowers and the trees;
Another will entice me on and on
Through almond blossoms and rich cinnamon,
Till in the bosom of a leafy world
120　We rest in silence, like two gems upcurled
In the recesses of a pearly shell.

And can I ever bid these joys farewell?
Yes, I must pass them for a nobler life,
Where I may find the agonies, the strife

Of human hearts—for lo! I see afar,
O'ersailing the blue cragginess, a car
And steeds with streamy manes–the charioteer
Looks out upon the winds with glorious fear.
And now the numerous tramplings quiver lightly
130 Along a huge cloud's ridge, and now with sprightly
Wheel downward come they into fresher skies,
Tipped round with silver from the sun's bright eyes,
Still downward with capacious whirl they glide.
And now I see them on the green hill's side
In breezy rest among the nodding stalks.
The charioteer with wondrous gesture talks
To the trees and mountains, and there soon appear
Shapes of delight, of mystery, and fear,
Passing along before a dusky space
140 Made by some mighty oaks; as they would chase
Some ever-fleeting music on they sweep.
Lo! how they murmur, laugh, and smile, and weep—
Some with upholden hand and mouth severe;
Some with their faces muffled to the ear
Between their arms; some, clear in youthful bloom,
Go glad and smilingly athwart the gloom;
Some looking back, and some with upward gaze.
Yes, thousands in a thousand different ways
Flit onward–now a lovely wreath of girls
150 Dancing their sleek hair into tangled curls,
And now broad wings. Most awfully intent,
The driver of those steeds is forward bent
And seems to listen. Oh, that I might know
All that he writes with such a hurrying glow.
The visions all are fled–the car is fled
Into the light of heaven, and in their stead
A sense of real things comes doubly strong,
And, like a muddy stream, would bear along
My soul to nothingness. But I will strive
160 Against all doubtings and will keep alive
The thought of that same chariot and the strange
Journey it went.

'I stood tip-toe upon a little hill'

[Extract]

O Maker of sweet poets, dear delight
Of this fair world and all its gentle livers,
Spangler of clouds, halo of crystal rivers,
Mingler with leaves and dew and tumbling streams,
120 Closer of lovely eyes to lovely dreams,
Lover of loneliness and wandering,
Of upcast eye and tender pondering!
Thee must I praise above all other glories
That smile us on to tell delightful stories.
For what has made the sage or poet write
But the fair paradise of Nature's light?
In the calm grandeur of a sober line
We see the waving of the mountain pine;
And when a tale is beautifully stayed,
130 We feel the safety of a hawthorn glade;
When it is moving on luxurious wings,
The soul is lost in pleasant smotherings—
Fair dewy roses brush against our faces
And flowering laurels spring from diamond vases;
O'er head we see the jasmine and sweet briar,
And bloomy grapes laughing from green attire;
While at our feet the voice of crystal bubbles
Charms us at once away from all our troubles,
So that we feel uplifted from the world,
140 Walking upon the white clouds wreathed and curled.
So felt he who first told how Psyche went
On the smooth wind to realms of wonderment;
What Psyche felt, and Love, when their full lips
First touched; what amorous and fondling nips
They gave each other's cheeks; with all their sighs,
And how they kissed each other's tremulous eyes;
The silver lamp–the ravishment–the wonder–
The darkness–loneliness–the fearful thunder;
Their woes gone by, and both to heaven upflown

150 To bow for gratitude before Jove's throne.
    So did he feel, who pulled the boughs aside
    That we might look into a forest wide
    To catch a glimpse of Fauns and Dryades
    Coming with softest rustle through the trees,
    And garlands woven of flowers wild and sweet,
    Upheld on ivory wrists or sporting feet:
    Telling us how fair trembling Syrinx fled
    Arcadian Pan, with such a fearful dread.
    Poor nymph, poor Pan—how he did weep to find
160 Nought but a lovely sighing of the wind
    Along the reedy stream, a half-heard strain
    Full of sweet desolation, balmy pain.

    What first inspired a bard of old to sing
    Narcissus pining o'er the untainted spring?
    In some delicious ramble he had found
    A little space, with boughs all woven round,
    And in the midst of all a clearer pool
    Than e'er reflected in its pleasant cool
    The blue sky here and there serenely peeping
170 Through tendril wreaths fantastically creeping.
    And on the bank a lonely flower he spied,
    A meek and forlorn flower, with naught of pride,
    Drooping its beauty o'er the water clearness
    To woo its own sad image into nearness.
    Deaf to light Zephyrus it would not move,
    But still would seem to droop, to pine, to love.
    So while the poet stood in this sweet spot,
    Some fainter gleamings o'er his fancy shot,
    Nor was it long ere he had told the tale
180 Of young Narcissus, and sad Echo's bale.
    Where had he been, from whose warm head out-flew
    That sweetest of all songs, that ever new,
    That ay refreshing pure deliciousness,
    Coming ever to bless
    The wanderer by moonlight? To him bringing
    Shapes from the invisible world, unearthly singing
    From out the middle air, from flowery nests,
    And from the pillowy silkiness that rests
    Full in the speculation of the stars.
190 Ah, surely he had burst our mortal bars,
    Into some wond'rous region he had gone
    To search for thee, divine Endymion!
    He was a poet, sure a lover too,

Who stood on Latmos' top, what time there blew
Soft breezes from the myrtle vale below,
And brought in faintness solemn, sweet and slow
A hymn from Dian's temple; while, upswelling,
The incense went to her own starry dwelling.
But though her face was clear as infant's eyes,
200 Though she stood smiling o'er the sacrifice,
The poet wept at her so piteous fate,
Wept that such beauty should be desolate.
So in fine wrath some golden sounds he won,
And gave meek Cynthia her Endymion.

Queen of the wide air! Thou most lovely queen
Of all the brightness that mine eyes have seen!
As thou exceedest all things in thy shine,
So every tale does this sweet tale of thine.
Oh, for three words of honey, that I might
210 Tell but one wonder of thy bridal night!

Where distant ships do seem to show their keels,
Phoebus awhile delayed his mighty wheels
And turned to smile upon thy bashful eyes,
Ere he his unseen pomp would solemnize.
The evening weather was so bright and clear
That men of health were of unusual cheer,
Stepping like Homer at the trumpet's call
Or young Apollo on the pedestal,
And lovely women were as fair and warm
220 As Venus looking sideways in alarm.
The breezes were ethereal and pure,
And crept through half-closed lattices to cure
The languid sick; it cooled their fevered sleep,
And soothed them into slumbers full and deep.
Soon they awoke clear-eyed, nor burnt with thirsting,
Nor with hot fingers, nor with temples bursting,
And springing up, they met the wondering sight
Of their dear friends, nigh foolish with delight,
Who feel their arms and breasts, and kiss and stare,
230 And on their placid foreheads part the hair.
Young men and maidens at each other gazed
With hands held back, and motionless, amazed
To see the brightness in each other's eyes;
And so they stood, filled with a sweet surprise,
Until their tongues were loosed in Poesy.
Therefore no lover did of anguish die,

But the soft numbers, in that moment spoken,
Made silken ties that never may be broken.
Cynthia! I cannot tell the greater blisses
240 That followed thine and thy dear shepherd's kisses:
Was there a poet born?—But now no more,
My wandering spirit must no further soar.

'After dark vapours have oppressed our plains'

After dark vapours have oppressed our plains
   For a long dreary season, comes a day
   Born of the gentle South, and clears away
From the sick heavens all unseemly stains.
The anxious month, relievèd of its pains,
   Takes as a long-lost right the feel of May;
   The eyelids with the passing coolness play
Like rose leaves with the drip of summer rains.
The calmest thoughts come round us; as of leaves
   Budding, fruit ripening in stillness, autumn suns
Smiling at eve upon the quiet sheaves,
Sweet Sappho's cheek, a sleeping infant's breath,
   The gradual sand that through an hour-glass runs,
A woodland rivulet, a poet's death.

To Leigh Hunt, Esq.

Glory and loveliness have passed away,
   For if we wander out in early morn
   No wreathèd incense do we see upborne
Into the east, to meet the smiling day;
No crowd of nymphs soft-voiced and young and gay,
   In woven baskets bringing ears of corn,
   Roses and pinks and violets, to adorn
The shrine of Flora in her early May.
But there are left delights as high as these,
   And I shall ever bless my destiny
That in a time, when under pleasant trees
   Pan is no longer sought, I feel a free,
A leafy, luxury, seeing I could please
   With these poor offerings a man like thee.

On Seeing the Elgin Marbles

My spirit is too weak—mortality
  Weighs heavily on me like unwilling sleep,
  And each imagined pinnacle and steep
Of godlike hardship tells me I must die
Like a sick eagle looking at the sky.
  Yet 'tis a gentle luxury to weep
  That I have not the cloudy winds to keep
Fresh for the opening of the morning's eye.
Such dim-conceivèd glories of the brain
  Bring round the heart an undescribable feud;
So do these wonders a most dizzy pain,
  That mingles Grecian grandeur with the rude
Wasting of old Time, with a billowy main,
  A sun, a shadow of a magnitude.

On the Sea

It keeps eternal whisperings around
   Desolate shores, and with its mighty swell
   Gluts twice ten thousand caverns, till the spell
Of Hecate leaves them their old shadowy sound.
Often 'tis in such gentle temper found
   That scarcely will the very smallest shell
   Be moved for days from where it sometime fell,
When last the winds of heaven were unbound.
O ye who have your eye-balls vexed and tired,
   Feast them upon the wideness of the sea!
     O ye whose ears are dinned with uproar rude,
   Or fed too much with cloying melody,
     Sit ye near some old cavern's mouth and brood
Until ye start, as if the sea-nymphs quired!

Endymion

from Book I

'O thou, whose mighty palace roof doth hang
From jagged trunks, and overshadoweth
Eternal whispers, glooms, the birth, life, death
Of unseen flowers in heavy peacefulness;
Who lov'st to see the hamadryads dress
Their ruffled locks where meeting hazels darken,
And through whole solemn hours dost sit, and hearken
The dreary melody of bedded reeds
240 In desolate places, where dank moisture breeds
The pipy hemlock to strange overgrowth,
Bethinking thee how melancholy loth
Thou wast to lose fair Syrinx—do thou now,
By thy love's milky brow,
By all the trembling mazes that she ran,
Hear us, great Pan!

'O thou, for whose soul-soothing quiet, turtles
Passion their voices cooingly 'mong myrtles,
What time thou wanderest at eventide
250 Through sunny meadows that outskirt the side
Of thine enmossèd realms. O thou, to whom
Broad-leavèd fig trees even now foredoom
Their ripened fruitage, yellow-girted bees
Their golden honeycombs, our village leas
Their fairest-blossomed beans and poppied corn,
The chuckling linnet its five young unborn
To sing for thee, low-creeping strawberries
Their summer coolness, pent-up butterflies
Their freckled wings, yea, the fresh budding year
260 All its completions—be quickly near,
By every wind that nods the mountain pine,
O forester divine!

'Thou, to whom every faun and satyr flies
For willing service, whether to surprise
The squatted hare while in half-sleeping fit;

Or upward ragged precipices flit
To save poor lambkins from the eagle's maw;
Or by mysterious enticement draw
Bewildered shepherds to their path again;
270   Or to tread breathless round the frothy main,
And gather up all fancifullest shells
For thee to tumble into naiads' cells,
And, being hidden, laugh at their out-peeping;
Or to delight thee with fantastic leaping,
The while they pelt each other on the crown
With silvery oak-apples and fir-cones brown—
By all the echoes that about thee ring,
Hear us, O satyr king!

'O hearkener to the loud-clapping shears
280   While ever and anon to his shorn peers
A ram goes bleating; winder of the horn
When snouted wild-boars routing tender corn
Anger our huntsmen; breather round our farms
To keep off mildews and all weather harms;
Strange ministrant of undescribèd sounds
That come a-swooning over hollow grounds
And wither drearily on barren moors;
Dread opener of the mysterious doors
Leading to universal knowledge—see,
290   Great son of Dryope,
The many that are come to pay their vows
With leaves about their brows!

'Be still the unimaginable lodge
For solitary thinkings—such as dodge
Conception to the very bourne of heaven,
Then leave the naked brain; be still the leaven,
That spreading in this dull and clodded earth
Gives it a touch ethereal, a new birth;
Be still a symbol of immensity,
300   A firmament reflected in a sea,
An element filling the space between,
An unknown—but no more! We humbly screen
With uplift hands our foreheads, lowly bending,
And giving out a shout most heaven-rending,
Conjure thee to receive our humble paean,
Upon thy Mount Lycean!'

from Book IV

'O Sorrow,
Why dost borrow
The natural hue of health, from vermeil lips?
To give maiden blushes
150   To the white rose bushes?
Or is it thy dewy hand the daisy tips?

O Sorrow,
Why dost borrow
The lustrous passion from a falcon-eye?
To give the glow-worm light?
Or, on a moonless night,
To tinge, on siren shores, the salt sea-spry?

O Sorrow
Why dost borrow
160   The mellow ditties from a mourning tongue?
To give at evening pale
Unto the nightingale,
That thou mayst listen the cold dews among?
O Sorrow,
Why dost borrow
Heart's lightness from the merriment of May?
A lover would not tread
A cowslip on the head,
Though he should dance from eve till peep of day—
170   Nor any drooping flower
Held sacred for thy bower,
Wherever he may sport himself and play.

To Sorrow
I bade good-morrow,
And thought to leave her far away behind.
But cheerly, cheerly,
She loves me dearly,
She is so constant to me, and so kind.
I would deceive her
180   And so leave her,
But ah, she is so constant and so kind!

Beneath my palm trees, by the river side,
I sat a-weeping. In the whole world wide
There was no one to ask me why I wept—

And so I kept
Brimming the water-lily cups with tears
Cold as my fears.

Beneath my palm trees, by the river side,
I sat a-weeping. What enamoured bride,
190 Cheated by shadowy wooer from the clouds,
But hides and shrouds
Beneath dark palm trees by a river side?
And as I sat, over the light blue hills
There came a noise of revellers. The rills
Into the wide stream came of purple hue–
'Twas Bacchus and his crew!
The earnest trumpet spake, and silver thrills
From kissing cymbals made a merry din–
'Twas Bacchus and his kin!
200 Like to a moving vintage down they came,
Crowned with green leaves, and faces all on flame—
All madly dancing through the pleasant valley,
To scare thee, Melancholy!
Oh, then, oh, then, thou wast a simple name!
And I forgot thee, as the berried holly
By shepherds is forgotten, when, in June,
Tall chestnuts keep away the sun and moon—
I rushed into the folly!

Within his car, aloft, young Bacchus stood,
210 Trifling his ivy-dart, in dancing mood,
With sidelong laughing;
And little rills of crimson wine imbrued
His plump white arms and shoulders, enough white
For Venus' pearly bite;
And near him rode Silenus on his ass,
Pelted with flowers as he on did pass
Tipsily quaffing.

Whence came ye, merry Damsels, whence came ye?
So many, and so many, and such glee?
220 Why have ye left your bowers desolate,
Your lutes and gentler fate?
"We follow Bacchus! Bacchus on the wing,
A-conquering!
Bacchus, young Bacchus! Good or ill betide,
We dance before him thorough kingdoms wide—
Come hither, lady fair, and joinèd be
To our wild minstrelsy!"

Whence came ye, jolly Satyrs, whence came ye?
So many, and so many, and such glee?
230 Why have ye left your forest haunts, why left
    Your nuts in oak-tree cleft?
"For wine, for wine we left our kernel tree;
For wine we left our heath and yellow brooms;
For wine we follow Bacchus through the earth—
Great God of breathless cups and chirping mirth!
Come hither, lady fair, and joinèd be
    To our mad minstrelsy!"

Over wide streams and mountains great we went,
240 And, save when Bacchus kept his ivy tent,
Onward the tiger and the leopard pants,
    With Asian elephants.
Onward these myriads—with song and dance,
With zebras striped and sleek Arabians' prance,
Web-footed alligators, crocodiles,
Bearing upon their scaly backs, in files,
Plump infant laughers mimicking the coil
Of seamen and stout galley-rowers' toil—
With toying oars and silken sails they glide,
250   Nor care for wind and tide.

Mounted on panthers' furs and lions' manes,
From rear to van they scour about the plains—
A three days' journey in a moment done.
And always, at the rising of the sun,
About the wilds they hunt with spear and horn,
    On spleenful unicorn.

I saw Osirian Egypt kneel adown
    Before the vine-wreath crown!
I saw parched Abyssinia rouse and sing
260   To the silver cymbals' ring!
I saw the whelming vintage hotly pierce
    Old Tartary the fierce!
The kings of Inde their jewel-sceptres vail,
And from their treasures scatter pearlèd hail.
Great Brahma from his mystic heaven groans,
    And all his priesthood moans,
Before young Bacchus' eye-wink turning pale.
Into these regions came I following him,
Sick hearted, weary—so I took a whim
270 To stray away into these forests drear
    Alone, without a peer.

And I have told thee all thou mayest hear.

> Young stranger!
> I've been a ranger
> In search of pleasure throughout every clime.
> Alas, 'tis not for me!
> Bewitched I sure must be,
> To lose in grieving all my maiden prime.

> Come then, Sorrow!
> Sweetest Sorrow!
> Like an own babe I nurse thee on my breast.
> I thought to leave thee
> And deceive thee,
> But now of all the world I love thee best.

> There is not one
> No, no, not one
> But thee to comfort a poor lonely maid.
> Thou art her mother,
> And her brother,
> Her playmate, and her wooer in the shade.'

Robin Hood

No, those days are gone away,
And their hours are old and gray,
And their minutes buried all
Under the down-trodden pall
Of the leaves of many years.
Many times have winter's shears,
Frozen north and chilling east,
Sounded tempests to the feast
Of the forest's whispering fleeces,
10 Since men knew nor rent nor leases.

No, the bugle sounds no more,
And the twanging bow no more.
Silent is the ivory shrill
Past the heath and up the hill.
There is no mid-forest laugh,
Where lone Echo gives the half
To some wight, amazed to hear
Jesting, deep in forest drear.

On the fairest time of June
20 You may go with sun or moon
Or the seven stars to light you,
Or the polar ray to right you.
But you never may behold
Little John, or Robin bold,
Never one, of all the clan,
Thrumming on an empty can
Some old hunting ditty, while
He doth his green way beguile
To fair hostess Merriment,
30 Down beside the pasture Trent,
For he left the merry tale,
Messenger for spicy ale.

Gone, the merry morris din;
Gone, the song of Gamelyn;
Gone, the tough-belted outlaw
Idling in the 'grenè shawe';

All are gone away and past!
And if Robin should be cast
Sudden from his turfèd grave,
40   And if Marian should have
Once again her forest days,
She would weep, and he would craze.
He would swear, for all his oaks,
Fallen beneath the dockyard strokes,
Have rotted on the briny seas.
She would weep that her wild bees
Sang not to her—strange that honey
Can't be got without hard money!

So it is—yet let us sing,
50   Honour to the old bow-string!
Honour to the bugle-horn!
Honour to the woods unshorn!
Honour to the Lincoln green!
Honour to the archer keen!
Honour to tight little John,
And the horse he rode upon!
Honour to bold Robin Hood,
Sleeping in the underwood!
Honour to maid Marian,
60   And to all the Sherwood-clan!
Though their days have hurried by
Let us two a burden try.

'Four seasons fill the measure of the year'

Four seasons fill the measure of the year;
   There are four seasons in the mind of man.
He has his lusty spring, when fancy clear
   Takes in all beauty with an easy span.
He has his summer, when luxuriously
   Spring's honeyed cud of youthful thought he loves
To ruminate, and by such dreaming nigh
   His nearest unto heaven. Quiet coves
His soul has in its autumn, when his wings
   He furleth close, contented so to look
On mists in idleness—to let fair things
   Pass by unheeded as a threshold brook;
He has his winter, too, of pale misfeature,
Or else he would forego his mortal nature.

To Homer

Standing aloof in giant ignorance,
  Of thee I hear and of the Cyclades,
As one who sits ashore and longs perchance
  To visit dolphin-coral in deep seas.
So wast thou blind. But then the veil was rent,
  For Jove uncurtained Heaven to let thee live,
And Neptune made for thee a spumy tent,
  And Pan made sing for thee his forest-hive.
Aye, on the shores of darkness there is light,
  And precipices show untrodden green;
There is a budding morrow in midnight,
  There is a triple sight in blindness keen;
Such seeing hadst thou, as it once befell
To Dian, Queen of Earth and Heaven and Hell.

Ode to May

Mother of Hermes! And still youthful Maia!
      May I sing to thee
As thou wast hymnèd on the shores of Baiae?
      Or may I woo thee
In earlier Sicilian? Or thy smiles
Seek, as they once were sought in Grecian isles
By bards who died content in pleasant sward,
      Leaving great verse unto a little clan?
Oh, give me their old vigour, and unheard,
      Save of the quiet primrose and the span
         Of Heaven and few ears,
Rounded by thee, my song should die away
         Content as theirs,
Rich in the simple worship of a day.

'Ah, ken ye what I met'

Ah, ken ye what I met the day
   Out oure the mountains,
A-coming down by craggies grey
   An mossie fountains?
Ah, goud-haired Marie yeve I pray
   Ane minute's guessing,
For that I met upon the way
   Is past expressing.
As I stood where a rocky brig
10   A torrent crosses,
I spied upon a misty rig
   A troup o' horses,
And as they trotted down the glen
   I sped to meet them
To see if I might know the men
   To stop and greet them.
First Willie on his sleek mare came
   At canting gallop—
His long hair rustled like a flame
20   On board a shallop.
Then came his brother Rab and then
   Young Peggy's mither,
And Peggy too—adown the glen
   They went togither.

I saw her wrappit in her hood
   Fra wind and raining—
Her cheek was flush wi' timid blood
   Twixt growth and waning.
She turned her dazèd head full oft,
30   For thence her brithers
Came riding with her bridegroom soft
   And mony ithers.
Young Tam came up an' eyed me quick
   With reddened cheek—
Braw Tam was daffèd like a chick,
   He coud na speak.
Ah, Marie, they are all gane hame

Through blustering weather,
An' every heart is full on flame
40   An' light as feather.
Ah, Marie, they are all gone hame
Fra happy wedding,
Whilst I–ah, is it not a shame?–
Sad tears am shedding.

To Ailsa Rock

Hearken, thou craggy ocean pyramid!
   Give answer from thy voice, the sea-fowls' screams!
   When were thy shoulders mantled in huge streams?
When from the sun was thy broad forehead hid?
How long is it since the mighty power bid
   Thee heave to airy sleep from fathom dreams—
   Sleep in the lap of thunder or sunbeams,
Or when grey clouds are thy cold coverlid?
Thou answer'st not, for thou art dead asleep.
   Thy life is but two dead eternities—
The last in air, the former in the deep,
   First with the whales, last with the eagle-skies.
Drowned wast thou till an earthquake made thee steep,
   Another cannot wake thy giant size.

'Where's the poet? Show him, show him'

Where's the poet? Show him, show him,
Muses nine, that I may know him!
'Tis the man who with a man
   Is an equal, be he king,
Or poorest of the beggar-clan,
   Or any other wondrous thing
A man may be 'twixt ape and Plato.
   'Tis the man who with a bird,
Wren or eagle, finds his way to
     All its instincts. He hath heard
The lion's roaring and can tell
   What his horny throat expresseth,
And to him the tiger's yell
   Comes articulate and presseth
On his ear like mother-tongue.

Fancy

Ever let the fancy roam,
Pleasure never is at home,
At a touch sweet Pleasure melteth,
Like to bubbles when rain pelteth.
Then let wingèd Fancy wander
Through the thought still spread beyond her;
Open wide the mind's cage-door,
She'll dart forth and cloudward soar.
Oh, sweet Fancy, let her loose!
10 Summer's joys are spoilt by use,
And the enjoying of the spring
Fades as does its blossoming.
Autumn's red-lipped fruitage, too,
Blushing through the mist and dew,
Cloys with tasting. What do then?
Sit thee by the ingle, when
The sere faggot blazes bright,
Spirit of a winter's night;
When the soundless earth is muffled,
20 And the cakèd snow is shuffled
From the ploughboy's heavy shoon;
When the night doth meet the noon
In a dark conspiracy
To banish even from her sky.
Sit thee there and send abroad,
With a mind self-overawed,
Fancy–high-commissioned send her!
She has vassals to attend her.
She will bring, in spite of frost,
30 Beauties that the earth hath lost.
She will bring thee, all together,
All delights of summer weather;
All the buds and bells of May,
From dewy sward or thorny spray;
All the heapèd autumn's wealth,
With a still, mysterious stealth.
She will mix these pleasures up

Like three fit wines in a cup,
And thou shalt quaff it. Thou shalt hear
40 Distant harvest-carols clear;
Rustle of the reapèd corn;
Sweet birds antheming the morn;
And, in the same moment—hark!
'Tis the early April lark,
Or the rooks with busy caw
Foraging for sticks and straw.
Thou shalt, at one glance, behold
The daisy and the marigold,
White-plumed lilies and the first
50 Hedge-grown primrose that hath burst,
Shaded hyacinth, alway
Sapphire queen of the mid-May,
And every leaf and every flower
Pearlèd with the self-same shower.
Thou shalt see the field-mouse peep
Meagre from its cellèd sleep,
And the snake all winter-thin
Cast on sunny bank its skin.
Freckled nest-eggs thou shalt see
60 Hatching in the hawthorn tree,
When the hen-bird's wing doth rest
Quiet on her mossy nest.
Then the hurry and alarm
When the bee-hive casts its swarm,
Acorns ripe down-pattering,
While the autumn breezes sing.

Oh, sweet Fancy! Let her loose;
Every thing is spoilt by use.
Where's the cheek that doth not fade,
70 Too much gazed at? Where's the maid
Whose lip mature is ever new?
Where's the eye, however blue,
Doth not weary? Where's the face
One would meet in every place?
Where's the voice, however soft,
One would hear so very oft?
At a touch sweet Pleasure melteth,
Like to bubbles when rain pelteth.
Let, then, wingèd Fancy find
80 Thee a mistress to thy mind,
Dulcet-eyed as Ceres' daughter,

Ere the God of Torment taught her
How to frown and how to chide,
With a waist and with a side
White as Hebe's, when her zone
Slipped its golden clasp, and down
Fell her kirtle to her feet,
While she held the goblet sweet,
And Jove grew languid.
                                    Break the mesh
90 Of the Fancy's silken leash,
Quickly break her prison-string
And such joys as these she'll bring.
Let the wingèd Fancy roam,
Pleasure never is at home.

Ode ['Bards of passion and of mirth']

Bards of passion and of mirth,
Ye have left your souls on earth!
Have ye souls in heaven too,
Double-lived in regions new?
Yes, and those of heaven commune
With the spheres of sun and moon;
With the noise of fountains wondrous,
And the parle of voices thund'rous;
With the whisper of heaven's trees,
10 And one another, in soft ease
Seated on Elysian lawns
Browsed by none but Dian's fawns,
Underneath large blue-bells tented,
Where the daisies are rose-scented
And the rose herself has got
Perfume which on earth is not,
Where the nightingale doth sing
Not a senseless, trancèd thing,
But divine melodious truth,
20 Philosophic numbers smooth,
Tales and golden histories
Of heaven and its mysteries.

Thus ye live on high, and then
On the earth ye live again;
And the souls ye left behind you
Teach us, here, the way to find you,
Where your other souls are joying,
Never slumbered, never cloying.
Here, your earth-born souls still speak
30 To mortals of their little week;
Of their sorrows and delights;
Of their passions and their spites;
Of their glory and their shame;
What doth strengthen and what maim.

Thus ye teach us, every day,
Wisdom, though fled far away.

Bards of passion and of mirth,
Ye have left your souls on earth!
Ye have souls in heaven too,
40   Double-lived in regions new!

The Eve of St Mark

Upon a Sabbath day it fell;
Twice holy was the Sabbath bell
That called the folk to evening prayer.
The city streets were clean and fair
From wholesome drench of April rains,
And, on the western window panes,
The chilly sunset faintly told
Of unmatured green valleys cold,
Of the green thorny bloomless hedge,
10   Of rivers new with spring-tide sedge,
Of primroses by sheltered rills,
And daisies on the aguish hills.
Twice holy was the Sabbath-bell;
The silent streets were crowded well
With staid and pious companies,
Warm from their fireside orat'ries,
And moving with demurest air
To even-song and vesper prayer.
Each archèd porch and entry low
20   Was filled with patient folk and slow,
With whispers hush and shuffling feet,
While played the organ loud and sweet.

The bells had ceased, the prayers begun,
And Bertha had not yet half done
A curious volume patched and torn,
That all day long from earliest morn
Had taken captive her two eyes
Among its golden broideries,
Perplexed her with a thousand things—
30   The stars of Heaven and angels' wings,
Martyrs in a fiery blaze,
Azure saints 'mid silver rays,
Aaron's breast plate, and the seven
Candlesticks John saw in heaven,
The winged Lion of Saint Mark,
And the Covenantal Ark
With its many mysteries,

Cherubim and golden mice.

Bertha was a maiden fair,
40   Dwelling in the old Minster Square;
From her fireside she could see,
Sidelong, its rich antiquity
Far as the Bishop's garden-wall,
Where sycamores and elm-trees tall,
Full-leaved, the forest had outstripped,
By no sharp north-wind ever nipped,
So sheltered by the mighty pile.
Bertha arose and read awhile
With forehead 'gainst the window-pane.
50   Again she tried, and then again,
Until the dusk eve left her dark
Upon the legend of St. Mark.
From pleated lawn-frill, fine and thin,
She lifted up her soft warm chin,
With aching neck and swimming eyes,
And dazed with saintly imageries.

All was gloom, and silent all,
Save now and then the still foot-fall
Of one returning homewards late,
60   Past the echoing Minster gate.

The clamorous daws, that all the day
Above tree tops and towers play,
Pair by pair had gone to rest,
Each in its ancient belfry nest,
Where asleep they fall betimes
To music of the drowsy chimes.

All was silent, all was gloom,
Abroad and in the homely room.
The maiden, lost in dizzy maze,
70   Turned to the fire and made a blaze;
Down she sat, poor cheated soul,
And struck a lamp from the dismal coal,
Leaned forward, with bright drooping hair,
And slant book full against the glare.
Her shadow, in uneasy guise,
Hovered about, a giant's size,
On ceiling beam and old oak chair,
The parrot's cage and panel square,

And the warm angled winter screen
80　On which were many monsters seen
Called doves of Siam, Lima mice,
And legless birds of Paradise,
Macaw and tender Av'davat,
And silken-furred Angora cat.
Untired she read, her shadow still
Glowered about, as it would fill
The room with wildest forms and shades;
As though some ghostly queen of spades
Had come to mock behind her back
90　And dance and ruffle her garments black.
Untired she read the legend page
Of holy Mark from youth to age,
On land, on sea, in pagan chains,
Rejoicing for his many pains.
Sometimes the learned eremite
With golden star or dagger bright
Referred to pious poesies
Written in smallest crow-quill size
Beneath the text; and thus the rhyme
100　Was parcelled out from time to time:
'Gif ye wol stonden, hardie wight,
Amiddës of the blackë night,
Righte in the churchë porch, pardie,
Ye wol behold a companie
Approchen thee full dolourouse.
For sooth to sain, from everich house,
Be it in city or village,
Wol come the phantom and image
Of ilka gent and ilka carle,
110　Whom coldë Deathë hath in parle,
And wol some day that very year
Touchen with foulë venime spear,
And sadly do them all to die:
Hem all shalt thou see verilie.
And everichon shall by thee pass,
All who must die that year, alas...
Als writith he of swevenis
Men han beforne they wake in blis,
Whanne that hir friendës thinke hem bound
120　In crimpede shroude farre under grounde;
And how a litling childe mote be
A saint er its nativitie,
Gif that the modre (God her blesse!)

228

Kepen in solitarinesse,
And kissen devoute the holy croce.
Of Goddis love, and Sathan's force,
He writith; and thinges many mo.
Of swichë thinges I may not show.
Bot I must tellen verilie
130   Somdel of Saintë Cicilie,
And chieflie what he auctorith
Of Saintë Markis life and dethe.'

At length her constant eye had come
Upon the fervent martyrdom,
Then lastly to his holy shrine,
Exalt amid the tapers' shine
At Venice . . .

To Sleep

O soft embalmer of the still midnight,
  Shutting with careful fingers and benign
Our gloom-pleased eyes, embowered from the light,
  Enshaded in forgetfulness divine:
O soothest Sleep! If so it please thee, close,
  In midst of this thine hymn, my willing eyes,
Or wait the 'Amen', ere thy poppy throws
  Around my bed its lulling charities.
Then save me, or the passèd day will shine
Upon my pillow, breeding many woes;
  Save me from curious conscience, that still hoards
Its strength for darkness, burrowing like a mole;
  Turn the key deftly in the oilèd wards,
And seal the hushèd casket of my soul.

Ode to Psyche

O Goddess! Hear these tuneless numbers, wrung
  By sweet enforcement and remembrance dear,
And pardon that thy secrets should be sung
  Even into thine own soft-conchèd ear.
Surely I dreamt to-day, or did I see
  The wingèd Psyche with awakened eyes?
    I wandered in a forest thoughtlessly,
  And, on the sudden, fainting with surprise,
Saw two fair creatures, couchèd side by side
10   In deepest grass, beneath the whispering roof
    Of leaves and trembled blossoms, where there ran
      A brooklet, scarce espied.
'Mid hushed, cool-rooted flowers, fragrant-eyed,
  Blue, silver-white and budded Tyrian,
They lay calm-breathing on the bedded grass;
  Their arms embracèd, and their pinions too;
  Their lips touched not, but had not bade adieu,
As if disjoinèd by soft-handed slumber,
And ready still past kisses to outnumber
20   At tender eye-dawn of aurorean love.
      The wingèd boy I knew;
  But who wast thou, O happy, happy dove?
      His Psyche true!
O latest born and loveliest vision far
  Of all Olympus' faded hierarchy!
Fairer than Phoebe's sapphire-regioned star,
  Or Vesper, amorous glow-worm of the sky;
Fairer than these, though temple thou hast none,
    Nor altar heaped with flowers;
30 Nor virgin-choir to make delicious moan
      Upon the midnight hours—
No voice, no lute, no pipe, no incense sweet
  From chain-swung censer teeming;
No shrine, no grove, no oracle, no heat
  Of pale-mouthed prophet dreaming.

O brightest, though too late for antique vows!
Too, too late for the fond believing lyre,

When holy were the haunted forest boughs,
Holy the air, the water and the fire.
40 Yet even in these days so far retired
From happy pieties, thy lucent fans,
Fluttering among the faint Olympians,
I see, and sing, by my own eyes inspired.
So let me be thy choir and make a moan
Upon the midnight hours—
Thy voice, thy lute, thy pipe, thy incense sweet
From swingèd censer teeming;
Thy shrine, thy grove, thy oracle, thy heat
Of pale-mouthed prophet dreaming.

50 Yes, I will be thy priest, and build a fane
In some untrodden region of my mind,
Where branchèd thoughts, new grown with pleasant
pain,
Instead of pines shall murmur in the wind:
Far, far around shall those dark-clustered trees
Fledge the wild-ridgèd mountains steep by steep;
And there by zephyrs, streams, and birds, and bees,
The moss-lain Dryads shall be lulled to sleep;
And in the midst of this wide quietness
A rosy sanctuary will I dress
60 With the wreathed trellis of a working brain,
With buds, and bells, and stars without a name,
With all the gardener Fancy e'er could feign,

Who breeding flowers will never breed the same:
And there shall be for thee all soft delight
That shadowy thought can win,
A bright torch, and a casement ope at night,
To let the warm Love in!

'If by dull rhymes our English must be chained'

If by dull rhymes our English must be chained,
And, like Andromeda, the Sonnet sweet
Fettered, in spite of painèd loveliness,
Let us find out, if we must be constrained,
Sandals more interwoven and complete
To fit the naked foot of Poesy.
Let us inspect the lyre, and weigh the stress
Of every chord, and see what may be gained
By ear industrious, and attention meet;
Misers of sound and syllable, no less
Than Midas of his coinage, let us be
Jealous of dead leaves in the bay wreath crown;
So, if we may not let the Muse be free,
She will be bound with garlands of her own.

'This living hand'

This living hand, now warm and capable
Of earnest grasping, would, if it were cold
And in the icy silence of the tomb,
So haunt thy days and chill thy dreaming nights
That thou would wish thine own heart dry of blood
So in my veins red life might stream again,
And thou be conscience-calmed. See here it is—
I hold it towards you.

Extracts from Letters, III

22. To J.H. Reynolds, 18 April 1817

I find that I cannot exist without poetry, without eternal poetry. Half a day will not do, the whole of it. . . I began with a little, but habit has made me a leviathan.

23. To Benjamin Bailey, 8 October 1817

I have heard Hunt say, and I may be asked–Why endeavour after a long poem? To which I should answer–Do not the lovers of poetry like to have a little region to wander in where they may pick and choose, and in which the images are so numerous that many are forgotten and found new in a second reading; which may be food for a week's stroll in the summer? Do not they like this better than what they can read through before Mrs Williams comes downstairs–a morning work at most? Besides, a long poem is a test of invention, which I take to be the polar star of poetry, as fancy is the sails and imagination the rudder. Did our great poets ever write short pieces–I mean in the shape of tales? This same invention seems indeed of late years to have been forgotten as a poetical excellence.

24. To George and Thomas Keats, 21 December 1817

It is a wonderful picture when West's age is considered. But there is nothing to be intense upon–no women one feels mad to kiss, no face swelling into reality. The excellence of every art is its intensity, capable of making all disagreeables evaporate from their being in close relationship with beauty and truth. Examine *King Lear*, and you will find this exemplified throughout. But in this picture we have unpleasantness without any momentous depth of speculation excited, in which to bury its repulsiveness...

10   I had, not a dispute, but a disquisition with Dilke on various subjects. Several things dovetailed in my mind, and at once it struck me what quality went to form a man of achievement, especially in literature, and which Shakespeare possessed so enormously. I mean *Negative Capability*—that is, when a man is capable of being in uncertainties, mysteries, doubts, without any irritable reaching after fact and reason. Coleridge, for instance, would let go by a fine isolated verisimilitude caught from the penetralium of mystery from being incapable of remaining content with half-knowledge.

20   This, pursued through volumes, would perhaps take us no further than this—that with a great poet the sense of beauty overcomes every other consideration or rather obliterates all consideration.

25. To J.H. Reynolds, 3 February 1818

We hate poetry that has a palpable design upon us, and, if we do not agree, seems to put its hand in its breeches pocket. Poetry should be great and unobtrusive, a thing which enters into one's soul and does not startle it or amaze it with itself but with its subject.

26. To John Taylor, 27 February 1818

In poetry I have a few axioms, and you will see how far I am from their centre. 1st. I think poetry should surprise by a fine excess and not by singularity. It should strike the reader as a wording of his own highest thoughts and appear almost a rememberance. 2nd. Its touches of beauty should never be half-way, thereby making the reader breathless instead of content. The rise, the progress, the setting of imagery should, like the sun, come natural to him—shine over him and set soberly, although in magnificence, leaving him in the luxury

10   of twilight. But it is easier to think what poetry should be

than to write it. And this leads me to another axiom—that if poetry comes not as naturally as the leaves to a tree, it had better not come at all.

27. To Benjamin Bailey, 13 March 1818

I am sometimes so very sceptical as to think poetry itself a mere Jack a lanthern to amuse whoever may chance to be struck with its brilliance. As tradesmen say every thing is is worth what it will fetch, so probably every mental pursuit takes its reality and worth from the ardour of the pursuer, being in itself a nothing. Ethereal things may at least be thus real, divided under three heads—things real, things semi-real, and no things: things real—such as existences of sun, moon, and stars and passages of Shakespeare; things semi-*10* real—such as love, the clouds, etc., which require a greeting of the spirit to make them wholly exist; and nothings, which are made great and dignified by an ardent pursuit, which, by the by, stamps the burgundy-mark on the bottles of our minds, insomuch as they are able to 'consecrate whate'er they look upon'.

28. To Charles Wentworth Dilke, 21 September 1818

His identity presses on me so all day that I am obliged to go out, and although I intended to have given some time to study alone, I am obliged to write and plunge into abstract images to ease myself of his countenance, his voice, and feebleness; so that I live now in a continual fever. It must be poisonous to life, although I feel well. Imagine 'the hateful siege of contraries'. If I think of fame of poetry it seems a crime to me, and yet I must do so or suffer.

29. To James Augustus Hessey, 8 October 1818

It is as good as I had power to make it—by myself. Had I been

237

nervous about its being a perfect piece and with that view asked advice and trembled over every page, it would not have been written, for it is not in my nature to fumble. I will write independently. I have written independently *without judgment*; I may write independently, and *with judgment*, hereafter. The genius of poetry must work out its own salvation in a man. It cannot be matured by law and percept, but by sensation and watchfulness in itself. That which is creative must create itself.

30. To Richard Woodhouse, 27 October 1818

As to the poetical character itself (I mean that sort of which, if I am any thing, I am a member, that sort distinguished from the Wordsworthian or egotistical sublime, which is a thing per se and stands alone), it is not itself–it has no self. It is everything and nothing. It has no character. It enjoys light and shade; it lives in gusto, be it foul or fair, high or low, rich or poor, mean or elevated, It has as much delight in conceiving an Iago as an Imogen. What shocks the virtuous philosopher delights the camelion poet. It does no harm from its relish of the dark side of things any more than from its taste for the bright one, because they both end in speculation. A poet is the most unpoetical of any thing in existence, because he has no identity. He is continually [informing] and filling some other body. The sun, the moon, the sea, and men and women, who are creatures of impulse, are poetical and have about them an unchangeable attribute. The poet has none, no identity. He is certainly the most unpoetical of all God's creatures. If then he has no self, and if I am a poet, where is the wonder that I should say I would write no more? Might I not at that very instant have been cogitating on the characters of Saturn and Ops? It is a wretched thing to confess but is a very fact that not one word I ever utter can be taken for granted as an opinion growing out of my identical nature. How can it, when I have no nature? When I am in a room with people, if I ever am free from speculating on creations of my own brain, then not myself goes home to myself, but the identity of every one in the room begins so to press upon me that I am in a very little

time annihilated. Not only among men; it would be the same
in a nursery of children. I know not whether I make myself
wholly understood. I hope enough so to let you see that no
dependence is to be placed on what I said that day.

In the second place, I will speak of my views and of the life
I purpose to myself. I am ambitious of doing the world some
good. If I am spared, that may be the work of maturer years.
In the interval I will assay to reach as high a summit in poetry
as the nerve bestowed upon me will suffer. The faint conceptions I have of poems to come brings the blood frequently
into my forehead. All I hope is that I may not lose all interest
in human affairs, that the solitary indifference I feel for
applause even from the finest spirits will not blunt any
acuteness of vision I may have. I do not think it will. I feel
assured I should write from the mere yearning and fondness
I have for the beautiful, even if my night's labours should
be burnt every morning and no eye ever shine upon them.
But even now I am perhaps not speaking from myself but
from some character in whose soul I now live.

31. To George and Georgiana Keats, 31 December 1818

I never can feel certain of any truth but from a clear perception of its beauty; and I find myself very young-minded
even in that perceptive power, which I hope will increase.

32. To Fanny Brawne, February 1820

'If I should die,' said I to myself, 'I have left no immortal
work behind me, nothing to make my friends proud of my
memory; but I have loved the principle of beauty in all
things, and if I had had time. I would have made myself
remembered.'

33. To Thomas Keats, 27 June 1818

What astonishes me more than anything is the tone, the

colouring, the slate, the stone, the moss, the rock-weed, or, if I may say so, the intellect, the countenance of such places. The space, the magnitude of mountains and waterfalls, are well imagined before one sees them; but this countenance or intellectual tone must surpass every imagination and defy any remembrance. I shall learn poetry here and henceforth write more than ever for the abstract endeavour of being able to add a mite to that mass of beauty which is harvested from these grand materials by the finest spirits and put into ethereal existence for the relish of one's fellows.

I cannot think with Hazlitt that these scenes make man appear little. I never forgot my stature so completely. I live in the eye, and my imagination, surpassed, is at rest.

34. To the Same, 9 July 1818

On our walk in Ireland we had too much opportunity to see the worse than nakedness, the rags, the dirt, and misery of the poor, common Irish. A Scotch cottage, though in that sometimes the smoke has no exit but the door, is a palace to an Irish one. We could observe that impetiosity in man, boy, and woman.

We had the pleasure of finding our way through a peat bog, three miles long at least, dreary, black, dank, flat and spongy. Here and there were poor dirty creatures and a few strong men cutting or carting peat.

We heard, on passing into Belfast through a most wretched suburb, that most disgusting of all noises, worse than the bagpipe, the laugh of a monkey, the chatter of women *solus*, the scream of a macaw—I mean, the sound of the shuttle. What a tremendous difficulty is the improvement of the condition of such people. I cannot conceive how a mind 'with child' of philanthropy could grasp at possibility; with me it is absolute despair.

At a miserable house of entertainment half way between Donaghadee and Belfast were two men sitting at whisky, one a labourer and the other I took to be a drunken weaver. The labourer took me for a Frenchman, and the other hinted at bounty money, saying he was ready to take it. On calling for the letters at Portpatrick, the man snapped out, 'what regiment?'

On our return from Belfast we met a sedan–the Duchess of Dunghill. It is no laughing matter though. Imagine the worst dog-kennel you ever saw placed upon two poles from a mouldy fencing. In such a wretched thing sat a squalid old woman, squat like an ape half-starved from a scarcity of biscuit in its passage from Madagascar to the Cape, with a pipe in her mouth and looking out with a round-eyed, skinny-lidded inanity–with a sort of horizontal idiotic movement of her head. Squab and lean she sat and puffed out the smoke while two ragged, tattered girls carried her along. What a thing would be a history of her life and sensations!

35. To the Same, 26 July 1818

The finest thing is Fingal's Cave. It is entirely a hollowing-out of basalt pillars. Suppose now the Giants who rebelled against Jove had taken a whole mass of black columns and bound them together like bunches of matches, and then with immense axes had made a cavern in the body of these columns. (Of course, the roof and floor must be composed of the broken ends of the columns.) Such is Fingal's Cave, except that the sea has done the work of excavations and is continually dashing there, so that we walk along the sides of the cave on the pillars, which are left as if for convenient stairs.

The roof is arched somewhat Gothic-wise, and the length of some of the entire side-pillars is fifty feet. About the island you might seat an army of men, each on a pillar. The length of the cave is one hundred and twenty feet, and from its extremity the view into the sea through the large arch at the entrance [is very grand]. The colour of the columns is a sort of black with a lurking gloom of purple therein. For solemnity and grandeur it far surpasses the finest cathedral. At the extremity of the cave there is a small perforation into another cave, at which, the waters meeting and buffetting each other, there is sometimes produced a report as of a cannon, heard as far as Iona, which must be twelve miles.

As we approached in the boat there was such a fine swell of the sea that the pillars appeared rising immediately out of the crystal. But it is impossible to describe it.

36. To the Same, 3 August 1818

The whole immense head of the mountain is composed
of large, loose stones—thousands of acres. Before we got half-
way up, we passed large patches of snow, and near the top
there is a chasm, some hundred feet deep, completely glutted
with it.

Talking of chasms, they are the finest wonder of the whole.
They appear great rents in the very heart of the mountain,
though they are not, being at the side of it. But other huge
crags arising round it give the appearance to Nevis of a
shattered heart or core in itself. These chasms are fifteen
hundred feet in depth and are the most tremendous places
I have ever seen. They turn one giddy if you choose to give
way to it. We tumbled in large stones and set the echoes at
work in fine style. Sometimes these chasms are tolerably
clear; sometimes there is a misty cloud which seems to steam
up; and sometimes they are entirely smothered with cloud.

After a little time the mist cleared away, but still there were
large clouds about, attracted by old Ben to a certain distance
so as to form, as it appeared, large dome curtains, which kept
sailing about, opening and shutting at intervals here and
there and everywhere; so that, although we did not see one
vast wide extent of prospect all round, we saw something
perhaps finer—these cloud-veils opening with a dissolving
motion and showing us the mountainous region beneath as
through a loop-hole, these cloudy loop-holes ever varying
and discovering fresh prospect east, west, north, and south.
Then it was misty again, and again it was fair. Then puff
came a cold breeze of wind and bared a craggy chap we had
not yet seen, though in close neighbourhood. Every now
and then we had overhead blue sky, clear and the sun pretty
warm.

I do not know whether I can give you an idea of the
prospect from a large mountain top. You are on a stony
plain, which of course makes you forget you are on any but
low ground. The horizon, or rather edges of this plain, being
above four thousand feet above the sea, hide all the country

242

immediately beneath you; so that the next objects you see all round next to the edges of the flat top are the summits of mountains of some distance off. As you move about, on all sides you see more or less of the near-neighbouring country according as the mountain you stand upon is in different parts steep or rounded; but the most new thing of all is the sudden leap of the eye from the extremity of what appears a plain into so vast a distance.

Lighter Verse

To Mrs Reynold's Cat

Cat, who hast passed thy grand climacteric,
  How many mice and rats hast in thy days
  Destroyed? How many titbits stolen? Gaze
With those bright languid segments green, and prick
Those velvet ears—but prithee do not stick
  Thy latent talons in me, and upraise
  Thy gentle mew, and tell me all thy frays
Of fish and mice, and rats and tender chick.
Nay, look not down, nor lick thy dainty wrists—
  For all the wheezy asthma, and for all
Thy tail's tip is nicked off, and though the fists
  Of many a maid have given thee many a maul,
Still is that fur as soft as when the lists
  In youth thou enter'dst on glass-bottled wall.

Lines on the Mermaid Tavern

Souls of Poets dead and gone,
What Elysium have ye known,
Happy field or mossy cavern,
Choicer than the Mermaid Tavern?
Have ye tippled drink more fine
Than mine host's Canary wine?
Or are fruits of Paradise
Sweeter than those dainty pies
Of venison? Oh, generous food,
10   Dressed as though bold Robin Hood
Would, with his Maid Marian,
Sup and bowse from horn and can.

I have heard that on a day
Mine host's sign-board flew away,
Nobody knew whither, till
An astrologer's old quill
To a sheepskin gave the story,
Said he saw you in your glory,
Underneath a new old sign
20   Sipping beverage divine,
And pledging with contented smack
The Mermaid in the Zodiac.

Souls of Poets dead and gone,
What Elysium have ye known,
Happy field or mossy cavern,
Choicer than the Mermaid Tavern?

'Oh, I am frightened with most hateful thoughts'

Oh, I am frightened with most hateful thoughts!
Perhaps her voice is not a nightingale's,
Perhaps her teeth are not the fairest pearl.
Her eye-lashes may be, for aught I know,
Not longer than the may-fly's small fan-horns.
There may not be one dimple on her hand.
And freckles many! Ah, a careless nurse,
In haste to teach the little thing to walk,
May have crumped up a pair of Dian's legs,
And warped the ivory of a Juno's neck.

'Over the hill and over the dale'

Over the hill and over the dale,
And over the bourn to Dawlish,
Where gingerbread wives have a scanty sale
And gingerbread nuts are smallish.

Rantipole Betty she ran down a hill,
And kicked up her petticoats fairly.
Says I, 'I'll be Jack if you will be Jill.'
So she sat on the grass debonairly.

'Here's somebody coming, here's somebody coming!'
10 Says I, ''Tis the wind at a parley.'
So without any fuss, any hawing and humming,
She lay on the grass debonairly.

'Here's somebody here and here's somebody *there*!'
Says I, 'Hold your tongue you young gipsy.'
So she held her tongue and lay plump and fair
And dead as a Venus tipsy.

Oh, who wouldn't hie to Dawlish fair,
Oh, who wouldn't stop in a meadow?
Oh, who would not rumple the daisies there
20 And make the wild fern for a bed do?

'Old Meg she was a gipsy'

Old Meg she was a gipsy,
  And lived upon the moors,
Her bed it was the brown heath turf,
  And her house was out of doors.

II

Her apples were swart blackberries,
  Her currants pods o' broom,
Her wine was dew of the wild white rose,
  Her book a churchyard tomb.

III

Her brothers were the craggy hills,
10   Her sisters larchen trees –
Alone with her great family
  She lived as she did please.

IV

No breakfast had she many a morn,
  No dinner many a noon,
And 'stead of supper she would stare
  Full hard against the moon.

V

But every morn of woodbine fresh
  She made her garlanding,
And every night the dark glen yew
20   She wove, and she would sing.

VI

And with her fingers old and brown
  She plaited mats o' rushes,
And gave them to the cottagers
  She met among the bushes.

VII

Old Meg was brave as Margaret Queen
   And tall as Amazon,
An old red blanket cloak she wore,
   A chip hat had she on.
God rest her agèd bones somewhere –
30   She died full long agone!

The Cap and Bells or,
The Jealousies

[Extract]

LXXI

This as a falsehood Crafticanto treats,
And as his style is of strange elegance,
Gentle and tender, full of soft conceits
(Much like our Boswell's), we will take a glance
At his sweet prose and, if we can, make dance
His woven periods into careless rhyme.
O little fairy Pegasus, rear—prance—
Trot round the quarto—ordinary time!
March, little Pegasus, with pawing hoof sublime!

LXXII

640   Well, let us see—*tenth book and chapter nine*—
Thus Crafticant pursues his diary:
''Twas twelve o'clock at night, the weather fine,
Latitude thirty-six; our scouts descry
A flight of starlings making rapidly
Toward Thibet. Mem.—birds fly in the night.
From twelve to half-past—wings not fit to fly
For a thick fog—the Princess, sulky quite,
Called for an extra shawl and gave her nurse a bite.

LXXIII

Five minutes before one—brought down a moth
650   With my new double-barrel—stewed the thighs
And made a very tolerable broth.
Princess turned dainty; to our great surprise,
Altered her mind, and thought it very nice.
Seeing her pleasant, tried her with a pun;
She frowned. A monstrous owl across us flies
About this time—a sad old figure of fun.
Bad omen—this new match can't be a happy one.

LXXIV

From two till half-past, dusky way we made,
Above the plains of Gobi – desert, bleak;
660   Beheld afar off, in the hooded shade
Of darkness, a great mountain (strange to speak)
Spitting, from forth its sulphur-baken peak,
A fan-shaped burst of blood-red, arrowy fire,
Turbaned with smoke, which still away did reek,
Solid and black from that eternal pyre,
Upon the laden wind that scantly could respire.

LXXV

Just upon three o'clock a falling star
Created an alarm among our troop,
Killed a man-cook, a page, and broke a jar,
670   A tureen, and three dishes, at one swoop,
Then passing by the Princess, singed her hoop.
Could not conceive what Coralline was at –
She clapped her hands three times and cried out
    'Whoop!'
Some strange Imaian custom. A large bat
Came sudden 'fore my face and brushed against my hat...

LXXX

About this time, making delightful way,
Shed a quill-feather from my larboard wing –
Wished, trusted, hoped 'twas no sign of decay –
Thank heaven, I'm hearty yet! – 'twas no such thing.
At five the golden light began to spring
With fiery shudder through the bloomèd east.
At six we heard Panthea's churches ring –
The city all her unhived swarms had cast,
720   To watch our grand approach and hail us as we passed.

LXXXI

As flowers turn their faces to the sun,
So on our flight with hungry eyes they gaze,
And, as we shaped our course, this, that way run,
With mad-cap pleasure, or hand-clasped amaze.
Sweet in the air a mild-toned music plays,
And progresses through its own labyrinth.
Buds gathered from the green spring's middle-days
They scattered – daisy, primrose, hyacinth—
Or round white columns wreathed from capital to
    plinth.

LXXXII

730   Onward we floated o'er the panting streets,
That seemed throughout with upheld faces paved.
Look where we will, our bird's eye vision meets
Legions of holiday: bright standards waved,
And fluttering ensigns emulously craved
Our minute's glance; a busy thunderous roar
From square to square among the buildings raved,
As when the sea, at flow, gluts up once more
The craggy hollowness of a wild-reefed shore.

LXXXIII

And "Bellanaine for ever," shouted they,
740   While that fair Princess, from her wingèd chair,
Bowed low with high demeanour, and, to pay
Their new-blown loyalty with guerdon fair,
Still emptied, at meet distance, here and there,
A plenty-horn of jewels. And here I
(Who wish to give the devil her due) declare
Against that ugly piece of calumny
Which calls them Highland pebble-stones not worth
    a fly.

LXXXIV

Still "Bellanaine" they shouted, while we glide
'Slant to a light Ionic portico,
750   The city's delicacy, and the pride
Of our Imperial Basilic. A row
Of lords and ladies, on each hand, make show
Submissive of knee-bent obeisance,
All down the steps; and, as we entered, lo!
The strangest sight, the most unlooked-for chance,
All things turned topsy-turvy in a devil's dance.

'Stead of his anxious Majesty and court
At the open doors, with wide saluting eyes,
Congées and scape-graces of every sort,
760   And all the smooth routine of gallantries,
Was seen, to our immoderate surprise,
A motley crowd thick gathered in the hall,
Lords, scullions, deputy-scullions, with wild cries
Stunning the vestibule from wall to wall,
Where the Chief Justice on his knees and hands doth
    crawl.

Counts of the palace and the state purveyor
Of moth's-down to make soft the royal beds,
The common council and my fool Lord Mayor
Marching a-row, each other slipshod treads.
770   Powdered bag-wigs and ruffy-tuffy heads
Of cinder wenches meet and soil each other.
Toe crushed with heel ill-natured fighting breeds,
Frill-rumpling elbows brew up many a bother,
And fists in the short ribs keep up the yell and pother.

LXXXVII

A poet, mounted on the Court-Clown's back,
Rode to the Princess swift with spurring heels,
And close into her face, with rhyming clack,
Began a Prothalamion. She reels,
She falls, she faints! while laughter peals
780   Over her woman's weakness. "Where," cried I,
"Where is his Majesty?" No person feels
Inclined to answer; wherefore instantly
I plunged into the crowd to find him or to die.

LXXXVIII

Jostling my way I gained the stairs and ran
To the first landing, where, incredible!
I met, far gone in liquor, that old man,
That vile impostor Hum——'
                So far so well,
For we have proved the Mago never fell
Down stairs, on Crafticanto's evidence,
790   And therefore duly shall proceed to tell,
Plain in our own original mood and tense,
The sequel of this day, though labour 'tis immense!

Extracts from Letters, IV

37. To George and Thomas Keats,
24 January 1818

I left off short in my last, just as I began an account of a
private theatrical. Well, it was of the lowest order, all greasy
and oily, in so much that if they had lived in olden times,
when signs were hung over the doors, the only appropriate
one for that oily place would have been a guttered Candle.
They played *John Bull*, *The Review*, and it was to conclude
with *Bombastes Furioso*. I saw from a box the first Act of *John
Bull*, then I went to Drury and did not return till it was over,
when, by Wells's interest, we got behind the scenes.

10   There was not a yard all the way round for actors, scene-
shifters, and interlopers to move in, for, 'Nota Bene', the
green-room was under the stage, and there was I threatened
over and over again to be turned out by the oily scene-
shifters. There did I hear a little painted trollop own, very
candidly, that she had failed in Mary, with a 'damned if
she'd play a serious part again as long as she lived'; and at the
same time she was habited as the Quaker in *The Review*.
There was a quarrel, and a fat good-natured looking girl
in soldier's clothes wished she had only been a man for
20 Tom's sake.

    One fellow began a song, but an unlucky finger-point from
the gallery sent him off like a shot. One chap was dressed to
kill for the King in *Bombastes*, and he stood at the edge of
the scene in the very sweat of anxiety to show himself, but
alas the thing was not played. The sweetest morsel of the
night moreover was that the musicians began pegging and
fagging away at an overtune. Never did you see faces more
in earnest. Three times did they play it over, dropping all
kinds of correctness, and still did not the curtain draw up.
30 Well, then they went into a country dance, then into a

region they well knew–into their old boonsome pothouse. And then to see how pompous o' the sudden they turned, how they looked about and chatted, how they did not care a damn, was a great treat.

38. To J.H. Reynolds, 14 March 1818

I escaped being blown over and blown under, and trees and houses being toppled on me. I have, since hearing of Brown's accident, had an aversion to a dose of parapet; and, being also a lover of antiquities, I would sooner have a harmless piece of herculaneum sent me quietly as a present than ever so modern a chimney-pot tumbled on to my head.

Being agog to see some Devonshire, I would have taken a walk the first day, but the rain would not let me; and the second, but the rain would not let me; and the third, but the rain forbade it. Ditto 4, ditto 5, ditto... So I made up my mind to stop indoors, and catch a sight flying between the showers; and behold I saw a pretty valley, pretty cliffs, pretty brooks, pretty meadows, pretty trees–both standing as they were created, and blown down as they were un-created.

The green is beautiful, as they say, and pity it is that it is amphibious. Mais but alas! the flowers here wait as naturally for the rain twice a day 'as the mussels do for the tide, so we look upon a brook in these parts as you look upon a dash in your country. There must be something to support this–aye, fog, hail, snow, rain, mist, blanketing up three parts of the year. This Devonshire is like Lydia Languish, very entertaining when at smiles, but cursedly subject to sympathetic moisture. You have the sensation of walking under one great lamplighter; and you can't go on the other side of the ladder to keep your frock clean and cosset your superstition.

Buy a girdle, put a pebble in your mouth, loosen your braces, for I am going among scenery whence I intend to tip you the Damosel Radcliffe. I'll cavern you, and grotto you, and waterfall you, and wood you, and water you, and immense-rock you, and tremendous-sound you, and

solitude you. I'll make a lodgment on your glacis by a row
of pines and storm your covered way with bramble bushes.
I'll have at you with hip and haw small-shot, and cannonade
you with shingles. I'll be witty upon salt fish, and impede
your cavalry with clotted cream.

39. To George and Georgiana Keats, 19 February 1819

Now I like claret. Whenever I can have claret I must drink
it–'tis the only palate affair that I am at all sensual in.
Would it not be a good spec to send you some vine shoots–
could it be done? I'll inquire. If you could make some wine
like claret to drink on summer evenings in an arbour! For
really 'tis so fine. It fills one's mouth with a gushing freshness, then goes down cool and feverless; then you do not
feel it quarrelling with your liver. No, it is rather a peace-
maker and lies as quiet as it did in the grape. Then it is as
10 fragrant as the queen bee; and the more ethereal part of it
mounts into the brain, not assaulting the cerebral apart-
ments like a bully in a bad-house looking for his trull and
hurrying from door to door, bouncing against the wainscot,
but rather walks like Aladin about his own enchanted
palace so gently that you do not feel his step. Other wines
of a heavy and spirituous nature transform a man to a
Silenus. This makes him a Hermes, and gives a woman the
soul and immortality of Ariadne, for whom Bacchus always
kept a good cellar of claret–and even of that he could never
20 persuade her to take above two cups.
     I said this same claret is the only palate passion I have.
I forgot game–I must plead guilty to the breast of a par-
tridge, the back of a hare, the backbone of a grouse, the
wing and side of a pheasant, and a woodcock *passim*.

Notes

Joy and Sorrow

ENDYMION, IV.512–48.
This long narrative poem, written between April and Nov. 1817, contains several passages of what Keats would probably have called a 'speculative' kind, and of these the one on the Cave of Quietude is perhaps the finest. The hero, Endymion, is now in the depth of despair; and in this passage Keats envisages a state of exceptional spiritual calm, of 'content'–not to be gained by conscious effort–that may lie on the other side of the intensest suffering. This state also offers release from pleasure that inevitably palls. These insights are further crossed (and perhaps weakened) by the Keatsian sense of 'indolence' and by the mood of 'half in love with easeful Death'. (See Middleton Murry's discussion in *The Mystery of Keats*, pp. 118–50.)

514–15. trace its own existence: this probably means something like 'discover–and in a way create–its own essential nature or "identity"'. See Letter 9 (p. 107).

515. remotest: perhaps in the sense of 'extreme'.

523. native hell: a hell-like state that man is born to.

530–1. A reference to the superstition that the tick of the death-watch beetle foretells death.

534–7. One of several occasions in Keats's poetry when some 'draught' initiates a new state of being.

536. Semele was the mother of Bacchus.

537–42. Perhaps this cluster of oxymorons expresses the idea that 'quietude' reconciles, or transcends, various contrary and conflicting states.

539. by due: probably means 'rightly', 'appropriately'.

540. infest: trouble, vex (compare *Lamia* II. line 166, p. 164). The general idea is that in this state of 'quietude' we do not attempt to live on hopes.

543–5. In its depths the soul has this all-saving resource, this 'den' of 'quietude'.

545. gentle Carian: Endymion.

547. feud: conflict within himself.

IN DREAR-NIGHTED DECEMBER (December 1817).
This lyric constitutes something of an antithesis to the Cave of
Quietude passage. Keats seems to be saying that quietude–'the
feel of not to feel' and 'numbèd sense'–is unattainable. Unlike the
rest of nature, man, because of his memory, cannot forget the
happiness that has gone by.
7. *frozen thawings:* the buds are frozen, thawed, frozen again.
12. *Apollo's summer look:* here the god Apollo is associated with
the sun.
14. *crystal fretting:* the foaming, etc., of the brook.
15. *petting:* being querulous about, complaining.
21. *feel:* feeling; *it:* the 'passèd joy'.
22. *none:* might mean 'no person to give comfort', or, alternatively,
'no compensatory feeling'.
23. *numbèd sense:* probably something like the 'indolence' described in Letter 9 (p. 105).

ON SITTING DOWN TO READ 'KING LEAR' AGAIN (22 January 1818).
In this sonnet, stimulated by the searing experience of re-reading
King Lear, Keats is momentarily dismissing the poesy of 'Romance', of beautiful, remote dreams and idealizations of life,
and once more affirming an aspiration towards Shakespearian
poetry concerned with 'the agonies, the strife/Of human hearts'.
2. *Fair plumèd:* 'Romance', personified, is seen with a plumed,
knight's helmet.
6. *damnation:* here means 'suffering like that endured in hell'.
7. *burn:* with line 13, this word communicates the intensity of
Keats's reading. *assay:* try by tasting, know by experience.
8. *bitter-sweet:* a hint of one of Keats's fundamental conceptions
of human experience.
9. *clouds of Albion:* this, and the following phrase, *old oak forest*,
admirably suggest that primeval British atmosphere that characterises *King Lear*.
12. *barren dream:* presumably the world of Romance.
14. *Phoenix wings:* the legendary phoenix bird renewed itself in
fire.

WHEN I HAVE FEARS THAT I MAY CEASE TO BE (late January 1818).
In this sonnet, his first in the Shakespearian form, Keats is
considering some of the chief deprivations that an early death
would entail. One of his reflections reveals a hankering after 'high
romance', and would therefore seem to contradict to some extent
what he had recently written in the *King Lear* sonnet. On the
other hand, at the end of the poem he speaks of a feeling of
detachment brought about by his thought of death, and perhaps

this remoteness has some connection with the quietude described in the previous *Endymion* extract. In such detachment his hunger for love and fame becomes insignificant.

3. charactery: probably means 'handwriting'.

8. magic hand of chance: Keats is probably referring to those felicitous expressions that come spontaneously.

9. fair creature: usually thought to be the unidentified young woman celebrated in *Time's Sea* (p. 117).

11–12. What Keats meant by 'unreflecting' is not clearly established by the context. Possibly he was thinking of a love that was enchanted because of its rare freedom from doubts, uncertainty, etc.

TO J. H. REYNOLDS, ESQ. (25 March 1818).

1–12. Keats begins, light-heartedly, with the unbeautiful aspects of dream and reverie, particularly their chaotic incongruities. There is also some satirical hit at the trivializing, unheroic aspects of his own time.

10. Miss Edgeworth was a contemporary novelist strongly disliked by Hazlitt.

11. Junius Brutus may be either the founder of the Roman republic or a Shakespearian actor of the period, Junius Brutus Booth; *so so*: intoxicated.

13–66. Much of this section, composed 'in fair dreaming wise', is inspired by Claude's painting, *The Enchanted Castle*. But much of the detail springs from Keats's own fancy. Note the prevalent suggestion of serenity and harmony.

14. whose... wings: something like 'who possess composure of spirit'.

18. Aeolian harps: stringed instruments that produced musical sounds when the air passed over them. They became a symbol of Romantic inspiration. But it is difficult to imagine them 'personified'.

20–2. There is no Titian painting of such a sacrifice; but these lines, which foreshadow stanza IV of the *Ode on a Grecian Urn* (p. 86), may have been suggested by Claude's *Landscape with the Father of Psyche*.

29. Urganda: an enchantress in the medieval romance *Amadis of Gaul*.

34. Merlin's Hall: i.e. like some building conjured up by the magician Merlin.

40. some giant: there are various legends of giants buried underground.

41–8. This passage follows the mixed architectural styles of the castle in Claude's picture.

41. see: residence.

42. Santon: a Muslim holy man.

44. Cuthbert de Saint Aldebrim: some imaginary medieval knight.

46. Lapland witch: suggested by *Paradise Lost* II.664–5. *maudlin*: fearful; or, penitent.

57. lightening moment-whiles: momentarily flashing as they come out of the water.

67–71. In this opening of the reflective section of the poem the *wish* Keats expresses is clear enough. (Lines *68–9* allude to Wordsworth's *Tintern Abbey*, 95–7.) But his description of 'dreamings' in their reality is less obvious. Perhaps he is saying that when they visit the soul in its state of greatest awareness they often plunge it into a kind of dark, distressful night, in which it is lost, as in a void. In this reading the 'dreamings' that 'shadow' the soul would probably be the 'horrid moods' he later describes.

71–2. For... jostle: perhaps, in this broken-off sentence, we have to understand that the 'world' referred to is the one described in the letter to Reynolds of 3 May 1818 as 'full of misery and heartbreak, pain, sickness, and oppression' (see Letter 6, p. 104).

73–6. As words like 'philosophize', 'high reason', and 'lore' indicate, the intellect and speculative thought, as well as imagination, come into that comprehending acceptance of all the mixed joy and suffering of human experience that was Keats's ultimate poetic ideal.

73. admiral: ship of the admiral, the flag-ship.

76–7. Things... thought: something like 'life is not what we should desire it to be, and the thought about this human predicament perplexes us to the point where thinking reaches a dead end'.

78–82. Apart from the general doubt expressed about the workings of the 'imagination', this is another obscure passage. Is Keats suggesting that the imagination needs to be linked to some acceptable system of beliefs, values, etc., whether of human or religious origin? In the letter to Reynolds he goes on to say that some of Milton's strength arose from his 'resting places and seeming sure points of reasoning'.

83. bourn: confines–i.e. of the immediate happiness we are experiencing.

88. lampit: limpet.

106. Moods of one's mind: Wordsworth's general title for a group of poems in his 1807 volumes.

107–13. An attempt to wrest the poem back to the style of its opening.

111. new romance: *Isabella* (pp. 118–31), which Keats was writing at the time.

112. centaine: consisting of one hundred (lines).

ON VISITING THE TOMB OF BURNS (1 July 1818).
This sonnet, which, Keats said, was 'written in a strange mood, half asleep', has an unKeatsian spareness and austerity. It poses some complex problems of interpretation that can only be roughly indicated in the following notes–one of these turning on the question of whether line 8 ends with a stop or not.

1–8. There is a persistent suggestion of coldness in these lines, and for Keats coldness was commonly associated with the painful and with death, as warmth was with joy.

6. ague: a shivering fit.

7. sapphire warm: Keats is probably thinking of the warm, blue summer skies of his more usual meridional poetic landscape.

9–14. In the last line Keats admits that the impression he has given of Scotland is wrong; and this distortion would seem to have been due to the workings of a 'Sickly imagination', investing the scene with a 'dead hue'.

9. Minos was a judge of the underworld. Here he probably stands for a totally detached, objective attitude.

10. real: perhaps 'essence', or 'idea', or 'truth'.

11. Sickly imagination: the last part of the next poem (and also the echo in lines 11–12 of *Hamlet*, III.i.84–5) may throw some light on this phrase.

LINES WRITTEN IN THE HIGHLANDS (around 18 July 1818).
To some extent much of this strange poem, a description of Keats's feelings as he walked towards Burns's cottage on 11 July, may be related to the passage on 'oneness' and 'self-destroying' in *Endymion* (pp. 115–16).

1–2. Compare *Endymion* 1,791–2 (p. 115).

7–24. This is a sustained poetic elaboration of the comment he had made to Reynolds in his letter of 11–13 July 1818. 'One of the pleasantest means of annulling self is approaching such a shrine as the cottage of Burns.' And to understand his reaction we have also to appreciate the quite extraordinary effect on him of what he once called 'the overpowering idea of our dead poets' (letter to Miss Jeffrey, 9 June 1819).

8. smart: possibly in the sense of 'intensity' or 'force'.

20. convulsed: agitated or alarmed (by the eagles).

22. palmer: pilgrim.

25–48. In the rest of the poem Keats expresses a fearful apprehension of the possible closeness to insanity of the kind of oblivion he has been describing. The sentiment is an odd one since there is nothing in the letters to suggest that he ever suffered from this fear.

36. fill: In their editions E. de. Sélincourt and H. W. Garrod print the variant word 'pain'. This variant might throw some light on the similar passage in the opening of the *Nightingale* ode (p. 82).

29. Scanty . . . steps: perhaps this phrase, repeated in line 31, carries an understood 'should be' after it.

41–4. The thought here would seem to be that any momentary self-oblivion is nothing compared with the active spiritual destiny a man has to fulfil.

WELCOME JOY AND WELCOME SORROW (October 1818).
In this poem of sharply juxtaposed opposites there is (to say nothing of the effect of its lilting metre) too much theatrically exaggerated perversity of a conventional Romantic kind for us to take it very seriously. But, while mainly a contrived poetical exercise, it may also intimate something of Keats's more intent engagement with the human enigma of intermingled joy and sorrow.

2. Lethe: the underworld river of oblivion; *Hermes*: (Mercury) the messenger of the gods, represented with wings and winged heels. The contrast is probably between torpor and a buoyant elasticity of spirit.

21. Momus: a god associated with jesting.

HYPERION (Autumn 1818–April 1819).
Book I. *1–14*. 'No English poem of any length since Milton . . . begins with more majesty and sureness of phrase than *Hyperion*' (W. J. Bate, *John Keats*, p.393).

1. shady: the first intimation of the persistent sensation of coldness in the poem.

4. Saturn was the Chief of the first gods, the Titans. He had been overthrown by his own rebellious children, led by Jupiter; *stone*: probably statue.

13. Naiad: the naiads were classical spirits associated with streams, fountains, etc.

18. This heaping up of epithets is Miltonic.

21. ancient Mother: in classical mythology the Titans were the children of Heaven (Coelus), the father, and of Earth (Tellus), the mother.

26. Thea, the wife of Saturn's brother, Hyperion, the sun god.

26–33. One of the chief imaginative impressions of *Hyperion* is that of magnitude and vastness. This is not confined to such physical descriptions of the Titans as we find in this passage.

30. Ixion: a god punished by being bound to an ever-turning wheel.

60. Conscious . . . command: the command of Jupiter.

61. reluctant: this use of adjective for adverb is Miltonic.

72–8. Though this device of the extended simile (one of several in the poem) is imitated from Milton, the sensibility that informs it is thoroughly Keatsian.

72. trancèd: enchanted or, possibly, inducing a state of trance.

74. The enchantment comes from the stars as they shine intently ('earnest') through the oak branches.

85–8. An explicit example of the sculpturesque effect, perhaps influenced by Dante and Milton, that is common in Books I and II. For another obvious example see II.33–5.

86. cathedral cavern: a memory of Keats's recent visit to Fingal's Cave. See Letter 35 (p. 241).

94. horrid: (in the Latin sense–and as used by Milton) bristling; *aspen*: the slightest stir of air will agitate the leaves of the aspen tree.

102–5. Saturn is not represented simply as a figure of anguished dejection. He is frantically baffled (see also II.129–155) by the question *why* such affliction and suffering should be.

102. front: forehead.

105. nervous: vigorous.

114 Perhaps to be related to Keats's idea that it is the men of power who possess a strong identity and individuality. The poetical character lacks such identity. See Letter 30 (p. 238).

125–33. It is this refusal to accept his painful situation, this entertainment of pointless hope, that constitutes Saturn's great–and all too human–weakness. This is underlined by Coelus's key speech in lines 329–36.

129. gold clouds metropolitan: Miltonic in inversion and in the polysyllabic 'metropolitan'.

135–8. One of several examples of the sensation of strain, contortion, and convulsion that is very strong in the poem. See I.93–4; I.259–63; II.23–8; II.45–7.

146. Olympus was the mountain home of the classical gods.

147. rebel three: Jupiter, Neptune, and Pluto.

156–7. Probably another recollection of the Scottish tour.

172–3. familiar... passing-bell: visits paid by family relatives ('familiar') to a dying man.

174. It is not certain what omen Keats had in mind here.

176–80. This description of Hyperion's palace contributes to the overall impression of immensity.

192. For: instead of.

206–8. Very Miltonic in expression; but the surprising floral image of the door in lines *209–12* is pure Keats.

216. Hours: female spirits who presided over the passage of the seasons.

229. Notice how the persistent sensation of cold is linked even with the sun god.

232. essence: being (as in II.331 and III.104). See also the note on *Endymion*, line 779.

236. clime: region; or, possibly (as in II.263), atmosphere.

238. fanes: temples.

246. Tellus... robes: the earth (Tellus) and the sea.

256. For the effect of cumulative detail note *cold* and also, in line 268, *chilly*.

274. colure: an astronomical term from *Paradise Lost*, IX.66.

281–2. save... gone: except as meaningless inscriptions on stone relics.

292–3. Even Hyperion cannot alter the 'course of Nature's law' (II.181).

297. sail: make sail.

311. powers: Coelus himself and Tellus.

326. wox: became (an archaism).

329–36. Notice how in this sad reproof of the ungodlike passions and reactions of the Titans Coelus includes 'hope' (compare line 540 in the Cave of Quietude passage.) Nevertheless, Coelus encourages Hyperion to resistance.

349. region: of the sky.

Book II. *4.* Cybele, also called Ops (line 78) or Rhea, was the wife of Saturn.

7. for: because of.

17. Stubborned: made hard, unyielding.

19–81. This passage is modelled on the assembly of the fallen angels in *Paradise Lost*, I.376–521. The names of the various Titans were derived by Keats from several different sources.

22. Typhon, for instance, was supposed to be imprisoned under the volcano of Aetna.

28. boiling gurge: a reference to lava eruption (see *Paradise Lost*, XII.41–2); *gurge*: whirlpool.

29. Mnemosyne (Memory) was the mother of the Muses. Apollo meets her in Book III.

33–8. Another recollection of Keats's summer journey in the north.

39. shroud: shrouded.

52. at horrid working: rolling etc. in a terrifying way.

53. The legendary mountain of Caf had associations with the Caucasus.

61. anchor: the traditional symbol of hope.

64. shelve: slope.

66. Enceladus was an especially warlike Titan who later delivers the speech in lines 309–45.

76. Clymene is later to describe her hearing of Apollo's music in lines 252–99.

92–8. A key passage. See the Introduction (p. 9).

98. disanointing: i.e. annulling Saturn's original consecration as supreme ruler of the Titans.

102. fevered: in various forms, a common–and significant–Keatsian word.

120. utterless: unutterable.

125. these fallen: the fallen Titans.

129–345. This section of the poem is based on the model of *Paradise Lost*, Book II, in the first half of which several of the fallen angels and Satan deliver their speeches at the council of Pandemonium.

133. spirit-leavèd: probably suggestive of some divine, prophetic inspiration.

134. Uranus was another name for Coelus.

144–7. This suggests some world-shattering (explosive?) storm. Perhaps, with 'sulphur' as one link, there is some echo of *King Lear*, III.ii.1–7.

161. engine... wrath: give our rage (or, transform our rage into) some effective weapon of war.

168. Athenian grove: a reference to the Athenian Academy where Plato taught.

192. intestine broil: civil war (from *Paradise Lost*, II.1001).

196. its own producer: i.e. chaos and darkness.

199. The Heavens and the Earth: Coelus and Tellus.

208. show beyond: appear superior to.

232. young... Seas: Neptune. What follows is the usual classical picture of him.

244. posed: pretended.

262–89. In imagery and sentiment this passage is more in the style of *Poems 1817* and *Endymion*.

270. mouthèd shell: presumably some kind of conch.

309–45. In several ways this fiery speech parallels that of Moloch in *Paradise Lost*, II.51–105.

341. wingèd thing: Victory was traditionally represented as a figure with wings.

371. Numidian: African.

372–5. A striking image of immensity.

374. Memnon was the son of Aurora, the dawn goddess. His statue in Egypt was supposed to give out a sound when struck by the rays of the rising or setting sun.

Book III. *10. Delphic*: the oracle of Apollo, the god of poetry, was at Delphi.

12. Dorian: one of the modes of Greek music.

24. Delos was the reputed birthplace of Apollo.

31–2. mother. . . twin sister: Latona and Diana.

43. golden bow: Apollo was traditionally represented with this weapon.

46. awful Goddess: Mnemosyne.

66. pain and pleasure: note this description of the effect of Apollo's music (i.e. poetry).

86–8. Compare '*Why did I laugh to-night?*' lines 6–8 (p. 80).

119. bright elixir peerless: again this Miltonic word order. *elixir*: some magical potion.

128. immortal death: perhaps in the sense of death as the common eternal lot.

130. life: immortal life (?); *anguished*: suffered anguish.

136. In the transcript of the poem made by Keats's friend Woodhouse this line is completed by the pencilled words 'glory dawned, he was a god'.

WHY DID I LAUGH TO-NIGHT? (March 1819).

This 'strange, profound, and unhappy sonnet' as R. Gittings calls it (*John Keats: the Living Year*, p.98) offers clear poetic evidence of Keats's deeply troubled, perhaps desperate, state between late February and early April 1819. Whatever the nature of the enigmatic laugh (was it one of cynicism?), the main drift of the poem is clear enough. The sonnet is closely linked with the *Ode to a Nightingale*, especially to stanza VI and its sentiment of 'half in love with easeful Death'. Keats is momentarily trying to persuade himself that death is a desirable consummation, an intenser experience than any of the blisses of life, which he has fully enjoyed–at least in imagination. Compare, from the letters, his remark to Bailey–'I am never alone without rejoicing there is such a thing as death' (10 June 1818), and to Fanny Brawne– 'I have two luxuries to brood over in my walks, your loveliness and the hour of my death' (25 July 1819). See Letters 7, p. 104, and 15, p. 179.

11. on. . .cease: compare *Ode to a Nightingale*, line 56 (p. 83).

12. ensigns: banners (presumably symbols of the 'fame' mentioned in the next line).

13. Verse. . . beauty: These, if we include love with beauty, are to be central terms of reference in the following odes; *intense*: affording the most strongly felt experience. For this key Keatsian word see, for example, Letter 24, (pp. 235–6).

HOW FEVERED IS THE MAN (April 1819).

Dismissing the itch for fame as a damaging, feverish sort of self-consciousness, this sonnet is linked with '*Why did I laugh to-night?*' and the *Ode on Indolence* (p. 80 and pp. 88–9). But in tone, and to some extent in thought, it is less hectic and more genuinely assured than '*Why did I laugh to-night?*'

4. Perhaps suggests a certain tarnishing of reputation.

7. elf: creature, being. See *Isabella*, line 453 (p. 130), and other examples.

13. grace: perhaps something like 'favourable acknowledgement' –almost 'recognition'.

14. miscreed: i.e. the belief in fame.

ODE TO A NIGHTINGALE (May 1819).

1–6. Perhaps, with the words 'My heart aches', Keats is alluding once more to the pain that may arise from an excess or over-intensity of joy; and this interpretation would seem to fit with the meaning of line 6. 'drowsy numbness' is probably his familiar sensation of 'indolence', which, if usually pleasurable, could sometimes produce pain. Lines 23–4 of the *Ode on Melancholy* (p. 87) ('aching Pleasure...sips') may throw some light on the interpretative problems that this opening passage presents.

2. hemlock: used as a drug as well as a poison.

7. Dryad: a wood nymph in classical mythology.

13. Flora: the goddess of flowers.

14. Possibly a reference to festivities at the grape harvest.

16. Hippocrene: a fountain on mount Helicon sacred to the Muses. This reference unobtrusively connects wine with poetic inspiration.

23. An echo of Wordsworth's *Tintern Abbey*, lines 52–3.

26. Almost certainly a reference to the recent death of Keats's brother Tom.

29–30. Compare *Ode on a Grecian Urn*, lines 19–20 and 25–30 (p. 85), and *Ode on Melancholy*, lines 21–3 (p. 87).

32. Bacchus: the god of wine. Like the lines in *Endymion* (IV. 240–1), this line is a recollection of Titian's picture *Bacchus and Ariadne*.

34. See the previous lines 27–8.

37. fays: fairies.

38–50. Apart from the revealing word 'embalmed', the whole of this passage might be taken as an image of 'rich' burial, similar to that of Adonis in *Endymion* (II.407–27), so leading to the explicit confession of the following stanza. And compare lines 38–41 with *To Sleep*, lines 1–4 (p. 230).

51. darkling: (bird) in darkness. See *Paradise Lost*, III.38–40.

53. many... rhyme: not to be taken quite literally; but see '*Why did I laugh to-night?*' (p. 80).

55. rich: in Keats this word commonly indicates intensity of sensation, of 'luxury'.

60. high requiem: i.e. the song would change from living 'ecstasy' to funeral chant.

61–70. Possibly the nightingale's song now becomes a symbol of something that does transcend human mortality—of solacing, enchanting poetry.

62. hungry generations: a haunting phrase, but the line is difficult to interpret. A cross-reference to line 46 of the *Ode on a Grecian Urn* (p. 86) may offer some illumination.

64. clown: peasant.

65–7. Ruth here epitomizes the exile. See the biblical *Book of Ruth*, especially 1:9 and 2:13–17.

68–70. Part of the inspiration for these lines may have been Claude's painting *The Enchanted Castle*. See *To J. H. Reynolds, Esq.*, lines 49–51 (p. 53).

71–2. Probably the repetition of the word 'forlorn' is no more than a rhetorical device—with some shift of meaning. In line 70 'forlorn' may mean 'unfrequented' perhaps synonymous with 'desolate' used to describe the little town in the *Ode on a Grecian Urn* (p. 86). In line 71 'forlorn' indicates a state of feeling, wretched, pitiable, etc.

72. toll: note the deathly association of this word.

74. elf: see '*How fevered is the Man*', line 7 (p. 81). But possibly the word is used here in the more familiar sense.

75. plaintive: suggestive of the fading of the bird's song and corresponding with the change in the poet's mood.

79–80. The interrogatives—and ambiguities—of these lines end the poem on a note of uncertainty that to some extent modifies the explicit statement of lines 73–4.

ODE ON A GRECIAN URN (May 1819, probably immediately following the *Ode to a Nightingale*).
Though the urn is mainly an imaginary one, Keats almost certainly took some of his ornamental detail from surviving Greek works of art, like the Sosibos vase in the Musée Napoléon in Paris, and from certain paintings. For a summary of most of the chief interpretations of the ode see E. C. Pettet, *On the Poetry of Keats*, pp.375–81.

1. unravished: intact (presumably with time as the potential ravisher). The urn is united to 'quietness', which, though primarily signifying that tranquillity of spirit which, in place of fever, was coming to be so important for Keats, might also carry the meaning of 'silence'. While the sexual paradox 'unravished bride' may be open to question, at least the expression is in keeping with lines 8–9, 19, and 26.

2. It is time, the long silent process of history, that has fostered this child of its original artist creator. Silence, always so congenial to Keats's sensibility and linked for him both with natural objects and 'quietude', continues to be associated with the urn (lines 11–14, 39, 44).

3–4. These lines should always be remembered in considering any subtle metaphysical interpretation of the poem. *historian*: story-teller; *Silvan*: because of the 'flowery tale' and 'leaf-fringed legend,' etc.

7. Tempe and Arcady: parts of classical Greece celebrated for beauty and joyful living.

17–20. This is an ideal sexual love, not a frustration, because it is new and because it is a desire and an anticipation that stops short of consummation. There is the same, if repetitious, sentiment in lines 25–7. Such love avoids the inevitable cloyment (line 29) of actual human love.

23. unwearièd: this might imply both unflagging poetic energy and freedom from wearing material worries. Keats had himself recently experienced a spell of poetic sterility, while he was only too familiar with the other possible sense of 'unwearièd'.

27. panting: perhaps not a happily chosen word, but reinforces 'still to be enjoyed'.

28. breathing: living, mortal.

29. cloyed: see *Fancy*, lines 68–76 (p. 222).

30. burning forehead: compare the love-destroyed knight in *La Belle Dame Sans Merci*, lines 9–10 (p. 144).

31–40. As with *To J. H. Reynolds, Esq.*, lines 20–2 (p. 52), the first four lines of this stanza were probably suggested by Claude's painting *Landscape with the Father of Psyche*. With Keats's conception (expressed elsewhere) of a Golden Age existing in early Greek times, most of this stanza could be taken as intimating an ideal of joyful communal living. See the *Ode to May* (p. 216), and note also the link between 'pious morn' and 'happy pieties' in the *Ode to Psyche* (p. 232).

The last three lines, with an effect possibly comparable to that of 'forlorn' at the end of the seventh stanza of the *Nightingale* ode, may express the intrusion of reality into this dream.

41. brede: something interwoven; embroidery.

44–5. See *To J. H. Reynolds, Esq.*, lines 76–7 (p. 53). The 'silent form' embodies a dream of what life might be if things *could* 'to the will/Be settled'. It is the disparity between dreamful desires and actuality (and the unanswerable questions this poses) that perplex and baffle thought.

45. Cold: this word appears to contradict most of what has gone before and what immediately follows. Is Keats momentarily referring back to lines 38–40? Or is he voicing–to reject it–a possible, unimaginative response to the urn?

49–50. Comment on these lines is immense and interminable. Apart from the meaning of the aphorism, there is doubt about the placing of the quotation marks and the problem of who is addressing whom. For what they are worth, the summary views of the present editor are (1) that both lines are spoken by the urn; (2) that the emphasis is on Beauty; and (3) that an assertion is being made that the beautiful imaginings embodied in the urn pictures have a validity, which is their 'truth'. These lines repeat the article of Romantic faith that Keats had declared in his letter to Bailey of 22 November 1817: 'what the imagination seizes as beauty must be truth–whether it existed before or not' (Letter 2, p. 99).

ODE ON MELANCHOLY (May 1819).
Much of the inspiration for this poem came from Keats's re-reading of Burton's *Anatomy of Melancholy*. There is extant a cancelled first stanza, which explains the abrupt opening of the published version:

> Though you should build a bark of dead men's bones,
> And rear a phantom gibbet for a mast,
> Stitch creeds together for a sail, with groans
> To fill it out, blood-stainèd and aghast;
> Although your rudder be a dragon's tail
> Long severed, yet still hard with agony,
> Your cordage large uprootings from the skull
> Of bald Medusa, certes you should fail
> To find the Melancholy–whether she
> Dreameth in any isle of Lethe dull. . .

1–10. The first stanza is mainly a rejection of the melancholy that tempts to suicide.

2. Wolf's-bane: aconite.

3–4. This odd use of nightshade may have been suggested by Burton's prescriptions for *head*-melancholy.

4. Proserpine was the wife of Pluto and queen of the underworld.

6. death-moth: the death's-head moth (from its markings).

7. Psyche: in this context either loved one or soul's emblem.

9. Something like 'for a succession of drowsy, shadowy states of consciousness will follow one upon another'.

10. In the *Nightingale* ode, lines 1–4 (p. 82), Keats's heart-ache is not drowned by 'drowsy numbness'. For those readers who sense a feverish spirit in this poem 'wakeful anguish' must seem a symptomatic, masochistically suggestive phrase.

12–14. Since the 'droop-headed flowers' may be flowers that symbolize grief etc. (see *Endymion*, IV. 170–1), there is no certainty that this simile is intimating a creative force in melancholy, as some critics have maintained. And even if there is such an intimation, it hardly sustains the poetic recipe for a self-conscious, exquisite contrivance of melancholy that follows.

15–17. rose...rainbow...peonies: all indicative of shortlived beauty; *rainbow*: this also refers to an irridescent effect of the light.

21. She: i.e. Melancholy.

23. aching: compare *Ode to a Nightingale* line 1 (p. 82) and *The Eve of St. Agnes* line 279 (p. 139).

25–30. This paradoxical assertion that melancholy is to be most intensely experienced in the intensity of joy (and perhaps sensuous gratification) constitutes one of Keats's most striking expressions of the inter-relationship of joy and sorrow. Lines 27–8 offer a notable example of contrast between great sensuous vitality and what some readers may consider the perversity and debility of the underlying sentiment.

25–8. These lines curiously prefigure, summary-wise, a substantial section of *The Fall of Hyperion*, lines 19–107 (pp. 91–3).

30. cloudy trophies: trophies of victory were hung up in classical temples; *cloudy*: perhaps something like 'shadowy', 'dimly seen'.

ODE ON INDOLENCE (May 1819).

The subject of this ode, a 'dreamy urn', obviously connects it closely with the *Ode on a Grecian Urn* (p. 85); and there are many correspondences of phrasing, imagery, and sensation with the other odes. Much of Keats's immediate inspiration must have come from a reading of the 19 March passage in his journal-letter to George and Georgiana (Letter 9, p. 105).

4. placid: possibly in the sense of 'soft-sounding'. See 'hush', line 12.

10. Phidean: Phideas, the most famous of Greek sculptors, carved the Elgin Marbles.

12. masque: a dumb-show of masked performers. And note the typical stress on silence.

15–18. Here the state of drowsy, benumbed 'indolence' is without pain, but it obviously corresponds in many respects with the sensations described in lines 1–4 of the *Ode to a Nightingale* (p. 82).

23–4. This desire is contradicted by the sentiments of the following stanza. Even this hour of indolence has not smothered the conflict within Keats.

30. demon: though the pejorative sense of this word should not be over-stressed, it certainly suggests an irresistible, tempting spirit who may bring some baneful effects.

34. fever: note this word, and especially the connection with '*How fevered is the man*' (p. 81).

43–4. i.e. Keats would have been self-obliterated in his immediate surroundings.

52. A frequent sensation in Keats's poetry. See, for example, *Ode to Psyche* line 15 (p. 231).

54. On 9 June 1819 Keats wrote to Miss Sarah Jeffrey: 'I hope I am a little more of a philosopher than I was, consequently a little less of a versifying pet-lamb.'

57–8. Since Poesy is one of the three dismissed phantoms, it would seem that Keats is speaking of 'visions' that are not to be expressed in verse.

TO AUTUMN (on or about 19 September 1819).

The immediate inspiration of this poem is indicated in a letter to J. H. Reynolds of 21 September 1819: 'How beautiful the season is now, how fine the air—a temperate sharpness about it. Really, without joking, chaste weather—Dian skies. I never liked stubble fields so much as now; aye, better than the chilly green of spring. Somehow a stubble plain looks warm, in the same way that some pictures look warm. This struck me so much in my Sunday's walk that I composed upon it.'

1–11. Even in Keats's poetry this first stanza, evoking all the ripeness and fulness of autumn, is quite outstanding for its gravid melodic beauty and for its packed richness of sensuous effect—an effect by no means limited to the visual. It admirably illustrates the 'axioms' that he set down in a letter to Taylor (Letter 26. pp. 236–7), and also something of what he meant when he advised Shelley (in a letter of 16 August 1820) to 'load every rift of your subject with ore'.

4. thatch-eves: this phrase, together with 'mossed cottage-trees' and the later reference to the robin, suggests some recollection of Coleridge's *Frost at Midnight*, lines 68–71.

5. mossed: for some curious reason moss appealed strongly to the sensibility of Romantic painters and poets. There are numerous small references to moss in Keats's poetry.

9–10. The chief metrical difference between *To Autumn* and the four May odes is the addition of an extra line to the stanza—this producing the rhymed couplet of lines 9–10. The effect of this couplet is 'to sustain the approaching close at a momentary crest before the stanza subsides in the final line' (W. J. Bate, *John Keats*, p. 581).

10. The significance of this line is not limited to the immediate context of the bees' activity. It insinuates (to be held in suspense, as it were) a vain, fanciful hope that the ode is ultimately to reject.

What the final stanza is to affirm, in a spirit of serene acceptance, is that warm days *will* cease.

12–22. Much of the total effect of these personifications of autumn is admirably described by Bate's phrase–'energy caught in repose' (*ibid.* p. 584). Some of the descriptive detail may derive from paintings Keats knew. See I.Jack, *Keats and the Mirror of Art*, pp. 236–8.

15. soft-lifted: 'soft', a key word to Keats's sensibility and repeated twice in stanza 3, occurs at least once in all the odes.

16. furrow: as a small indication of Keats's attention to the melodic effect of his poetry it is interesting to note that that 'furrow' replaces the inappropriately hard-sounding word 'field' in his first draft.

17. poppies: wild poppies, and other 'twinèd flowers', once commonly grew in cornfields.

18. swath: in days when corn was hand cut, the swath was the width covered by the sweep of the advancing mower's sickle or reaping-hook.

23–33. Though the first two stanzas might be taken mainly, even entirely, as a description of autumn, of its ripeness and repose, with the last stanza the ode perceptibly deepens, becoming an expression–oblique but none the less strong–of a profoundly felt attitude to certain aspects of human experience. The images, still autumnal, relate to change, transience, mortality, and to the contraries and opposites involved in them. As A. Davenport wrote: 'The music of Autumn which ends the poem is a music of living and dying, of staying and departure, of summer-winter' (*John Keats: A Reassessment*, p. 98). And, with the theme modulated from earth's physical maturity to a maturity of spirit, everything is simply, unfeverishly accepted.

So far as Keats's sensibility is concerned, this last stanza is highly characteristic of his fondness for remote, subdued sounds.

25. bloom: this uncertain word is perhaps to be linked with 'rosy hue'; and the suggestion may be that the redness of the clouds gives an appearance of life and health to what might otherwise be the pallor of the dying day.

27. wailful. . .mourn: the sadness of the gnats may be for their brief existence and the passing of 'warm days'.

28. sallows: willows.

30. hilly bourn: boundary formed by the hills.

33. To appreciate the span and movement of the ode we may contrast the thin, flat sound and rhythmical restlessness of this line with the measured mellifluousness of the opening line, and its sense of impermanence and inevitable winter with all the substantial satisfactions of 'mellow fruitfulness'.

THE FALL OF HYPERION (probably between July and 21 September 1819).

Though Keats made some fairly substantial alterations to the original text of the first Book of *Hyperion*, the main difference between *The Fall of Hyperion*, as the revised version is now known, and the poem abandoned in the previous April is the addition of an introductory allegorical vision (lines 1–293). This vision concerns the Poet, to whom the story of the Titans is ultimately unfolded.

1–18. There are two points to be noticed about this prelude. (1) Here at least Keats is asserting that dreams, virtually synonymous with imagination, are the essence of poetry. (2) He does not appear to be making any very high claims for poetry: the main superiority of the poet's dreams over those of the religious enthusiast (the 'fanatic') and of primitive man is that they are perpetuated in verse.

3. loftiest... sleep: i.e. his most visionary dreams.

9–11. Imagination is dumb, under some baneful spell, as it were, unless released by the magic of poetic utterance. *sable*: this word has associations with death.

12. Keats is putting a dismissive interjection into the mouth of some imaginary hostile critic: 'You are no poet, Keats; therefore you should not attempt to tell your dreams.'

22–4. This is probably a fused recollection of *Paradise Lost*, IV.325–7 and V.348–9.

26–7. Compare the *Ode to Psyche*, lines 46–7 and 60–1 (p. 232).

28–9. See *Paradise Lost*, V.391–2.

31. angel: the archangel Michael (a precise reference here to *Paradise Lost*).

34. whose... know: in these enigmatic words Keats may be hinting that he himself could never experience this innocent, primitive sensuous delight in its wholeness and full perfection.

35. fabled horn: the cornucopia of Ceres. See *Lamia* II, 186–7 (p. 164).

37. The goddess Proserpine was allowed to return from the underworld to the earth in spring.

41–56. This drinking of the 'transparent juice' has often been given an allegorical interpretation. Frequently it has been related to the chambers of consciousness passage in the letter to Reynolds of 3 May 1818 (Letter 6, pp. 103–4), and read as the Poet's initiation into speculative thought that brings the world of 'luxury' to an end. But the references to poppy and poison and the 'cloudy swoon' are strongly against this interpretation. It seems much more likely that, as in the first four lines of the *Ode to a Nightingale*, Keats is chiefly describing that drugged intoxication that supervenes on intense sensuous gratification. Alternatively, he may be repeating the idea and imagery of the last stanza of the *Ode on Melancholy*, for the Poet is soon to encounter 'veiled melancholy' (Moneta) at her 'sovereign shrine'.

45. Keats always found an intoxicating inspiration in the great poetic names of the past.

47. elixir: potion or drug (here of a poisonous kind).

48. Caliphat: the ruling Caliphs of Bagdad.

50. scarlet conclave: the red-robed cardinals electing a new Pope.

56. Silenus: see *Endymion* IV.215 (p. 209) and the note.

59. wings: a common Keatsian image for poetic inspiration and renewal.

61–93. Though one or two details of this account of the 'old sanctuary' may be taken in a symbolic way, most of the passage can probably be read as straightforward description. The sanctuary might stand for knowledge (including memory), but this is sufficiently embodied in Moneta, soon to appear.

68. superannuations: ruins of what has decayed through age.

70. faulture: ruin, decay, weakness.

74. asbestos: here it is the resistance of the material to decay that is relevant.

77. imageries: designs. Compare *The Eve of St Agnes*, line 209 (p. 137).

79–80. Articles of religious ritual.

88. An image: of Saturn, as lines 224–6 later make plain.

96. One ministering: the goddess-priestess Moneta (Mnemosyne in *Hyperion*).

97–101. This singularly vivid simile intimates the Poet's potential revival. The sensuous imagery has a restraint that characterises the whole of the introductory vision.

103. Maian incense: the scent of spring flowers (Maia, the goddess of spring).

116. gummed leaves: leaves of aromatic plants used in classical rituals.

135–6. See Jacob's dream in *Genesis*, 28:12.

141–5. These lines may suggest that the poet of real greatness must experience suffering in his own personal life as well as imaginatively.

144–5. thou... doom: thou hast extended thy (poetic) life; *dated on*: postponed.

151. thoughtless: note the significance of this word.

154–65. In answer to the Poet's question, lines 154–60, Moneta replies that the majority of those who love their fellow men and strive to improve their lot are practical men of action, not poets, not 'visionaries' or 'dreamers weak'.

167–76. In view of the Poet's triumphant ascent of the altar steps and Moneta's apparent acknowledgement of his achievement, it may at first seem contradictory that she is now belittling the poet as a dreamer and visionary. The explanation is probably that the definition of the poet as dreamer has changed from the implicit definition in lines 1–18. In contrast with the practical, active humanitarian even the poet who has become imaginatively responsive to the misery of the world remains a dreamer in the sense that he is totally ineffective in mitigating it.

180. suffered in: allowed into.

184. sickness not ignoble: the Poet does not deny the sickness ('fever') allegation, but insists that this springs from worthy–if mistaken–intentions and attitudes.

186–210. It is fairly certain that Keats intended to cancel or at least revise this passage. See the comment in the Introduction (p. 23).

190. humanist: humanitarian.

203. Pythia's spleen: Pythia, often in a rageful temper, was the woman who uttered the oracles of Apollo.

207–8. Keats almost certainly had Byron very much in mind here.

222–4. This refers to the war of the Titans (not related by Keats) against Jupiter and the new race of gods.

231. mourn: mourning, lamentation.

243. My power: including particularly her vivid, comprehensive vision of all the 'scenes' of the past.

245. globèd: a curious epithet that may derive from Keats's medical studies.

246. electral: akin to 'electrical' and probably suggesting vivid illumination.

248. This line raises at least two problems: (1) why, unlike Moneta, the Poet should be free from pain; and (2) how consistent this line is with lines 171–6.

249–54. In so far as Moneta is offering a revelation of the highest kind of poetic activity, it is important to notice that the Poet's reaction is an ambivalent one: she brings a mother's comfort, but at the same time she seems to him invested with a certain terror.

256–71. A whole essay might be written on this memorable and complex passage. In brief, if the vision of Moneta's face symbolizes the supreme poetry that Keats aspired to, the first part of the description would seem to signify the suffering and sorrow such poetry must reflect, the second (lines 264–70) its sustaining solace. But it may be that in the first part of the vision Keats is confusing an ideal of poetry with the state of the Poet–with his own spiritual 'sickness' and 'fever'.

257. pined: perhaps in the sense of 'wasted'.

267. visionless: unregarding, taking no notice of.

269–71. The moon is often associated in Keats's poetry with solace and benison.

274. sullen: gloomy, sombre.

288. omega: last one (literally, the final letter of the Greek alphabet).

Letters I

LETTER I.

Keats first met Benjamin Haydon (1786–1846), the painter and something of a celebrity at the time, at Leigh Hunt's Hampstead cottage in October 1816. For two years or so they were fairly close friends; later their friendship decidedly cooled. Their correspondence is a mixture of high art concerns and money matters.

8. my poem: *Endymion*.

16. 'leave...behind': *The Tempest*, IV.i.156.

25. Alfred: for Keats King Alfred was a kind of myth figure, a great champion of liberty.

LETTER 2.

Benjamin Bailey (1791–1853) was at this time an undergraduate of Magdalen College, Oxford, where Keats stayed with him during September 1817, when he completed Book 3 of *Endymion*. Though their friendship was a brief one, Keats seems to have had a high regard for Bailey, to whom he wrote some of his most deeply considered letters of the period.

4–6. What... not: apart from its general importance, this statement about the imagination has an obvious particular bearing on the *Ode on a Grecian Urn*.

9. first Book: Keats almost certainly means Book 1 of *Endymion* rather than the poem as a whole; *little song*: 'O sorrow', *Endymion* IV. 146–181.

12. Adam's dream: *Paradise Lost*, VIII.452–90.

18–19. O...thoughts: two points should be noted about this often quoted remark: first, that 'sensations' means feelings (and probably imaginative intuitions); and secondly, that it expresses an attitude that Keats was soon to reject decisively. See the second of of extracts of the letter to Taylor of 24 April 1818 (Letter 5, pp. 102–3) and the first of the letter to Reynolds of 3 May 1818 (Letter 6, p. 103).

46–7. philosophic mind...: from Wordsworth's *Immortality* ode, line 190–a poem Keats knew well.

53. startles: here in the sense of 'moves', 'stirs'.

61. abstraction: a state of being withdrawn from feeling.

2–3. '*By...drachmas*': a loose quotation from *Julius Caesar*, IV.iii. 72–3.

LETTER 4.

John Hamilton Reynolds (1794–1852), who had already published several poems when Keats first met him in the Leigh Hunt circle in 1816, was one of Keats's first literary friends, and their acquaintance remained close throughout his life. Reynolds's tombstone proclaims him 'the friend of Keats.'

8–9: 10. '*the...palaces*'; '*voyage of conception*': unidentified quotations.

15. '*an...isle*': *The Tempest*, I.ii.223.

16. '*girdle...earth*': *A Midsummer-Night's Dream*, II.i.175.

19–20. '*spirit...good*': Wordsworth's *The Old Cumberland Beggar*, line 77.

24. like the spider: the passage on the spider and bee that follows probably owes something to Pliny and Swift.

44. heath of furze: possibly an echo of *The Tempest*, I.i.71–2.

52. guerdon: reward, recompense.

59. passive and receptive: an allusion to Wordsworth's idea of 'wise passiveness' in *Expostulation and Reply*, line 24.

LETTER 5.

John Taylor (1781–1864) was Keats's second and chief publisher and always a good and generous friend, helping him in numerous ways.

1–2. I...Endymion: Keats is referring to the final corrections of *Endymion*, which had just appeared in print.

14. '*get...understanding*': *Proverbs*, 4.5.

LETTER 6.

3. '*burden...mystery*': Wordsworth's *Tintern Abbey*, line 38.

8. ten...deep: *Paradise Lost*, II.934.

9–10. bare-shouldered creature: possibly an echo of *King Lear*, III.iv. 112.

11. fledge: (fledged) having feathered wings.

13. This...benefit: one meaning of the now archaic expression 'run one's rigs on' was 'to run riot'. Possibly Keats is saying, dismissively, something like 'This is going too far in a general (or theoretical) consideration'.

19–20. '*that...to*': *Hamlet*, III.i.63.

34. breathing: a somewhat obscure word here; it may refer back to 'atmosphere'.

41–2. We...mist: compare the *Epistle to J. H. Reynolds*, lines 74–80, written a few weeks before.

8. 'burden of society': an unidentified quotation. It was the desperate financial state of the Keats brothers that induced George to try his fortune in America. With his newly married bride, Georgiana Wylie, he left England a fortnight after this letter–on June 24.

8–9. the other: Tom Keats, already seriously ill.

10. early...parents: Keats was eight when his father was killed, fourteen when his mother died.

12. 'passing...women': 2 *Samuel*, 1:26.

15. sister: the reference (in a kind of parenthesis) is probably to Fanny Keats, but it could be to his sister-in-law, Georgiana.

Mrs Wylie was the mother of George's wife, Georgiana. Still on his Scottish tour, Keats wrote this letter from Inverness.

The two extracts are from a long journal letter, probably the most important of all Keats's letters, covering the period 14 February to 3 May 1819: hence the two separate dates given.

7. as I am*: in his asterisk note to the letter Keats refers for the second time to a black eye received while playing cricket.

11–15. Neither...disguisement: it was the re-reading of this passage that inspired the *Ode on Indolence*.

18. Haslam: though there are only three extant letters to William Haslam (1795?–1851), his friendship with Keats was a long-standing one. Keats spoke of him as 'always doing me some good turn', 'a most kind and obliging and constant friend'. It was Haslam who, at the last minute, persuaded Severn to accompany Keats to Italy in 1820.

32–9. In the first...life: on the evidence of this letter, Keats did not share the common Romantic idealization of the 'noble savage'.

41. 'A poor forked creature': a loose quotation from *King Lear*, III.iv.113.

46–7. heaven with its stars: probably this refers to inevitable Fate or destiny–the 'mischances' previously mentioned.

70. in spite: in the sense of 'contrary to hostile worldly elements'.

104. horn-book: a leaf of paper containing the ABC (and sometimes other matter like the Lord's Prayer) protected by a sheet of transparent horn, from which children once learnt to read.

114. identical: this must mean 'possessing identity', not 'the same'.

Though James Rice (1792?–1832) was not among Keats's more distinguished friends and suffered from continual bad health, he was much admired by Keats as a wit and for his good sense–'he makes you laugh and think'. He and Keats stayed together at Shanklin in the Isle of Wight for most of July 1819.

10–13. sixth...sensation: when Keats speaks of being 'taken ill', he is almost certainly referring to the severe haemorrhage on 3 February 1820 that marked the beginning of his fatal illness. This confession, which must therefore cover most of the second half of 1819, is an extremely revealing one in several ways.

20. Like poor Falstaff: *Henry V*, II.iii.17.

La Belle Dame Sans Merci

HAPPY IS ENGLAND: (Winter 1816).
Though this early poem is not among the pick of Keats's sonnets, the sestet expresses something of the sentimental, vaguely idealizing attitude towards women and love that fills so much of *Endymion*. Compare his later remarks on 'Charmian', Letter 12 (pp. 174–5).

ON A LEANDER GEM (March 1817).
This sonnet marks the first intimation–probably a subconscious one–of that sense of love's fatality that was to remain so strongly persistent in Keats's poetry. In the classical story Leander was drowned as he swam the Hellespont to meet his beloved, Hero.

The title refers to one of the imitation paste gems, engraved with some classical subject, that were made by James Tassie and very popular at the time. The gift was from Miss Reynolds.

10. swooning: this word, though usually expressing ecstasy, is common in Keats's love poetry.

11. against: anticipating.

12–14. An effective climax–vivid, condensed, and with appropriately abrupt phrasing.

ENDYMION, I.777–842.
As one of his letters shows, Keats attached great importance to this speculative passage; and it has frequently been used to support elaborate allegorical interpretations of the poem. But, taken in its context, it may be directly read as Endymion's high-flown defence of 'earthly love' (line 843) against his sister's previous reproof of his love-lorn, downcast state.

At the centre of this defence is a conception of happiness as a 'self-destroying', an empathic 'oneness' with the world and others. Keats elaborates this idea through the ascending gradations of what he called 'a kind of pleasure thermometer'. Nature in its sensuous beauties, music, friendship–all these may induce a sense of self-oblivion, a liberating 'oneness'; but this kind of happiness is to be experienced at its most intense in sexual love–love that is, however, no mere 'commingling of passionate breath'. Hence love, which is also celebrated as a force prompting towards wider good as well as the vital, generative element of all life, is the predominant theme here. See E. C. Pettet, *On the Poetry of Keats*, pp. 155–60.

778. divine: Keats had a fondness for religious words, Christian or pagan, and no special meaning should be read into 'divine' or the following 'clear religion of heaven'.

779. essence: This word, which carries no metaphysical significance, has misled many commentators. In Keats's occasional, individual use of the term it usually means 'being', 'existence'. Here it means 'all being', and particularly those 'thing(s) of beauty' referred to in the first line of the poem. In an earlier, cruder version of lines 777–81 Keats speaks more clearly of 'blending pleasurable' and 'delight'.

780. alchemized: something like 'spiritualized', 'sublimated'–the state of the 'floating spirit, line 797.

783–94. What Keats seems to be mainly thinking of here is imaginary music associated with certain places. Perhaps the sentiment is the one later expressed in the *Ode on a Grecian Urn*, lines 11–12 (p. 85).

786. lucid: a baffling word–'translucent', or, possibly 'clear in sound' (?).

787. enclouded: perhaps 'hazily seen'.

790. Apollo is here as the god of song and music.

791. bruit: sound.

794. Orpheus was a legendary Greek poet and musician.

795–7. Summarizing lines. The essential condition of this 'oneness' is that we feel intensely 'these things' of beauty, these 'essences'.

813–15. Keats is here stating that love is the essential force of life–its 'proper pith'.

815. This refers to the mythical belief that the pelican fed its young with its own blood.

816. unsating: uncloying.

817. men: i.e. potential reformers, etc.

826–35. The idea intimated here, that love is a force working indirectly towards a spirit of benevolence and humanity, is fully worked out in Book III of the poem.

831. Possibly an echo of 'gray-hooded Ev'n' in Milton's *Comus*, line 188.

835–42. The thought in these lines is not of course to be taken literally; nor is it quite so 'sentimental' as Byron believed. Keats is probably intending to suggest that love is the essential life-force in all fruitful conjunctions and harmonies.

TIME'S SEA (4 February 1818).
The subject of Keats's recollection here is usually taken to be a young woman he had fleetingly seen in the Vauxhall Gardens in the summer of 1814. See also '*When I have fears*', line 9 (p. 51). The sonnet is his second of the Shakespearian type; and there are many words and phrases reminiscent of Shakespeare's sonnets.

2. A reference to the sand- or hour-glass. Compare '*After dark vapours*', line 13 (p. 202).

9–12. Because the budding flower reminds the poet of the girl's lips, he waits for it to utter some 'love-sound' instead of enjoying the flower's scent and colour.

14. A typically Keatsian juxtaposition of joy and grief.

ISABELLA (February or March to 27 April 1818).
This poem arose from an abortive scheme of Keats and his friend Reynolds to compose a collection of verse tales based on some of Boccaccio's stories. Partly because he followed the first English translation of 1620, he treated the Boccaccio original quite freely.

A year later he expressed some strongly adverse comment on the poem, and generally–with Charles Lamb as one notable exception –it has been considered the least successful of his narratives. But it contains many fine lines and stanzas; its narrative, in marked contrast with that of *Endymion*, is substantial, compact, and swift moving; and Lamb was surely right in his high commendation of the description of Lorenzo's disinterment.

The stanza form, new to Keats, is the *ottava rima* (abababcc).

2. young... eye!: a young pilgrim with love as his dedicated mission.

8. to... dream: dream about each other.

13–15. Note the typical fondness of Keats for soft, subdued sounds.

21. vespers: evening prayers.

23. sick longing: one of the many touches in the opening stanzas that remind us of the mawkish treatment of love in *Endymion*.

34. Became pallid where there should have been a rosy bloom.

39. If... love-laws: if her looks show that she is under the power of love.

46. Fevered...conceit: wrought his imagination to fever-pitch.

49. anguished: felt anguish (throughout the night).

52. symbol: sign, indication.

56. For the *Endymion* parallel it is interesting to note that in one of his cancelled expansions at this point Keats described Lorenzo, like Endymion, losing his pleasure in hunting.

62. fear: frighten.

64. shrive: confess (Keats has changed the usual meaning).

67–76. blossoms, flower, roses: note the sustained linkage of imagery.

70. dewy: perhaps for a suggestion of freshness, newness.

75. close: secretly (as again in lines 81 and 85).

85. From the first this 'bower' image is recurrent in Keats's poetry.

89–104. There are three other author-intrusions–lines 121–60, 385–92, and 433–48.

94. Possibly a reminiscence of *Romeo and Juliet*, v.iii.299.

95–6. An exception because, in classical story, Ariadne had been deserted by the hero Theseus after helping him kill the Minotaur, the Cretan monster.

99. The allusion comes from Virgil's *Aeneid*, vi.434–76. In her undying grief Dido, who had killed herself when deserted by Aeneas, haunted a wood in the underworld.

101–2. An anticipation of the story to come–of Lorenzo's burial in the forest.

103. almsmen: men endowed to pray for the souls of others. The suggestion is of murmured prayer.

104. Compare *Ode to Melancholy* lines 23–4 (p. 87).

105–120. The vivid vigour of these two stanzas, describing the exploitations of the two merchant brothers, contrasts notably with most of the writing that has gone before.

107. swelt: swelter (a word borrowed from Spenser).

109. proud-quivered: a typical Keatsian compound that probably means 'once proud, now quivering'. But it could, alternatively, refer to conquered natives who once proudly wore their quivers of arrows.

120. peel: (literally) to strip the skin from.

124. lazar-stairs: stairs of a leper-house.

131. close: probably, secretive; or, concealing themselves; *land inspired*: Palestine.

132. Paled in: fenced in.

133. hawks...forests: The meaning of this is not clear: possibly something like 'always alert to pounce on the likely profits that merchant-ships brought'.

135. Possibly 'quick to get their claws on those whose (over) generosity had got them into debt'.

136. Spanish... Malay: languages useful for their commercial activities.

140. Hot Egypt's pest: the plague of darkness on the Egyptians (*Exodus*, 10:21–3)

147. myrtles: plants emblematically associated with love.

150. ghittern: a guitar-like instrument.

155. assail: attempt, endeavour.

156. old prose: Boccaccio's *Decameron* was written in prose.

159. stead: serve.

168. olive-trees: a wealthy possession in Italy.

169. jealous: perhaps chiefly in the sense of 'apprehensive', 'troubled by suspicious fears'.

187–8. ere... eglantine: i.e. before the hot sun dries up the dew-drops on the eglantine. The metaphor is of counting the beads of a rosary.

209. murdered man: probably the most frequently cited example of prolepsis (anticipatory statement) in English poetry.

215–16. The nature of the rhyme makes this an appalling couplet, marring a good stanza.

219. when... win: i.e. by release of a brutal, unnatural death.

221. break-covert: perhaps 'no longer concealed', 'coming out into the open'.

236. luxury: an instance of Keats's use of this word for intense sentiment or sensation.

242. single: her heart could really hold only one feeling, love.

243. for: (in longing) for: *golden hour*: Lorenzo's return.

246. zest: sharper, intenser feelings (not of course of enjoyment).

248. rude: of hardship, discomfort.

249–55. A simile of earth's declining, death-stricken beauty in autumn.

258. eye all pale: Not a happy phrase. Did Keats mean something like 'lustreless'?

259. dungeon climes: regions, countries where he was detained (not literally imprisoned).

262. like... vale: i.e. like an abomination (2 *Chronicles*, 27:3).

268. feathered pall: death.

269–72. A somewhat obscure reference from a book Keats knew from school-library days, Robertson's *History of America*. It may allude to a surprise attack in Red Indian warfare, or to the Indians' torture of prisoners or of themselves.

287. under-song: probably indicating some kind of echoing effect.

288. sepulchral: graveyard.

292. woof: (metaphorical) woven pattern.

297–304. Surely one of the finest stanzas in the poem.

306. Upon... dwelling: on the fringe of human habitation (and human life).

307. In fact, in the Catholic service only the priest chants the mass.

312. A most poignant line.

320. essence: being. See note on *Endymion*, 1.779.

322. atom: possibly, if we take this word in conjunction with line 326, it signifies a darkness fragmented by flashes of light.

331–2. Compare *The Fall of Hyperion* lines 173–5 (p. 95).

344. forest-hearse: burial-place. An obviously forced rhyme.

347. champaign: an expanse of countryside.

353–60. Another good stanza spoilt by the conclusion, especially by the jarring colloquialism of 'this is holiday'.

354. demon: possibly for the underground association.

385–92. Something of an apology for lacking the simplicity of Boccaccio's 'old tale'. The construction is deliberately broken off after 'To speak'. Probably we can understand that continuation would have meant further reference to 'wormy circumstance'.

393. Persean sword: In classical story Perseus cut off the head of the Gorgon, a monster.

398. impersonate: embodied in a human being.

401–8. A rare example in Keats's poetry of that fascination of the loathsome-beautiful, the repulsive-attractive, that is a feature of much Romantic poetry and art.

409. dews: distillations, liquid perfumes.

412. serpent-pipe: curved distillation pipe.

416. Sweet basil: an aromatic plant.

432. leafits: little leaves.

433–44. In general Keats is apostrophizing various spirits to mourn the coming death of Isabella. But some of the detail is not clear. Are the 'spirits in grief', line 437, human mourners as line 485 seems to suggest?

442. Melpomene: the classical muse of tragedy.

451. Baälites of pelf: worshippers of the false god of money.

465. sift: get to the bottom of.

467. chapel-shrift: confession to priest.

491. chuckle: probably in the sense of a bird's cry to its young.

THE EVE OF ST AGNES (18 January–2 February 1819; revised in September 1819).
This simple narrative poem of a triumphant, happy love (in this and other respects the antithesis of *Isabella*) was a combination of the superstition of St Agnes' Eve and the ancient *Romeo and Juliet* motif of elopement against a background of family hostility. Not surprisingly, it contains many echoes of Shakespeare's play.

It is also Keats's most important expression of his persistent, idealized vision of the Middle Ages, that major element in English Romanticism; and appropriately, in further exploration of narrative verse forms, he adopted the Spenserian stanza of *The Faerie Queene*, employing it, on the whole, with considerable skill and effectiveness.

1. The superstition about St Agnes' Eve (20 January) was that on this night, by fasting and other observances, a girl might have a vision of her future husband.

5. *Beadsman*: a man endowed to pray for the soul of his benefactor —much the same as 'almsman' in *Isabella*, line 103 (p. 120).

6. frosted breath: This might pictorially suggest the Beadsman's own departing spirit.

14–18. In fancy the effigies become the dead knights and ladies dumbly praying.

21. Flattered: delighted? beguiled?–the meaning is uncertain.

26. reprieve: redemption.

31. silver: This colour appears repeatedly in the poem.

33. glowing: This word, a product of revision, begins to suggest the contrasting warmth inside the castle.

34. carvèd angels: ornamentations to the cornice around the walls.

39–41. Lines applicable to the early Keats himself.

39. fairily: as an enchantment.

56. Something like 'divine music of poignant-sweet longing'.

58. train: i.e. of skirts.

69. This implication of hostility among the guests is probably one of the many reminiscences of *Romeo and Juliet* in the poem.

70. amort: dead.

71. Lambs were associated with the story of St Agnes, and at the Feast of St Agnes's Day two unshorn lambs were brought to the altar and blessed.

90. beldame: old woman. Though in many respects unlike the Nurse in *Romeo and Juliet*, the beldame Angela plays something of the same reluctant-helper role.

98–108. In this dialogue–and its later continuation–there is some naturalness and vigour.

105. gossip: This word has a special Elizabethan flavour, but the modern meaning will do.

115–17. After the Feast of St Agnes the wool of the lambs was woven by nuns into a pallium, an ecclesiastical vestment.

120. hold... sieve: once believed in as a practice for magical purposes.

124. conjuror: in the sense of one who calls up spirits or visions.

125. deceive: not an easy word to understand. Perhaps the deception she hopes for is that Madeline will be allowed to remain in her dreams. See later lines 141–3.

126. mickle: much.

133. brook: restrain.

138. purple: a reference to the blood beating in his heart.

168. legioned fairies: fairies of a good protective kind; 'legioned', and perhaps 'paced', suggest that they are massed on soldierly duty.

171. Demon: probably refers to Nimue. Merlin's lover, and *debt* to his magic secrets that he revealed to her; *monstrous* would refer to her treachery in using these enchantments to imprison him. But the comparison is an odd one in the context.

173. cates and dainties: Elizabethan words for various delicacies.

174. tambour-frame: embroidery frame shaped like a tambour (drum).

185. dim espial: being just seen in the 'dusky gallery'.

188. covert: concealment; *amain*: to the extreme.

189. agues: Literally an 'ague' was a fever or shivering fit.

198. frayed: alarmed, timorous.

208–16. Two points may be noted of this famous stanza so outstandingly rich in imagery and sound: (1) that it was much worked over before Keats arrived at the final version: and (2) that its details contain several reminiscences, notably of Scott's *Lay of the Last Minstrel* (II.stanza 11), a poem echoed elsewhere in *The Eve of St Agnes*.

215. emblazonings: heraldic devices.

216. scutcheon: coat of arms; *blushed with blood*: i.e. the 'gules' (heraldic red).

241. Probably 'shut (within herself) as a Christian prayer-book would be in a Muslim ("Paynim") country'.

247. This might suggest a breathing of love-sighs.

257. drowsy Morphean amulet: sleep-inducing charm. Morpheus was the god of sleep.

262–70: This stanza was even more heavily worked over in revision than stanza xxiv.

262. azure-lidded: referring to Madeline's blue-veined eyelids.

266. soother: smoother (a word-coinage).

268. Manna: Probably Keats meant some rare fruit.

270. Samarkand was famous for its silks.

277. eremite: hermit, religious devotee. See *Bright Star*, line 4 (p. 172).

288. woofèd: woven, imaginatively elaborated.

292. La belle dame sans mercy was the title of a poem by Alain Chartier (1386–1458).

316–22. Keats meant us to understand that the love was physically consummated, and in a revision of lines 314–22, which his publisher Taylor refused to accept, he made his meaning clearer.

322. Solution: blending; fusion.

325. flaw: a sudden (short) gust of wind.

333. unprunèd: unpreened (a suggestion of despoilment, etc.).

334–42. Several probable echoes here, like 'shrine' and 'take my rest', of *Romeo and Juliet*.

344. haggard: wild.

349. Rhenish: wine from the Rhineland.

352–69. Again there may be some reminiscence of *The Lay of the Last Minstrel* (II.stanza 26) and also of Byron's *Siege of Corinth*, lines 620–7.

370–8. This concluding note of mortality, which recalls the opening, must not be overlooked in our overall impression of the poem.

377. thousand aves: repetitions of the *Ave Maria* prayer 'told' to the rosary beads.

AS HERMES ONCE (April 1819).
Though in the second half of this fine sonnet, which has several important links with *La Belle Dame Sans Merci*, Keats imaginatively identifies himself with the tormented, restless spirits of Paolo and Francesca, destroyed by passion, almost certainly because the poem is to be connected with his love for Fanny Brawne, so full of contradictory emotions, this identification contains some sensation of joy. However, joy–and warmth–were much more strongly present in the dream, described as 'one of the most delightful enjoyments I ever had in my life' (letter to George and Georgiana Keats, 16 April 1819), which was the genesis of the sonnet.

1–2. In classical story Hermes (winged Mercury) lulled the hundred-eyed monster Argus to sleep by his reed music and so rescued Io, the beloved of Jupiter.

3–5. In general Keats is speaking of poetry as an imaginative escape from the world, particularly from those he felt to be prying into his private affairs. *Delphic reed*: poetry. Delphi was the site of the oracle of Apollo, the poet-god.

7–8. Mount Ida and the beautiful vale of Tempe were famous in classical story. Jove (Jupiter) was certainly grieved for the loss of Io, but the connection of this with Tempe is uncertain.

11–12. lovers... sorrow: some ambiguity in this expression, but the association of love and sorrow is clear.

LA BELLE DAME SANS MERCI (21 April 1819).
To what has already been said in the Introduction a general comment of Wilson Knight may be added here: 'Keats's pagan sensuousness does not forget that there is something subtly wrong with human love: that it is subject to tragic necessity, and that ugliness... may be at the core of its luscious bloom' (*The Starlit Dome*, p.275).

For all its uniqueness, the poem is singularly full of echoes, great and small, from Keats's reading–of old ballads like *Thomas of Ercildoune*, the enchantresses Florimel and Phaedria in Spenser's

The Faerie Queene, Dante's *Inferno*, Canto v, Burton's *Anatomy of Melancholy*, and so on. This fact has two points of significance: first, it reminds us how effortlessly and harmoniously Keats was able to combine his various 'influences' (see the sonnet *How many Bards* p. 191); and secondly, that works of great originality may sometimes, paradoxically, owe a great debt to tradition.

4. Possibly an echo of 'Let no birds sing' (William Browne's *Britannia's Pastorals*, ii. line 245).

10. fever-dew: feverish sweat.

18. fragrant zone: a girdle of flowers.

20. moan: For Keats's slightly unusual use of this word see also *Ode to Psyche*, line 30 (p. 231) and *Lamia*, i. line 75 (p. 152).

26. Possibly an echo of Coleridge's *Kubla Khan*, line 53.

32. kisses four: Several suggestions have been offered about this detail. But there seems little reason for looking beyond Keats's own light-hearted explanation: 'I was obliged to choose an even number that both eyes might have fair play: and to speak truly, I think two apiece quite sufficient' (letter to George and Georgiana Keats, 21 April 1819).

37–8. pale: Compare *As Hermes Once*, lines 12 and 13 (p. 143).

41. gloam: twilight.

OTHO THE GREAT, v.v.55–193 (early July to late August 1819). This play, hastily written and largely in the unfulfilled hope of a quick and substantial financial return, was composed during approximately the same period as *Lamia*. For the first four Acts Keats's friend, Charles Brown, sketched out the scenes, while Keats's own contribution was mainly confined to the writing of the dialogue. The fifth Act was Keats's own work.

As those fortunate enough to see the unique performance in 1950 were able to appreciate, the play is by no means worthless, in spite of its preposterous, complex, and often obscure plot. This plot may be roughly summarized as follows. At the beginning, supported by Duke Conrad, Ludolph, the hero, is in opposition to his father, the emperor Otho—partly because he wishes to marry Conrad's sister, Auranthe, while Otho wishes him to wed his cousin, Erminia. Auranthe, a 'she-devil', besides the hinted incestuous relationship with her brother, is having an affair with a knight named Albert. By a deception she has also succeeded in besmirching the moral character of the virtuous Erminia. When Otho, knowing only of the alleged disgrace of Erminia, is reconciled with Ludolph, he encourages the wedding of his son and Auranthe to take place.

By chance a letter revealing Auranthe's intrigues falls into Erminia's hands. She entrusts it to Albert to present to Otho, but instead he uses it to bring pressure on Conrad and Auranthe, insisting that Auranthe flee the country with him. Just as the flight appears to be taking place there is a fight between Albert and Conrad in which both are killed. Ludolph recaptures his wife, but he has been driven out of his mind by her infidelity and treachery.

In a letter to Fanny Brawne of 5 August 1819 Keats wrote: 'I leave this minute a scene in our tragedy and see you... through the mist of plots, speeches, counterplots and counter speeches. The lover is madder than I am.' Whether or not Keats was really saying here a little more than he intended, it seems highly probable that something of his attitude towards Fanny at this difficult time went into the expression of Ludolph's infatuation for Auranthe, his growing suspicions, and his devastation.

55. three more: i.e. Conrad, Albert, and Auranthe. The first two are in fact dead.

58–70. Many of the details of this picture of Auranthe–the blue eyes, the apparently pale complexion, the small nostrils, the thin ('tenderly'?) but attractively moulded cheeks–fit closely with the information we have of Fanny Brawne's appearance, including Keats's own description of her in Letter 13 (p. 176).

61. ebon brows: a Shakespearian echo (?).

80. Sigifred was an officer and friend of Ludolph.

85–6. glistened... caskets: Keats is of course referring to jewels taken from their caskets.

87. lawn: fine linen or cambric.

90. Margravines: the feminine of the old German title, Margrave.

98. Gersa was a captured Hungarian prince well treated by Otho and charged to look after Ludolph in the latter part of the play.

111. Ethelbert was an abbot who, in the course of the play, had attempted to expose the intrigues of Auranthe, especially against Erminia, and so incurred the hostility of an outraged Ludolph.

116–125. An unmistakable Keatsian passage–for its general sensuous richness, its reference to pledging in wine, and for certain words like 'ripe', 'goblet', 'pulpy'. And if the final conceit about Bacchus is strained, it fits the demented speaker.

116. certes: assuredly (an archaism from Spenser). See *Lamia* II. line 80 (p. 162).

141. do... sad: Ludolph thinks that his father's tears will weaken his own murderous resolve against Auranthe: he wants his father to put on the 'judge's brow', etc.

148–9. The compression here may cause some misunderstanding. Presumably Ludolph is inviting Otho to 'denounce' the crime, the punishment for which will be 'executed' by himself alone.

161. fell: fierce, ruthless.

164. pight: settled, determined (probably borrowed from Shakespeare).
184. (stage direction): in her hopeless' situation Auranthe has killed herself.

LAMIA (late June to early September 1819).
Keats seems to have regarded this work, based on an anecdote from one of his favourite books, Burton's *Anatomy of Melancholy*, as the best of his narrative poems, and there are strong grounds to support his preference. The poem has almost as much sensuous richness as *The Eve of St Agnes*, though this is more diffused; it relates a swiftly moving story that is dramatic with conflict and psychological interest–a notable advance in this respect on his previous narrative pieces. Also, thanks partly to a study of Dryden's versification, he achieves an immense improvement in his handling of the pentameter couplets, though the poem is flawed here and there by some odd stylistic lapses.

All the same, as many critics have felt, *Lamia* is in several ways a baffling and contradictory poem. Most of all our response is likely to be confused by Keats's treatment of the heroine, for she is an enigmatic, ambiguous figure. One the one hand, she *is* serpent and a deadly, deceptive enchantress who destroys Lycius. On the other, she is endowed with some good qualities, while in Part II especially she seems a woman, a passive victim almost, helplessly fated to bring destruction to Lycius rather than an active agent of evil and destruction.

Lamia is certainly not to be read as straight autobiography, but probably the main explanation of these ambiguities (including the unsympathetic treatment of the 'trusty guide and good instructor' Apollonius, who may in some respects represent Charles Brown) lies in Keats's tortured and contradictory attitude towards Fanny Brawne in the months of voluntary separation from her when the poem was being written. There is probably no more illuminating clue to it than his confession 'You absorb me in spite of myself.' See the Letters (p. 179).

Part I.
1–6. Here Keats imagines a time when the English fairies, under their King, Oberon, expelled the classical rural spirits– nymphs, satyrs, dryads, fauns.
7. ever-smitten Hermes: Hermes (Mercury) was notoriously amorous. This initial episode of Hermes and the nymph, 1.7–145, serves several purposes. As a reward for her help, Lamia is changed from a snake into a woman. There is the intimation of an ideal 'dream' of love that, for the gods, persists, 1.126–8; and with the invisible nymph and the transformation of Lamia, there

is an introduction of the hallucinations, false appearances, etc. that dominate the poem.

16. withered: i.e. because the Tritons were sea spirits.

39–41. These lines indicate the sensual kind of love that Lamia is to embody.

46. cirque-couchant: lying coiled in a circle (a bold compound coinage).

47. gordian: intricately coiled. See the classical story of King Gordius.

55–6. These lines, with Lamia's snake form, a symbol of evil, establish her manacing ill; *penanced lady elf*, along with lines 117–18, would seem to suggest that she had once been a woman who had been punished for some evil-doing.

58. Ariadne's tiar: When Dionysus married Ariadne he gave her a crown which was placed among the stars. There may be a reminiscence of Titian's painting *Bacchus and Ariadne*.

67. stooped: about to swoop down.

75. A suggestively lengthened line (an alexandrine)–one of several in the poem.

76. purple flakes: dawn-reddened clouds.

78. Phoebean dart: shaft of sunlight. 'Phoebus' (bright) was an epithet for Apollo as sun god.

81. star of Lethe: Hermes guided the dead beyond the river Lethe into the underworld.

89. serpent rod: a rod, entwined with serpents, was an emblem carried by Hermes.

100–3. Contradictorily, here Lamia is a protectress against the lustful loves of satyrs, etc.

107. weird syrups: magic liquid.

114. psalterian: probably from 'psalter' (a prayer-book or book of psalms) and therefore suggesting a solemn, sacred oath.

115. Circean: This identifies Lamia with Circe, the destructive enchantress through her power of stimulating intense sensual love.

125. near: probably in the sense of 'close by'.

133. lithe Caducean charm: Hermes' rod, called the Caduceus, had magic powers; 'lithe' would suggest the entwined snakes. Hermes is starting the metamorphosis of Lamia.

145. A contrasting, key line, indicating the sorrows (transience?) of human love.

155. volcanian yellow: sulphur-like.

158. brede: a word for something woven. See the *Ode on a Grecian Urn*, line 41 (p. 86).

163. rubious-argent: silver tinged with red (a typical Keats compound-formation).

174. Cenchreas was the port of Corinth, situated on the Isthmus.

176. founts: sources.

178. cloudy wrack: mass or bank of cloud.

183. passionèd: a word-coinage: the pool reflects the physical signs of her intense feelings.

185. happy: This early word further intimates something of the complex contradictions of the poem.

189–96. Difficult but important lines: *yet... core* would seem to suggest an essentially sensuous, passionate love, though not in any deprecatory way. Her ability to keep bliss and pain apart is surely (for Keats) an admirable power and wisdom. See *The Fall of Hyperion*, lines 172–6 (p. 95).

191. sciental: having knowledge, wisdom.

192, unperplex: keep from bewildering (and distressing) contact with (?).

193, pettish: irksome; *estrange*: separate, keep apart (?).

197–9. Triple-rhymed. Poor lines, with the namby-pamby–and protracted – 'Cupid's college' simile, and the forced feminine rhyme. *unshent*: unspoilt.

204. list: pleased.

206. faint Elysium: the faintly seen abode of the blessed.

207. Nereids: sea-nymphs. One was Thetis, mother of Achilles.

211. palatine: connected with a palace; or, splendid, palatial.

212. Mulciber (Vulcan): the god of fire; *piazzian*: in a colonnade.

217. envious: inciting competitive feelings.

219. swooning: Note this familar Keatsian word in the context of love.

229. vows: probably prayers etc., for a happy marriage.

235–6. His imagination ('fancy') lost itself in the serene mysteries of Platonism.

238. indifference drear: the indifference of Lycius is 'drear' to Lamia.

248. In the classical story Orpheus, who was leading Eurydice away from the underworld, lost her because in his love he broke the condition of not looking back to see that she was following. Because of the contradictions of the poem, this sombre reference is not out of place in this otherwise joyous encounter.

265. Pleiad: one of the seven daughters of Asia who became stars when they died.

266–7. An allusion to the legendary music of the 'spheres' on which the stars were once supposed to turn.

271–86. Lamia in her first speech to Lycius begins with the lie, later withdrawn, that she is a goddess.

275. nice: exact, perhaps in the sense of 'vivid'.

285. sleights: craft (but not in any pejorative sense here).

287–97. This enchantment of Lycius is very reminiscent of what happens in *La Belle Dame Sans Merci* (pp. 144–5).

288. lone complain: Lamia has just complained that she cannot be with Lycius on earth.

293. amenity: complaisance.

300. The fancy here is that the stars stop twinkling as they listen to the song.

320. The Adonian feast was a festival to commemorate Adonis, the youth loved by Venus and killed by a boar.

321. adore: join in the festival and Venus worship.

327. unperplexed: pure in the special sense indicated by 1.192.

328–33. A bad lapse, especially the vulgar, colloquial 'such a treat... As a real woman'. Possibly, in a quite unsuitable context, Keats was momentarily aping a Byronic manner.

329. Peris: good spirits in Persian tales.

333. Pyrrha's pebbles: After a great flood Deucalion and Pyrrha repeopled the world by throwing pebbles, which changed into men and women, behind them.

347. comprised: absorbed.

352. lewd: given to licentious practices. This association of Corinth is to be noted.

377. folly: of Lycius's folly–a momentary admission of truth and guilt.

386. Aeolian: like music of the Aeolian harp.

394. flitter-wingèd: possibly an apologetic term–'verse not of vigorous flight'.

397. of more incredulous: another uncertain phrase. Perhaps 'incurious to know more'.

Part II

1–10. Whether or not reflecting another moment of Byronic influence, this is a curious passage expressing a pessimistic and slightly cynical view of love that, for rich and poor alike, inevitably turns to distrust and hate, even perhaps to wifely nagging! It may be worth remembering that Part II was started a month after the completion of Part I.

6. non-elect: those who have not been granted the necessary knowledge.

8. a fresh frown: something like 'another forbidding testimony'.

9. clenched: proved.

11–15. The image here would seem to be of Cupid frightening away intruders.

12. jealous: possibly in the sense of 'apprehensive about'.

16. For all this: in spite of all this (i.e. Cupid's surveillance).

26–45. A key passage in the poem: even more important than the intrusion of the real world into the love-swooning enchantment, is the first awakening of thought in Lycius–of that rational faculty which must always be in opposition to the blindness and illusion of passion. The 'penetrant' Lamia instantly realizes this, and the danger. See especially lines 37–9 and 41.

26. suburb: neighbouring.

31. A significant line that epitomizes much of the contradiction of the poem.

51. smart: This word may indicate intensity of feeling rather than anguish. See *Lines Written in the Highlands*, line 8 (p. 56).

53. labyrinth: difficult to gloss this unusual use of the word as a verb. Perhaps it suggests impossibility of escape.

64–9. It is to be noticed that Lamia opposes the idea of a public marriage, with its possible dangers. She is rather a victim of love and her own enchantment than an active, evil agent of destruction.

72–7. Another curious note–this time of sadism. But not unique: see *Ode on Melancholy*, lines 18–20. (p. 87). Note also 'luxurious', line 74, that common Keatsian word for sensuous indulgence.

76. sanguineous: deeply flushed.

80. The serpent: the monstrous Python that Apollo slew at Delphi. The allusion is ironical here.

102. blind and blank: something like 'obscure and meaningless'.

105. betrayed: This suggests that the sleep was induced by a spell.

114. pompousness: taste for ceremony, display, etc.

116. misery: This word presumably covers both Lamia's feelings and the situation generally.

118. subtle: probably signifies 'of spirit nature'. See 'viewless', II. line 136.

122–4. This suggestion that the roof is supported by music begins a strong prevalent impression of illusion and confusion–of things not being what they seem. And notice how in the following description of the chamber much of the architectural embellishment appears as vegetation; *mimicking*, line 125, is a key word.

135. Perhaps suggests a somewhat lifeless Lamia, unhappy about the situation but resigned to it.

142. faded at self-will: made herself vanish.

144. rude: boisterous.

148. silent-blessing fate: i.e. Fate had given him a happiness he could have enjoyed in quietness.

155. desmesne: palace.

160. daffed: resisted, daunted.

179–82. Note the double-seeing; and again the word 'mimicked'.

183. ensphered: surrounded.

185. libbard's: leopard's (archaic).

186. thrice told: three times the amount.

188. tun: cask.

190. image: a small statue.

224. These emblems epitomize the contradictions in *Lamia*. Willow was the traditional symbol of sorrow in love, especially of desertion; and 'adder's tongue' is sufficiently self-explanatory, though in actual fact this type of fern was used for soothing medicinal qualities.

226. thyrsus: the staff of Bacchus, with its entwined vine and ivy leaves, was a symbol of intoxication.

229–38. For philosophy in the sense of rational speculation about life Keats had an increasing regard. Here, in what may be to some extent a dramatic utterance appropriate to the situation, it is 'philosophy' in the sense of scientific, analytical investigation that is under attack. The rainbow reference is probably a reminiscence of a dinner at Haydon's (28 December 1817) in which, in a light-hearted, convivial spirit, Keats and Lamb had criticized Newton because his work on prismatic colours had destroyed the poetry of the rainbow.

236. gnomèd mine: gnomes, etc., were often legendarily associated with underground workings.

257. owned: acknowledged, responded to.

259. Some... absorbs: the beautiful Lamia is completely possessed by some consuming spell.

274–5. no... vision: there was no feeling to liven her glazed, sunken eyes.

277. juggling: in the sense of 'conjuring and controlling spirits'.

279. dreadful images: see II. 190.

289. demon eyes: To the infatuated Lycius, Apollonius has now become the demon. That is understandable. But Keats's representation of an entirely unsympathetic Apollonius in lines 291–2 is another matter.

301. perceant: piercing (an archaism from Spenser).

304. level: perhaps in the sense of 'unwavering', 'unaltered'.

307–11. This fatal end of Lycius is Keats's own addition to his source story.

THE DAY IS GONE (10 October 1819).
One of a small group of intimately personal poems addressed to Fanny Brawne in the late autumn of 1819. Keats and Fanny had been separated for nearly four months, and this sonnet was probably written immediately after their first meeting again on 10 October. In a letter to Fanny, dated 11 October, Keats wrote: 'I am living today in yesterday. I feel myself at your mercy... You dazzled me. There is nothing in the world so bright and delicate.' See also Letter 20 (pp. 182–3).

Keats has reverted to the Shakespearian sonnet form.

9. shut of eve: Keats hàd used a similar phrase in *Lamia* II, line 107 (p. 162).
10. holiday: the word carries its original sense.
13. I've... through: performed all the true love-observances. For a similar religious turn of expression see Letter 20 (pp. 182–3).

TO [FANNY] (15–31 October 1819).
This poem, confused and contradictory, communicates a mood very different from that of the quietly enraptured surrender of the sonnet *The day is gone*. Among other things it voices and then recants a rebellious outburst against an absorbing love that seems to frustrate poetic activity. There is also, in this highly personal poem, a sustained reference to Keats's brother and sister-in-law, whose situation in America at this time worried him deeply.

The form of the poem is an unusually free one for Keats.
4. Touch has a memory: a vividly memorable expression.
10–17. Besides their admission of a loss of poetic fire, these lines have another disturbing significance. See the Introduction, pp. 24–5.
10. particoloured: Perhaps Keats means that his poetry had lacked the full colouring he would have liked. An odd disclaimer.
17. throes: is violently agitated (verb).
25–6. A further example of religious vocabulary in Keats's love poetry.
31–43. See the Introduction.
35. urns: sources.
42. bud: possibly a text corruption, intended to be cancelled for the substituted word 'flowers'.
48–57. This conclusion, with its passionate invitation to the 'tender gaolers', contradicts the opening of the poem. But something of the conflict remains in the line, 'Oh, the sweetness of the pain'.

I CRY YOUR MERCY (October–November 1819).
This sonnet, also in the Shakespearian form, marks a return to the complete surrender of *The day is gone*. But it is much more intense, and perhaps for some readers hectic–'feverish', if we are inclined to use that Keatsian word.
2–5. Behind these lines we may detect that suspicious jealousy that was always part of the anguish of Keats's love for Fanny.
4. Unmasked: without concealment.
11–14. Compare *To [Fanny]*, lines 10–13 (p. 169).
14. gust: zest (with a suggestion of perceptive sharpness).

BRIGHT STAR (In spite of some past controversy, most probably composed October–November 1819).

This sonnet, expressing a yearning for a serene certainty and constancy in love, is the best of the final group of sonnets and without question one of the finest Keats ever wrote. Not to mention minor details of resemblance, its general movement and measured, resonant assurance of expression must remind us of Keats's first triumph in the sonnet form—*On First Looking into Chapman's Homer*.

1–4. There is probably a reminiscence here of the description of Windermere Keats has written to his brother Tom (25–27 June 1818)—especially of his words 'a sort of north star which can never cease to be open-lidded and steadfast over the wonders of the great Power'.

5–6. These lines, in which Keats represents the tides as performing a kind of religious cleansing, create a subtle shift in the development of the poem. The three preceding lines (2–4) are rhetorically negative and dismissive: in his desired state of love Keats does not wish to share the lonely isolation (and possibly not the sleeplessness) of the star. But with this further idea of purification—paralleled by the following reference to snow—the negative begins to turn into a positive, for now he is suggesting something that may be taken as part of his love ideal.

12. sweet unrest: a hint of the contraries involved in Keats's dream of love? At any rate there is a passing contradiction to the predominant yearning for a steadfast tranquillity.

14. With the key word 'swoon', this line is a striking reminder of how often in his poetry Keats associates the consummation of sexual love with death. See that revealing sentence in his letter to Fanny Brawne of 25 July 1819 (Letter 15, p. 179): 'I have two luxuries to brood over in my walks, your loveliness and the hour of my death.'

Letters II

LETTER 11.

19. among women: Keats was probably thinking particularly of the sisters of Reynolds.

31–2. 'with...power': Milton's *Comus*, line 816.

39. five feet high: Keats was 5 ft. ¾ in. in height. But he was broad-shouldered and struck people as taller. Also, the average height was lower then.

LETTER 12.

In the first of the two extracts from the 14–31 October journal letter to George and Georgiana, Keats is speaking of Jane Cox, the daughter of Mrs Reynolds's brother. She was born in India.

1. Charmian: one of Cleopatra's attendants in Shakespeare's *Antony and Cleopatra*.

6. particular: 'being particular' was a current expression for flirting.

14. tune of Mozart's: Keats makes several references to his enjoyment of Mozart's music.

36. John Howard (1726?–90): a famous philanthropist and reformer. *Hooker* (1554?–1600): author of *Laws of Ecclesiastical Polity*, but not a bishop.

41. that same lady: Mrs Isabella Jones, whom Keats first met at Hasting in May or June of 1817. After the October meeting described in the journal letter, Keats certainly saw her occasionally during the next two or three months. But how intimate their relationship was is uncertain. (For further information on this elusive figure see R. Gittings. *John Keats: The Living Year* and *The Mask of Keats*.)

43. English Opera: this was the Lyceum Theatre in the Strand. Keats is referring to a visit in May 1818.

81. Winander mere: Lake Windermere in the Lake District.

82. feel: the dash after this word seems to indicate the sudden breaking-off of one expression and the substitution of another.

86–7. The mighty . . . things: these words are often quoted in discussions of Keats's fundamental attitude to life and poetry. But they contain some ambiguity.

LETTER 13.

Keats probably met Fanny Brawne for the first time in the middle of November 1818; and there is a brief, earlier reference to her (16 December) in this journal letter. In this reference Keats writes that she is 'I think beautiful and elegant, graceful, silly, fashionable, and strange. We have a little tiff now and then, and she behaves a little better; or I must have sheered off.'

2–3. She . . . feature: presumably this means that not *all* Fanny's features are expressive or striking.

9. not seventeen: in fact Fanny was eighteen in August 1818.

LETTER 14.

This is the first of the extant love-letters to Fanny Brawne. It expresses the feverish conflict that underlies most of the love-letters that follow—the contradiction between the side of Keats that resisted his intense absorption in Fanny and the side that hungered for it. Though we know little for certain of the relations between the two up to July, it is a reasonable guess that one of Keats's motives for leaving London in the summer and early autumn—first for the Isle of Wight and then for Winchester—was the hope that physical absence from Fanny might perhaps, in some sort of way, alleviate this conflict.

This letter also introduces another recurrent note in the ones that were to follow–Keats's groundless suspicious of Fanny and his fits of jealousy.

3. Héloïse: Rousseau's famous novel, *La Nouvelle Héloïse*.

11. laughed...another: see the remarks on Haslam in Letter 19 (p. 182).

13. cottage window: the cottage, in which Keats was staying with Rice, was at the south end of the High Street in Shanklin, Isle of Wight.

39. Pam: the knave of clubs, highest trump in the card game of loo.

49–54. To...expression: a loose quotation from Massinger's play, *The Duke of Milan*, I.iii.206–7.

LETTER 15.

6. abstract poem: probably a reference to Keats's revision of *Hyperion* rather than to *Lamia*.

18. Severn: the painter Joseph Severn (1793–1879), an early and lifelong friend of Keats, who accompanied him to Italy in 1820 and looked after him in his last illness. Severn did much for the early growth of Keats's reputation. (See also the reference in Letter 19.)

28. You...myself: a particularly revealing sentence.

LETTER 16.

1. here: at Winchester. Keats had left Shanklin.

4. last... tragedy: the last act of *Otho the Great* was entirely Keats's own work.

17. brace... longer: this hope was mainly fulfilled, and in the last two of the four months in which he was away from London Keats completed the last act of *Otho the Great* and Part II of *Lamia*.

34. Idalia: Venus, the goddess of Love (from Idalium in Cyprus, where she was worshipped).

LETTER 18.

On 10 September 1819 Keats heard from George that, in an unfortunate business venture, he had lost about half the money he had taken to America. George wished his brother to approach Richard Abbey, once their guardian and still controlling certain inheritance money that was due to them; and Keats immediately took the night coach to London. Though he was unable to see Abbey till Monday evening (13 September), he decided not to meet Fanny Brawne. The letter was written on Monday morning.

17. I... Walthamstow: to visit his sister Fanny, who lived with her guardian, Abbey.

LETTER 20.

23–4. 'to . . . love': from Ford's play '*Tis pity she's a Whore*, 1.iii. The line in Giovanni's speech reads: 'Reasoned against the reason of my love'.

LETTER 21.

6–7. You . . . new: compare *Fancy*, lines 69–76 (p.222).

Poems Various

TO MY BROTHER GEORGE (August 1816).
This verse letter, written from Margate, was one of three such pieces included in *Poems 1817*. (The other two were addressed to his friends G. F. Mathew and C. C. Clarke respectively.)

These epistles owe something to the example of the Elizabethan poets William Browne and Michael Drayton, and something to that of Leigh Hunt. They closely resemble one another in their mainly autobiographical and literary content, their familiar tone, and their loose treatment of the pentameter couplet. As early work, they all reveal a mixture of good, bad, and indifferent writing. Perhaps, for its subject matter, *To my Brother George* is the most interesting.

1–5. To a large extent the epistle is an attempt to break out of this frustrating deadness by writing—not for the first or last time—a poem about poetry.

7–8. Very Hunt-like in the feminine rhyme and use of 'divinely'. See also lines 15–16.

12. golden lyre: i.e. of the poet-god Apollo.

19. Poets were traditionally crowned with a wreath of bay (laurel) leaves.

24. Libertas: Leigh Hunt, signifying his liberal political views.

25–46. An expression of that dream of medieval chivalry, derived from Spenser and to some extent from Leigh Hunt, that inspired such early poems as *Specimen of an Induction to a Poem* and *Calidore* and culminated in *The Eve of St Agnes* (pp. 132–42).

38. fit for the silvering: This vague phrase would seem to suggest some shining quality of a divine dream.

40. bright spots: the stars (?).

46. rose: as a type of tangible, merely earthly, beauty.

50–3. Some of the more admirable lines of the poem.

56. A characteristically Keatsian sensation.

66. spell: cast a spell over.

73–6. Under Leigh Hunt's influence Keats had at this time quite a strong belief in the possible political significance of poetry. But

305

the effect of this belief is only slightly evident in his work, and the following passage (lines 81–103), concerned with 'lays' of 'dear delight', expresses a much more central and engrossing aspiration.

99. glistening circlet: eyeballs.

112. dearer to society: more social. But Keats was never an unsocial person–far from it.

126. tablet: the paper Keats was writing on.

130. scarlet coats: soldiers. Keats's Huntian, liberal views included a strong antimilitarism.

139. into the west: towards London, where George remained.

'HOW MANY BARDS' (1816, probably October).

One interest of this sonnet is that it probably intimates something of Keats's easy, spontaneous assimilation of his chosen literary 'influences'. The sestet also admirably expresses his particular sensitivity to soft, subdued, remote sounds.

1. gild: something like 'goldenly illuminate'. *lapses*: past periods.

12–*13. thousand . . . bereaves*: innumerable sounds not distinctly recognizable because of distance.

ON FIRST LOOKING INTO CHAPMAN'S HOMER (October 1816).

One evening Cowden Clarke read to Keats some passages of Homer in the translation of the poet and dramatist George Chapman (1559–1634). By ten o'clock next morning Clarke received the first draft of this sonnet. With its effortless strength, condensation, assurance, and faultlessness, it is the outstanding single piece in *Poems 1817*; and more than anything else in that volume, which contained much mediocre writing, it might have revealed to a prescient reader of the time firm promise of the major poetry to come.

1. Though the immediate reference is to poetry of supreme achievement (compare '*How many Bards*', line 1.), the metaphor later links up with the reference to exploration for the gold of the New World.

4. in fealty: as feudal under-lords.

7. serene: clear, perfect sky. Note, as an example of Keats's frequent revisionary improvements, his original version of this line–'Yet could I never judge what men could mean'.

9–*10*. Herschel's discovery of the planet Uranus in 1781.

11. It was Bilboa, not Cortez, who first caught sight of the Pacific from the Darien isthmus. But this slip does not seriously affect the sonnet's memorable conclusion.

TO MY BROTHERS (18 November 1816).

Though this sonnet has little poetic distinction, it is a charming (and, at the end, poignant) expression of Keats's deep and intimate relationship with his brothers, Tom and George. The three brothers had just taken lodgings together at 17 Cheapside.

3. household gods: a reference to the Roman belief in such deities (the Lares).

7. lore: of poetry; *voluble*: fluent, eloquent.

'GREAT SPIRITS NOW ON EARTH' (19 or 20 November 1816).
This is the second of three sonnets addressed to the painter, Benjamin Haydon, who, counteracting the recent influence of Leigh Hunt on Keats, 'did more than anyone else in the crucial year ahead to jolt Keats out of the restricted and coy approach to art with which he had inevitably been tempted' (W. J. Bate, *John Keats*, p. 86). The poem also expresses Keats's strong sense of the great artistic stirrings of his time.

2-4. A reference to Wordsworth.

5-6. Leigh Hunt, imprisoned 1813–15 for libel on the Prince Regent.

7-8. These lines suggest Haydon's inspiration ('whisperings') from Raphael.

13. At Haydon's admirable suggestion this line was shortened from the original 'Of mighty workings in a distant mart'.

SLEEP AND POETRY (October-December 1816).
Printed last in *Poems 1817*, this work of 404 lines was Keats's longest piece to date. Part of it was written in Leigh Hunt's Hampstead cottage, and it may be regarded as Keats's chief poetic memorial to Hunt. Though there are some admirable passages, the writing is still very uneven.

57-9. Luxury, signifying intense sensuous relish, is a key word in Keats's writing. *Intoxication* and *die a death* intimate the swooning, the oblivion, perhaps the latent death-wish, that he was more and more to associate with intensities of sensuous experience.

58. bays: as in *To my Brother George*, line 19 (p. 187), signifying the poet's laurel crown.

61-3. Keats appears to be saying here that to one inspired by poesy all places may yield beauty, their 'fair visions'.

63. bowery nook: as more extensively in lines 117–21, another example of this common image.

74. Meander: a winding river in Asia Minor.

81-4. As later, in lines 123–5, Keats seems to be glancing at a poetry of more serious intent.

83. tease: perhaps in the sense of 'agitate with perplexities'. Keats uses this word in several other poems (e.g. *Ode on a Grecian Urn* line 44, p. 86) with varying shades of meaning.

85–95. In this passage the brevity and precariousness of life is sharply set against its joys (if transient).

89. The river Montmorenci has a waterfall just before it joins the St Lawrence below Quebec.

96–162. See the Introduction for a discussion of this passage.

113–16. I. Jack in *Keats and the Mirror of Art* has suggested that this and several other details (e.g. lines 126–8) owe something to Poussin's painting *L'Empire de Flore*.

117–21. For an outstanding example of this typically Keatsian sensation of being smothered in vegetation see *Ode to a Nightingale* stanza 5 (p. 83). And note, as also in lines 68 and 74, the significance of silence.

'I STOOD TIP-TOE' (finished December 1816).

This long poem, the composition of which was probably spread over several months, moves from landscape description (some of which reveals touches of sensitive observation) to something like a shortened version of the Endymion story. In fact Keats did for a time call the poem *Endymion*.

Among other things the selected extract demonstrates his delight in classical myth and legend.

116–24. As image, and sometimes symbol, the moon persists throughout Keats's poetry.

125–40. In this passage Keats gives Romantic ideas about nature a somewhat unusual turn. He appears to suggest that various qualities of nature, its grandeur, its sustaining solace, its sensuous richness, influence a poet even when he is not directly writing about it.

129. stayed: This is our modern 'staid', but the intended meaning is uncertain.

132–6. Again the Keatsian sensation of a smothering in flowers, etc. This is in fact a description of what frequently happens in his *Endymion* when that tale moves 'on luxurious wings'.

141–204. The link between the preceding passage and the retold classical legends that follow is the idea, almost certainly derived from Wordsworth's *Excursion* (IV.847–87), that many of the classical deities were personifications of early man's imaginative response to various aspects of nature.

141–50. This story of the mortal woman Psyche, who was wooed by the god Eros, was 'first told' by the Latin writer Apuleius in *The Golden Ass*. Keats knew this work through Adlington's translation (1566), and he returned to the story in his ode *To Psyche* (see pp. 231–2).

147–50. These lines briefly summarize much of the story—Psyche breaking the condition of secret meetings in the dark, Eros's

temporary abandonment of her, their ultimate reunion in heaven.
157–62. This legend is told in Ovid's *Metamorphoses*. Pursued by
the love-smitten Pan, Syrinx changed into a marsh reed.
162. This line expresses a common Keatsian paradox, particularly
so far as love is concerned.
163–80. The story of Narcissus, who, spurning the love of Echo,
fell in love with his own water-reflected image and was then
transformed into a flower, was also related in Ovid's *Metamorphoses*.
168. *cool*: for 'coolness'.
175. *Zephyrus*: the classical name for the bland west wind.
182–3. This description of the Endymion story hardly indicates
the profound allegorical meanings that have been read by some
commentators into *Endymion*.
187–8. *flowery nests...pillowy silkiness*: Is Keats thinking, as so
often, of someone reclining on flowers or soft grass? Compare, for
example, *To my Brother George*, line 123 (p. 189).
189. *speculation*: sight (not implying meditation).
194. *Latmos*: the mountain in Asia Minor where the moon-goddess
(Diana or Cynthia) appeared to the mortal Endymion.
199–204. The idea is that the poet invented the love story out of
compassion for the loneliness of Diana.
203. *fine wrath*: the poetic 'furor' or frenzy.
205–10. Keats begins to tell of the auspicious wedding-night of
Cynthia and Endymion.
212. *Phoebus*: the sun-god, delaying the nightly descent of his
chariot.
217. *like Homer*: the point of this allusion is not clear.
218. *young Apollo*: a reference to the famous classical statue of
the Belvedere Apollo.
221–4. One of numerous references to the pleasant sensation of
cool breezes.
241. *Was... born?*: Was Keats thinking of his full-scale *Endymion*,
soon to be started?

'AFTER DARK VAPOURS' (31 January 1817).
This sonnet is particularly rich in characteristic images and
sensations, notably in the sestet's combination of soft sounds and
tranquil mood.
1–4. Compare *The Fall of Hyperion*, lines 97–101 (p. 93).
5. *month*: Possibly a misprint for 'mouth'.
10–11. Something of a prelude hint of the ode *To Autumn*.
12. *Sappho*: a famous Greek poetess. Hunt had a bust of her in his
cottage.
14. Note how these 'calmest thoughts' come to a strange climax in
'a poet's death'. The poet alluded to may be Chatterton.

TO LEIGH HUNT, ESQ. (late February 1817). This was the dedication sonnet addressed to Leigh Hunt in *Poems 1817*. It again expresses Keats's dream of the beauty of pagan rites and worship, and so perhaps bears on the meaning of the fourth stanza of *Ode on a Grecian Urn*.

5–8. Possibly another recollection of Poussin's *L'Empire de Flore*.
13. leafy luxury: This phrase, taken from the Preface to Hunt's *Nymphs*, epitomizes a predominant sensation in Keats's poetry.

ON SEEING THE ELGIN MARBLES (just before 3 March 1817).
This sonnet forms a sharp and significant contrast with the last. It was partly through such artistic works as these sculptures from the Parthenon, recently acquired by the British Museum, that Haydon weaned Keats from the Huntian cult of prettiness to grander conceptions of poetry–'Grecian grandeur', 'a shadow of a magnitude'.

1. mortality: human limitations, weakness.
7–8. This would seem to be a fanciful description of the eagle's activities.
13–14. billowy main...sun: images of magnitude and glory.
14. shadow: probably something like 'intimation'.

ON THE SEA (17 April 1817).
In part this sonnet, written in the Isle of Wight just before Keats started on *Endymion*, expresses something of the sense of vastness and majestic power alluded to in the previous one.

3–4. The reference here is to the turn of the tide, controlled by Hecate (one of the names of the moon-goddess).
4. shadowy sound: compare *The Fall of Hyperion*, line 6 (p. 91). The main emphasis of the poem is, characteristically, on such subdued sound.
14. quired: sang in a choir.

ENDYMION, I.232–306 and IV.146–290.
Whatever their strictures on the poem as a whole, most critics have praised two sustained passages–the songs to Pan and to Bacchus.
I.*232–306*.
At the beginning of the poem Endymion's Latmian people assemble for a religious festival in honour of Pan, the god of nature. After performing certain rites, the priests sing a hymn to the god.
232–3. In the poem the sides of Mount Latmos are represented as covered by a 'mighty forest' (line 64).
236. hamadryads: tree nymphs.
238–43. See '*I stood tip-toe*', lines 157–62 (p. 199).
241. pipy hemlock: Musical pipes were made from the substantial,

hollow stem of the hemlock. Pan was the reputed inventor of the
syrinx or reed pipe.

247–62. This stanza is particularly rich in packed, sensuous
impressions–characteristically, of growth and ripeness.

247. turtles: turtle doves.

248. Passion: give feeling to (an Elizabethan word).

254. leas: fields (normally for pasture).

256. chuckling: a clucking, nesting sound.

258. summer coolness: a rather odd, but very Keatsian, association
with strawberries; *pent-up:* still in the chrysalis stage.

261. The pine was emblematically associated with Pan.

288–9. From this point in the hymn onwards Pan is celebrated as
more than the god of fertility and of nature in the limited sense of
the word: he is an inspiration to that imaginative insight into
the 'burden of the mystery' that Keats increasingly sought.

290. In classical mythology Dryope was the mortal wife of Apollo
and the mother of Amphissius. Keats probably got this unusual
genealogy from Chapman's *Hymn to Pan.*

293. lodge: lodging-place, focus.

294–6. Very difficult lines to interpret. It has been suggested that
'solitary thinkings' are intuitive, imaginative insights and 'conception' a term for rational thought. But there is no certainty about
such an antithesis. 'Then leave the naked brain' is another
obscure expression.

295. bourne: boundary, limit.

306. Mount Lycaeus in Arcadia was sacred to Pan.

IV.*146–290.*
After his long, frustrated search after Cynthia, Endymion en-
counters a mysterious Indian maid, who sings this song to him. The
opening of Letter 2 (pp. 98–9) would seem to offer a clear lead to
the reading of the first part of the song. But unless we are to take it
that it is the beauty of the song itself that has been created by the
maid's grief, it is not entirely obvious how Keats's comment applies.
However, the familiar juxtaposition of joy and sorrow is evident
enough.

The opulent description of the procession of Bacchus furnishes a
good example of the way in which Keats's poetry was often
influenced by works of art–here, almost certainly, by Titian's
Bacchus and Ariadne.

157. Siren: a hint of delusive love? *spry:* spray.

178. kind: Perhaps more in the Elizabethan sense of 'kinship',
'bound by human ties'.

190–2. The idea expressed in these lines would fit the situation
of Endymion; and perhaps the Indian maid, who is really Cynthia,

is momentarily putting herself in his place.

194–5. The rills... hue: the river was tinged with streams of wine.

205. berried holly: emblematic of winter.

210. trifling: playing with.

215. Silenus, the foster-parent of Bacchus, is shown in *Bacchus and Ariadne* riding an ass.

228. Satyrs: classical demigods of the countryside, horned, hairy, and with goatish legs and feet.

232. kernel: see the previous line.

239–42. What is being represented is Bacchus's legendary conquest of the East.

241. In *Bacchus and Ariadne* Bacchus's chariot is pulled by leopards.

247. coil: bustle (an Elizabethan word).

256. spleenful: testy, or spirited, or impulsive. (Shakespeare has various meanings for the word.)

257. Osirian: Osiris was one of the chief gods of ancient Egypt.

261. whelming: conquering.

265. Great Brahma: in Hindu mythology the creator of the universe.

270. Compare the *Ode to a Nightingale*, line 20 (p. 82).

273–90. A return to the sorrow theme–and to the lyric stanzas of the opening.

ROBIN HOOD (February 1818).

This fairly light-hearted example of Keats's medievalism, slightly touched with the note of transience and mortality, was stimulated by two sonnets by Reynolds on Robin Hood. As in *Lines on the Mermaid Tavern* (p. 248), written about the same time, Keats uses a trochaic, four-stress couplet that was probably modelled on Milton's *L'Allegro* and *Il Penseroso* and Fletcher's *The Faithful Shepherdess*.

6–9. An image of sheep-shearing.

10. This flagrantly untrue reference to medieval conditions was probably intended as a jest, since Reynolds was training to become a solicitor, much concerned with such things.

13. ivory: i.e. the hunting-horn.

22. right: guide.

33. morris din: sound of the medieval morris dance.

34. song of Gamelyn: *The Tale of Gamelyn* was a well-known medieval romance.

36. 'grenè shawe': from Chaucer's *The Friar's Tale*, line 87; *shawe*: grove or small wood.

43–5. A realistic reference to the naval side of the recent Napoleonic wars.

55. tight: adroit, or vigorous, or perhaps well-made (several meanings possible).

62. burden: chorus.

'FOUR SEASONS FILL' (7–13 March 1818).
This sonnet, with a strong Shakespearian accent, expresses Keats's ideal of an unstrained, passive responsiveness.
7. nigh: come nigh (as verb).
12. threshold: near some dwelling.
13. misfeature: possibly something like 'ill-favoured appearance'.

TO HOMER (April-May 1818).
'I shall learn Greek... I long to feast upon old Homer as we have upon Shakespeare and as I have lately upon Milton' (to Reynolds, 27 April 1818). Indirectly, no doubt, the sonnet expresses a hope of the vision that may yet come to himself as a poet–at the moment 'Lost in a sort of Purgatory blind'.
2. Cyclades: Greek islands.
5. With the rest of the sonnet compare Keats's observation written on his copy of *Paradise Lost*: 'It can scarcely be conceived how Milton's blindness might here aid the magnitude of his conceptions.'
8. A reference to the Homeric *Hymn to Pan*, which Keats knew from Chapman's translation.
12. triple: probably of the heaven of the gods, the underworld, and earth.
14. Under her various classical names Phoebe (Cynthia), Diana, Hecate, the goddess had this triple dominion.

ODE TO MAY (1 May 1818).
One feature of the ancient Greek world that particularly attracted Keats was what he called in the ode *To Psyche* (p. 232) its 'happy pieties'. There is a hint of that feeling in this fragment, which, in form, can be seen as an experimentation towards the odes of 1819.
1. Maia, who gave her name to the month, was a wife of Jupiter and the mother of Hermes (Mercury). The early lines take her worship back in time.
3. Baiae: a town on the bay of Naples.
10. quiet primrose: as appropriate to the season. And note 'quiet'.

'AH, KEN YE WHAT I MET' (9 July 1818).
This was one of the poems written during the Scottish tour with Charles Brown. In the metre and sentiment (especially of the last four lines) there is perhaps some hint of the future *La Belle Dame Sans Merci* (pp. 144–5).
1. ken: know.
5. yeve: give.

11. rig: ridge.
18. canting: brisk.
20. shallop: a kind of boat.
35. daffed: a northern dialect word–'lacking in spirit' (?).

TO AILSA ROCK (10 July 1818).
Of the Romantic poets it was Shelley who did most to bring poetry into contact with science. But this sonnet, with its powerfully imaginative vision of geological evolution, is interesting for the speculation of what Keats might, just possibly, have done in this area of experience. He regarded it as the best of the five sonnets writtens during the Scottish tour.
6. fathom: fathoms deep.
13. steep: something like 'slope up' (?).

'WHERE'S THE POET?' (October 1818).
This can be regarded as a poetic version of some of the observations in Letter 30 (pp.238–9).
8–10. 'If a sparrow come before my window I take part in its existence and pick about the gravel' (Letter 2, p. 100).

FANCY (December 1818).
Essentially–though not to deny the existence of some fine lines– this poem is yet another catalogue of 'luxuries' of the kind Keats had composed so many times before, with a continuous emphasis on pleasure. It is a poetic product of those delightful 'imaginings' he had so often written about; and this time his word for such imagin- ings is 'Fancy'–a voluntary imaginative power capable of reviving past delights, of freely interchanging and intermingling times and places, and (so Keats would believe) devoid of the inevitable cloyment of the sensuous and erotic pleasures of actuality.
    In its metrical form, like its companion piece '*Bards of Passion*', the poem returns to the four-stress, trochaic couplets of *Robin Hood*.
1–4. Explained by lines 10–15 and later 68–78.
6. The word 'thought' makes this line a little obscure. The version of the poem that appears in his journal-letter to his brother and sister-in-law of 16 December 1818 to 4 January 1819 has the much clearer line 'Towards heaven still spread beyond her'.
13–15. Autumn is personified. The journal-letter has 'kissing' for 'tasting'.
15–18. Compare *Sleep and Poetry*, lines 71–3 (p. 195). The fire seems to be envisaged as some kind of household spirit.
21. shoon: archaic plural of 'shoe'.
22–4. The short winter day, with no gradual twilight.

26. Presumably this means that the 'mind', as intellectual activity, is suppressed.

34. dewy sward: All through Keats's poetry there is this association of vegetation with life-giving moisture; see also lines 53–4 and *The Eve of St Mark*, lines 10–11 (p. 226).

36. still: quiet (?). 'Still' is a key, though ambiguously elusive, word in Keats's vocabulary.

38. three: hereabouts Keats is describing an intermingling of spring, summer, and autumn.

69–76. Compare *Ode on a Grecian Urn*, lines 25–30 (p. 85).

79–89. This harks back to the young man's erotic dream, at the heart of *Endymion*, of some ideal lover. In the journal-letter version this eroticism is amplified.

81. Ceres' daughter: Proserpine. Compare *Lamia*, 1. 63 (p. 152).

82. God of Torment: Pluto, who carried Proserpine away into the underworld.

85. Hebe: a goddess and cup-bearer to the gods.

90. silken leash: Fancy is represented as a bird held by some light, silken tether.

'BARDS OF PASSION AND OF MIRTH' (probably December 1818).
This poem was also included in the journal-letter of 16 December –January 1819, and Keats explains–'it is on the double immortality of poets'.

8. parle: speech.

20. numbers: poetic utterance.

28. Never slumbered: i.e. never suffering that insensate kind of 'indolence' that Keats himself sometimes experienced. For something of a gloss on the phrase see *Hyperion* III, lines 86–91 (p. 78). It is also significant that the ideal heavenly life of the poets is 'never cloying'. This links the poem with much of the sentiment in its companion-piece, *Fancy* (pp. 221–3).

29–36. Keats is not suggesting that great immortal poetry is directly didactic. But he is describing it as something beyond delightful 'imaginings', dreams, and the sensuously pleasurable.

THE EVE OF ST MARK (13–17 February 1819; lines 101–16 probably added after 20 September 1819).
In spite of its title, some medieval colouring, the use of another popular superstition, and its date of composition, this fragment bears no important resemblance to *The Eve of St Agnes*. Partly because of the very different metrical form, the writing, in its cadences, constructions, and expression generally, is crisper and simpler; it is also much more restrained–delicate sometimes–in its sensuous suggestion. Further, there are some sophisticated, not

altogether serious touches of a kind not to be found in *The Eve of St Agnes*.

2. Twice holy: because the Sunday was also St Mark's Day, 25 April.

12. aguish: An ague is a shivering fit, but otherwise the meaning of the adjective is not clear.

16. orat'ries: Keats uses this word in *The Eve of St Agnes*, line 16 (p. 132). But here the implication is ironical.

25–38. As R. Gittings has shown (*John Keats: the Living Year*, pp. 87–9), many of the details of this illuminated book were taken from the stained-glass window of the chapel of Stanstead House on the Sussex–Hampshire border, which Keats had recently visited.

28. golden broideries: probably referring to the gold-leaf illustrations.

33–34. See Leviticus, 8:8. and *Revelation*, 1:20.

35. The lion was the emblem of St Mark.

36–8. See *Hebrews*, 9:4–5 and 1 *Samuel*, 6:4.

45. Because protected, the elms and sycamores were in unusually early leaf.

47. pile: of the cathedral or minster.

71. cheated: because of her difficulty of finding light.

79–84. A reference to a kind of Chinese screen still fashionable in Keats's time. Though such screens were very fancifully decorated, there may be a deliberately grotesque touch in the description that fits in with a playful, mocking, slightly ironic tone that delicately plays over the poem. Was it just accident that Keats linked his comic *The Cap and Bells* (pp. 253–6) with Bertha?

83. Av'davat: the avadavat is an Indian bird.

88–90. Perhaps a hint of sinister developments to come: the queen of spades stands for death.

95. learned eremite: the scholar-recluse who had written the *curious volume*.

96. star or dagger: signs to indicate the footnotes, which were in a much smaller script.

100. parcelled out: divided into smaller sections (as additional footnotes?)

101–32. This passage, in imitation Middle English, includes the St Mark's Eve superstition. This was the belief that during the midnight hours the spirits of those who were to die the following year could be seen passing into church. D. G. Rossetti surmised that Bertha was to be represented as a woman whose treatment of her lover led to his death.

109. carle: one of low birth (as opposed to *gent*).

110. in parle: perhaps 'in his power'.

117. Als: also; *swevenis*: dreams.

123. modre: mother.
131. auctorith: writes.
134. martyrdom: of St Mark.

TO SLEEP (probably April 1819).
One of the handful of experimental sonnets that Keats composed in the spring of 1819. It has obvious connections with *Ode to a Nightingale*, written shortly afterwards, and with the mood of 'half in love with easeful Death'.
1. embalmer: Note this significant word, and compare with line 43 of *Ode to a Nightingale* (p. 83); also compare 'still midnight' with line 56 of the ode.
7. wait the 'Amen': wait till the close of this hymn.
8. The original draft reads: 'Its sweet death-dews o'er every pulse and limb'.
11. curious: something like 'intently inquiring, probing, etc.'

ODE TO PSYCHE (between 21 and 30 April 1819).
At the beginning of his commentary on this first 1819 ode W. J. Bate (*John Keats*, pp. 487–95) rightly stresses its peculiar 'elusive' quality, the way it has 'always puzzled readers'.

The main puzzle is what kind and depth of meaning we are to read into it. From one point of view it might be regarded as an opulently described, semi-narrative 'imagining', like something from *Endymion* but quite unlike anything in the other odes, followed and completed by an extensive conceit, also without parallel in the other odes–a conceit in which a goddess who came too late for celebration as a classical deity is now celebrated in the poet's imagination and the present poem.

This would be to read it, like most of the older critics, as essentially a poem of embellishment and decorative writing, of detached artistic making, much nearer to *Fancy* than to the *Ode to a Nightingale;* and this approach might fit in with Keats's own confession of 'leisurely' composition, in a particularly 'peaceable and healthy spirit'.

From another point of view, taken by several modern critics, the ode may seem to hold some depth of conceptual meaning. Thus Bate, associating it closely with the 'chambers of consciousness' letter (6, pp. 103–4), interprets it as a 'credo' of Keats's resolution to devote his poetic imagination to an exploration of the modern human psyche as it now finds itself in those 'dark passages' that are also mentioned in the letter. (See also the essay by K. Allott in *John Keats: A Reassessment*, pp. 74–94.)

There is no space here to contest the Bate view. But if we are

317

to find some valid deeper meaning in the poem—at the same time paying due regard to its beginning and end—might it be that Keats, in the first ecstasy of his passion for Fanny Brawne, is simply celebrating the human spirit in and for its relationship with new-found love? Again, what of Roger Sharrock's conclusion that '*Psyche* suggests that human love may become a substitute for religious faith'?

1–4. A reminiscence of the opening of Milton's *Lycidas*, especially of line 6.

4. conchèd: shell-like.

14. Ancient Tyre was noted for the production of a purple dye.

20. eye-dawn: awakening; *auroran*: renewing itself like the dawn. (Aurora was the goddess of dawn.)

21. wingèd boy: Eros (Cupid).

27. Vesper: the goddess of the evening star.

30–5. Some reminiscence here of Milton's *Nativity Ode*, especially of lines 179–80 and 191.

34. heat: implying a feverish state of trance, divine inspiration, etc.

36. antique vows: worship accorded by classical antiquity. 'You must recollect that Psyche was not embodied as a goddess before the time of Apuleius, the Platonist, who lived after the Augustan age, and consequently the goddess was never worshipped or sacrificed to with any of the ancient fervour. . . I am more orthodox than to let a heathen goddess be so neglected' (journal-letter to George and Georgiana Keats, 14 February to 3 May 1819).

37. fond believing lyre: poets of the 'happy pieties', who would have voiced their devotion to Psyche.

41. lucent fans: shining wings.

42. faint: synonymous with 'faded' in line 25.

50–62. In this passage Keats represents his mind and imagination in terms of a place of worship for Psyche. The literal and the metaphorical constantly interchange and intermingle. Some of the descriptive details may have been suggested by Adlington's translation of the Psyche story; and in lines 54–5 Keats echoes an expression from one of his Scottish letters to his brother Tom.

52. branchèd: suggestive of a natural, organic, tree-like growth of poetic conceptions.

59–63. The image of the 'rosy sanctuary', very appropriate to a celebration of love, hardly fits Bate's interpretation of this last stanza. And 'Fancy' cannot signify imagination in any deep sense: it means the impulse that prompted the poem printed immediately after *To Psyche* in the 1820 volume—'Ever let the fancy roam'.

62. feign: invent (in the Elizabethan sense).

65. shadowy: perhaps 'vaguely suggestive' or 'indulging in fancy'.

66–7. In the legend Psyche's use of a bright torch to discover the

318

identity of the lover who visited her in darkness nearly brought disaster.

'IF BY DULL RHYMES' (probably between 30 April and 3 May 1819). This sonnet, the last of Keats's sonnet experiments in the spring of 1819, is a poetic statement of his dissatisfaction with both the Petrarchan and Shakespearian forms. In its rhyming and structure it breaks away from both.

2. In the classical story Andromeda was chained to a rock and later rescued by Perseus from a sea monster.

5. Sandals: the rhyme scheme (which, in this sonnet, is more 'interwoven' than usual).

11. Midas was a miserly king to whom Bacchus granted the power of turning all he touched into gold.

'THIS LIVING HAND' (probably November 1819). This fragment, possibly intended for use some time in a play, has a singular vividness of expression and plasticity of rhythm. It is an elaboration of the image in *The Fall of Hyperion*, line 18 (p. 91).

Letters III

LETTER 23.
In this extract Keats is writing with special reference to *Endymion*.
8. Mrs Williams: some imaginary woman.
10–11. fancy: imagination: usually synonymous for Keats.

LETTER 24.
1. a wonderful picture: *Death on the Pale Horse* by Benjamin West (1738–1820).
1–3. But...reality: Compare 'Whenever we look at the hands of Correggio's women or of Raphael's, we always wish to touch them' (W. Hazlitt, 'On Gusto'). Hazlitt's term 'gusto' is very close in meaning to 'intensity' and 'intense', which are key words in Keats's ideas about art and poetry.
10. Dilke: see Letter 28, note.
17. verisimilitude: truth.
18. penetralium: 'An admirable phrase!–if only penetralium were Latin' (Colvin, *John Keats*, p. 48 n); *penetralia*: inmost parts.

LETTER 25. In this extract Keats has Wordsworth particularly in mind. A few sentences before he asks: 'for the sake of a few fine imaginative or domestic passages are we to be bullied into a certain philosophy engendered in the whims of an egoist?' But at other times his attitude to Wordsworth's poetry is much more favourable. See, for example, Letter 6 (p. 104).

LETTER 26.
Historically speaking, Keats's first axiom is rather an odd mixture. The stress on 'excess' is Romantic. Samuel Palmer (1805–81), whose paintings often reveal a close kinship with Keats's poetry, wrote: 'Excess is the essential vivifying spirit... of the finest art'. But the rest of the axiom is pure eighteenth century doctrine, as we may see from Johnson's praise of Gray's *Elegy* in his *Lives of the Poets*.

LETTER 27.
2. Jack a lanthern: the will o'-the wisp–a misleading light.
9. passages of Shakespeare: typical of Keats's worship of Shakespeare to include him among 'Things real'.
13–14. stamps...minds: Keats means something like 'shows the high quality of our minds'.
14–15. 'consecrate...upon': an echo of Shelley's *Hymn to Intellectual Beauty'*, stanza 2.

LETTER 28.
Charles Wentworth Dilke (1789–1864) was at this period a civil servant with strong literary interests. For a time he shared the Hampstead house, Wentworth Place, with Charles Brown; and he was an early friend of Keats. He did much to establish the poet's reputation, as did his grandson, Sir Charles Wentworth Dilke.
1. His identity: i.e. of his dying brother Tom. For further understanding of 'identity' see Letter 30 (pp. 238–9).
3–4. abstract images: Keats is referring here to *Hyperion*.
6–7. 'the...contraries': *Paradise Lost*, IX.121–2.

LETTER 29.
James Augustus Hessey (1785–1870) was a partner in John Taylor's publishing business. Keats was on less intimate terms with him than he was with Taylor, the dominant partner. The extract refers to *Endymion*.

LETTER 30.
Richard Woodhouse (1788–1834) was the scholarly literary and legal adviser to Taylor and Hessey. In several ways he proved a kind and helpful friend to Keats, who had a considerable respect for him. Students of Keats will always be greatly indebted to him. 'He devoted much time to his Keatsiana, collecting and copying

every poem, letter, anecdote, proof-sheet he could lay his hands on'
(H. E. Rollins, *The Letters of John Keats*, 1, p. 92).

1. poetical character: in view of what follows, 'character' may be a
little misleading, since Keats's essential point is that the poet has no
character or self.

3. Wordsworthian...sublime: Keats is not saying anything deroga-
tory about Wordsworth.

4. per se...alone: *Troilus and Cressida*, 1.ii.15–16.

6. gusto: Keats may have owed this word, an intenser synonym of
the following 'delight' and 'relish', to Hazlitt. See Hazlitt's essay
On Gusto.

8. Imogen: the admirable heroine of *Cymbeline*.

11–12. because...speculation: compare the last sentence of the comment on West's *Death on the Pale Horse*, in Letter 24 (p. 236).

14. informing: a commonly accepted emendation for 'in for',
though Keats may have intended these two words.

19–20. I...more: at a dinner-party given by Hessey on 14 September 1818 Keats had made some such statement. Woodhouse took it
up in his letter of 21 October, to which Keats was now replying: 'I
understood you to say you thought there was now nothing original
to be written in poetry, that its riches were already exhausted and
all its beauties forestalled, and that you should, consequently,
write no more.'

21. Saturn and Ops: characters in *Hyperion*. Though Keats was
writing *Hyperion* at the time of this letter, he had not started it when
he originally made his statement.

24. identical: possessing an identity, as in Letter 9.

26–7. not...myself: the meaning is something like 'I am not then
brought to a consciousness of myself'.

27–8. identity...me: compare the beginning of Letter 28 (p. 237).

32. that day: at Hessey's dinner-party.

34–5. I...good: compare his remark to Taylor some six months
previously: 'I find there is no worthy pursuit but the idea of doing
some good for the world' (Letter 5, p. 103).

LETTER 32.

3–4. the principle...things: See Letter 12 (p. 176) (second extract).

LETTER 33.

Up to the time of his Scottish tour all Keats had directly known of
nature had been the soft, lush landscape of southern England. This
delighted discovery of the stone-hard qualities of the northern
landscape probably had some influence on the imagery of *Hyperion*, which is so different from that of all his preceding work.

10. finest spirits: probably Keats had Wordsworth especially in mind.

LETTER 34.
During their Scottish tour Keats and Charles Brown made a very brief visit to northern Ireland. After their crossing from Portpatrick they walked from Donaghadee to Belfast and back.
5. impetiosity: neither M. B. Forman nor H. E. Rollins comments on this word. The obvious correction 'impetuosity' would pro-produce a completely disconnected remark. Did Keats intend 'impecuniosity'?
17. with child: The Faerie Queene, I.V.I.
23. bounty money: given to a recruit on enlistment. This and the following sentence indicate the extent to which Irishmen were forced, through poverty, into military service.
26–7. Duchess of Dunghill: an imaginary name for the occupant of the sedan-chair.
30. squat: crouched down.
34. squab: means short and *stout*. Rollins thinks Keats intended to repeat 'squat'.

LETTER 35.
1. Fingal's Cave: on the island of Staffa.
17. is very grand: these words are supplied from a similar description in the September 17–27 journal-letter to George and Georgiana.

LETTER 36.
A description of Ben Nevis, the highest mountain in Great Britain.
19. dome curtains: perhaps recollected in *Hyperion*, 1.180–1, (p. 63).
26. discovering: in the old sense of uncovering, disclosing.

Lighter Verse

TO MRS REYNOLDS'S CAT (16 January 1818).
Mrs Reynolds was the mother of Keats's friend, John Reynolds.
13. the lists: in which knightly jousts were fought.

LINES ON THE MERMAID TAVERN (around 3 February 1818).
The Mermaid Tavern in Cheapside was reputedly the meeting place of certain Elizabethan poets and dramatists. This poem was included in a letter to Reynolds of 3 February 1818 along with *Robin Hood*: hence the reference in lines 9–12.
12. bowse: drink.
17. sheepskin: parchment.

19. new old sign:–the tavern sign-board was now hanging in heaven.

'OH I AM FRIGHTENED' (Spring 1818).
These lines were probably suggested by Shakespeare's sonnet CXXX.
9. crumped up: made bandy.

'OVER THE HILL AND OVER THE DALE' (23 March 1818).
This was written after a visit to Dawlish Fair during Keats's spring holiday in Devon.
2. bourn: stream.
5. Rantipole: expressive dialect for a 'fast' one.

OLD MEG (2 July 1818).
This ballad was one of the poems written during the Scottish tour. There is a slightly Wordsworthian ring about it.
28. A chip hat was a hat made out of thin wooden strips.

THE CAP AND BELLS (November–December 1819).
This uncompleted comic fairy poem of 794 lines was Keats's last substantial work. In its satirical hits at the love life of the Prince Regent, who was seeking a divorce from Princess Caroline, and in its general tone and treatment, it was obviously influenced by Byron's popular *Don Juan*. Though no comic masterpiece, it contains some amusing and vigorously written passages.

Much against the wishes of both parties concerned, a political marriage has been arranged between the fairy Emperor Elfinan and the fairy Princess Bellanaine. The royal chamberlain, Crafticant, is escorting the reluctant bride-to-be from her distant home in Imaus to Elfinan's capital, and the extract printed is supposed to come from his diary, describing the last stages of the journey.
631. This refers to the alleged death of Hum, a disreputable magician who is helping Elfinan to carry off his real love, the human Bertha of Canterbury. See lines 786–7.
637. Pegasus, the legendary winged horse, here symbolizes poetic inspiration.
657. new match: i.e. the wedding of Elfinan and Bellanaine.
671. hoop: hoop-skirt.
672. Coralline was the chief attendant of Bellanaine.
718. Panthea: was the capital of Elfinan's empire. It contains many features of London, including the new street gas-lighting.
721–9. This stanza has many characteristically Keatsian touches.
730–41. No doubt inspired by memories of some London royal procession.

737–8. Compare *On the Sea*, lines 2–3 (p. 205) and *Hyperion* II. 305–6 (p. 74).

744. plenty-horn: a reference to the legendary cornucopia.

751. Basilic: from 'basilica', a royal palace.

757. At this time Elfinan was on his way to Canterbury and Bertha.

759. Bowing and scraping (as we should now say).

770. Powdered bag-wigs: a kind of wig. Wigs would be worn by the more important persons present. *ruffy-tuffy*: with unkempt hair.

771. cinder wenches: presumably servants who cleared the fire-places.

778. A prothalamion was a type of poem to celebrate a wedding.

788. Mago: magician.

Letters IV

2. private theatrical: a performance put on by amateurs at their own expense, to which audiences were admitted free.

6–7. They...Furioso: *John Bull* was a comedy by George Coleman, the younger (1762–1836), *The Review* a musical farce in two acts, and *Bombastes Furioso* a burlesque tragic opera in one act.

8. Drury: the Drury Lane Theatre where Keats saw Kean in *Richard III*.

9. Wells: one of Keats's less intimate friends.

11. 'Nota Bene': 'take notice'. But could refer to a farce of the time with that title.

15. Mary: a character in *John Bull*.

19. in soldier's clothes: this identifies the 'girl' as a character in *The Review*.

20. Tom: probably the actor who played Tom Shuffleton in *John Bull*.

21. finger-point: a way of giving performers the 'bird'.

25–6. sweetest...night: *Henry IV, Part II*, II.iv. 396–7.

31. boonsome: a word coined by Keats; connected with 'boon companions'.

Keats spent March and April of 1818 at Teignmouth with his brother Tom. When he left London for Exeter on 4 March there was a tremendous storm, reputed to be one of the worst for years.

3. Brown's accident: several years before Brown's leg had been seriously injured by a falling parapet stone.